Democracy, Islam, and Secularism in Turkey

RELIGION, CULTURE, AND PUBLIC LIFE

Religion, Culture, and Public Life
Series Editors: Alfred Stepan and Mark C. Taylor

The resurgence of religion calls for careful analysis and constructive criticism of new forms of intolerance, as well as new approaches to tolerance, respect, mutual understanding, and accommodation. In order to promote serious scholarship and informed debate, the Institute for Religion, Culture, and Public Life and Columbia University Press are sponsoring a book series devoted to the investigation of the role of religion in society and culture today. This series includes works by scholars in religious studies, political science, history, cultural anthropology, economics, social psychology, and other allied fields whose work sustains multidisciplinary and comparative as well as transnational analyses of historical and contemporary issues. The series focuses on issues related to questions of difference, identity, and practice within local, national, and international contexts. Special attention is paid to the ways in which religious traditions encourage conflict, violence, and intolerance and also support human rights, ecumenical values, and mutual understanding. By mediating alternative methodologies and different religious, social, and cultural traditions, books published in this series will open channels of communication that facilitate critical analysis.

After Pluralism: Reimagining Religious Engagement, edited by Courtney Bender and
    Pamela E. Klassen
Religion and International Relations Theory, edited by Jack Snyder
Religion in America: A Political History, Denis Lacorne

Democracy, Islam, and Secularism in Turkey

EDITED BY

AHMET T. KURU

AND

ALFRED STEPAN

Columbia University Press   *New York*

Columbia University Press
Publishers Since 1893
New York   Chichester, West Sussex
Copyright © 2012 Columbia University Press
All rights reserved

Library of Congress Cataloging-in-Publication Data
Democracy, Islam, and secularism in Turkey / edited by Ahmet T. Kuru
and Alfred Stepan.
p.   cm. — (Religion, culture, and public life)
Includes bibliographical references and index.
ISBN 978-0-231-15932-6 (cloth : alk. paper)   ISBN 978-0-231-15933-3 (pbk. : alk. paper)
ISBN 978-0-231-53025-5 (e-book)
1. Turkey—Politics and government—20th century. 2. Turkey—Politics and
government—21st century. 3. Democracy—Turkey. 4. Islam and state—Turkey.
5. Secularism—Turkey. 6. Cultural pluralism—Turkey. I. Kuru, Ahmet T.
II. Stepan, Alfred C. III. Title. IV. Series.

JQ1805.D46   2012
320.9561—dc23

2011029163

Columbia University Press books are printed on permanent and durable acid-free paper.
This book is printed on paper with recycled content.
Printed in the United States of America

Contents

Contents

Democracy, Islam, and Secularism in Turkey

Introduction

AHMET T. KURU AND ALFRED STEPAN

The 1982 Constitution of Turkey was drawn up and passed in the immediate aftermath of the 1980 military coup d'état, under the "guardianship" of the military. Because Turkey is now engaged in the application process for membership in the European Union (EU), many key actors, both in the EU and in Turkey, feel that it is appropriate that a new, more democratic constitution be crafted, but there are also those who fear that the new constitution might lead to the domination in Turkish politics of the currently ruling Justice and Development Party (AKP). A lot is at stake for a great number of people. If Turkey is admitted, it would be the first Muslim-majority country to become a member of the EU, the second most populous member of the EU, and the member of the EU with the largest military force. Most importantly, what is at issue for many observers is whether the AKP, which is seen as an Islamically inspired, conservative, and democratic party, can, like the Christian Democratic Party in Germany before it, maintain some of its roots in religion, but build a welcome addition to the existing models of European democracy.[1]

The politics of revising the existing secular, but not sufficiently democratic, constitution has produced intense intellectual debates, and unprecedented *pro* and *con* social mobilization. To discuss this crucial issue, we organized several meetings, including two major conferences at Columbia

University in 2008 and 2009, and both of the editors held meetings with some of the contributors in Istanbul in 2009 and 2010. A key participant at our 2008 conference was the distinguished legal theorist and political scientist Ergun Özbudun—the president of an academic committee drafting a new constitution (and thus at the center of the debate). A year later, we organized a second, larger conference to analyze some of the most salient and controversial questions about Turkish politics: What are the historical roots and contemporary content of the Kemalist ideology that is now under challenge? Should, and could, Turkey's version of hard, controlling secularism be softened to allow greater space for religious actors in the public sphere, as in other democracies in Muslim-majority societies such as Indonesia and Senegal? How might the "guardian" role of the Turkish military in politics be reduced? Why have many once anti-Western Muslim groups become supportive of joining Europe, while the historically pro-Western military and its Kemalist allies have become Euro-skeptics? And finally: Can the constitutional crisis that began in 2007 and continues, as of this writing, result in a deepened democracy in a Muslim-majority democracy?

This volume aims to provide comparative insights into this critical period in Turkish and European history. We also believe that our analyses will aid in the more general discussion of one of the most important and fraught issues of our times: Islam, secularism, and democracy. But before undertaking an examination of contemporary politics in Turkey, our volume looks at two of the most important historical legacies of modern Turkey: the Ottoman Empire and Kemalism. Turkey is the successor of the Ottoman Empire, which ruled much of the Muslim world for centuries and in the process developed forms of interreligious toleration that accorded most minorities more liberties than were then available in western Europe. We are fortunate to be introduced to the question of toleration in the Ottoman Empire by Karen Barkey, the author of the prize-winning *Empire of Difference: The Ottomans in Comparative Perspective* (2008). In "Rethinking Ottoman Management of Diversity," Barkey examines why and how the Ottomans created this distinctive "premodern" form of religious and ethnic accommodation and toleration, and speculates on what parts of this heritage might possibly be of use if the relatively peaceful coexistence among the diverse languages and religions of the Ottoman Empire were allowed to reemerge. Such reemergence will not happen, of course, unless the post-Ottoman, Kemalist legacy is modified to grant more space in the public sphere to some of the newly emerging tolerant and democratic Islamic individuals and groups.

If there is one name that any comprehensive analysis of Turkish politics must include, it is that of Mustafa Kemal Atatürk (1881–1938), the founder of the Turkish Republic, and if there is one ideology that it must include, it is "Kemalism." M. Şükrü Hanioğlu's chapter, "The Historical Roots of Kemalism," is therefore crucial reading for any student of the major varieties of modernization theory and of Turkish politics. Hanioğlu is chair of the Department of Near Eastern Studies at Princeton University and a renowned authority on the political history of the late Ottoman era, especially the thought and activism of the Jeunes Turcs (Young Turks). His essay, in an unprecedentedly critical and deeply insightful way, traces the Young Turks' intellectual legacy within Kemalism. According to Hanioğlu, three intellectual movements (scientism, Westernism, and Turkish unitary nationalism) link Kemalism to late Ottoman thought and to the dominant ideology of the Turkish state; these are only now being challenged by the ruling, Muslim-inspired AKP. There is now much theoretical speculation in contemporary social science, and indeed in our globalized world, about "multiple modernities" and even "multiple secularisms." However, Hanioğlu documents how, why, and with what consequence Kemalist ideology insists that there is only a single modernity and a single (quite aggressive) secularism in any serious project of modernism in the contemporary world.[2] No comparative analysis of the consequences of Turkey's radical "nation-state"–building strategies in a de facto "multiethnic" and "multicultural" context is possible without an understanding of Kemalist ideas about modernity; this concept of modernity still has an important impact on many Turks' understanding of the "nation-state" and "secularism."

Like Hanioğlu, Ergun Özbudun puts what are called the six Kemalist "arrows" (republicanism, nationalism, populism, statism, secularism, and transformationism) at the center of his analysis in "Turkey—Plural Society and Monolithic State," with a special focus on populism and statism.[3] Özbudun—whose many books cover almost all important aspects of Turkish politics, such as civil–military relations, party politics, and constitutional crisis—provides a reinterpretation of Turkish state and society from the perspective of societal pluralism within state unitarism. Since the foundation of the republic, ethnic and religious groups such as the Kurds and the Alevis have made up about one-quarter of Turkish society. Özbudun argues that instead of recognizing this diversity with pluralistic policies, the Turkish state has tried to create a monolithic society in its own image. The "statist" aspect of the Kemalist ideology has led to the state's attempt to monopolize various spheres, including the economy, culture, education, language, and religion. He points out that continued pluralizing reforms of state policies are necessary for Turkey's democratic consolidation.

From a comparative and theoretical viewpoint it is worth noting that most long-standing, relatively peaceful democracies that have more than one major ethnic group within a geographical concentration (e.g., Spain, Canada, India, the United Kingdom, and Belgium) have attempted to manage this de facto "politically robust multinationalism" by two policies: legalizing more than one official (or regionally recognized) language (India has more than twenty-five official languages) and creating a federal system, or at least allowing sufficient devolution (in the United Kingdom, there are Scottish, Welsh, and Northern Irish parliaments in addition to the House of Commons in London).[4] Nonetheless, a few democratic countries, such as Greece, Bulgaria, and Turkey, have neither; they are unitary states, and still do not allow the full use of their minority languages (Turkish in Greece and Bulgaria, Kurdish in Turkey) in politics. Although all three have recently made significant reforms and efforts, in part due to EU scrutiny, to expand the basic human rights of their minorities at an individual level, they shy away from recognizing collective group rights for the Turks of western Thrace and southern Bulgaria, and the Kurds of southeastern Anatolia. The fact that over forty thousand citizens of Turkey have died in military conflicts with a Kurdish dimension makes it clear that in multiethnic contexts, hard monocultural nation-state building and democracy building are not mutually reinforcing—but mutually conflicting—logics. Perhaps to overcome this tension, the AKP government in Turkey initiated broadcasting in Arabic, Bosnian, Circassian, Kurdish, and Zaza from state television (TRT) in 2004, expanding this broadcast with an exclusively Kurdish-language state channel in 2009 and an exclusively Arabic state channel in 2010, which are important but still insufficient steps in solving Turkey's ethnic question.

Secularism obviously has always constituted an important pillar of Kemalist thought and practice in Turkey and is now a major part of the mobilization and conflicts over its alternative meanings and its future. To go beyond the clichés about "Turkey's unique secularism (*laiklik*)," we (Kuru and Stepan) compare *laïcité* in France, Senegal, and Turkey. Our essay, "*Laïcité* as an 'Ideal Type' and a Continuum," aims to reveal that *laïcité* is not a monolithic concept; rather, it has various understandings and implementations in different contexts. Although *laïcité* as a Weberian ideal type implies a secular legal system and the lack of an official religion, in reality it refers to a *continuum* of radically different possible state practices toward religion. This continuum ranges from states with religion-friendly, democratic, and relatively noncontrolling policies toward religion, to states with religion-unfriendly, authoritarian, and highly controlling policies toward religion. Among our three cases, Senegalese implementation of *laïcité* is the most accommodating and inclusionary toward religion, the Turkish practice of *laïcité* is the most controlling and exclusionary, and that of France is by and large in between. We explain this variation by means of some historical factors, especially the absence or existence of an ancien régime, which implied the alliance of a ruling, hereditary monarchy with a hegemonic religion against the republicans. The presence of an ancien régime (pre-revolutionary France with its ruling king and the established Catholic Church, and the Ottoman Empire with its ruling sultan supported by the *ulema* [organized body of Muslim scholars]) radicalized the original formation process of *laïcité* in France and Turkey, while the lack of a comparable ancien régime contributed to religion-friendly *laïcité* in Senegal. Our chapter also discusses the differences between France and Turkey with regard to their different historical and contemporary characteristics, especially the democratic roots of *laïcité* in France and the authoritarian (almost "secular fundamentalist") aspects of *laïcité* in Turkey.

As empirical comparativists, we are interested in causal relations and examine the influence of historical institutions on contemporary politics by analyzing both path-dependent and transformative processes. There are obviously other perspectives available for analyzing secular state policies. *Critical theory* deconstructs discourses on secularism; its recent and influential example is Talal Asad's *Formations of the Secular*.[5] This approach is based largely on a Foucauldian discourse analysis intended to reveal power relations behind the debates on secularism. From this perspective, some scholars argue that the Turkish state did not target Islam, but has instead tried to produce a particular version of Islam,[6] which is in turn generally called "privatized," "Republican," or "Kemalist" Islam. The second perspective is the *hermeneutical approach*, which aims to understand peculiarities of secularism in a particular case. Andrew Davison's *Secularism and Revivalism in Turkey* is a major example of this approach.[7] According to Davison, the Turkish state did not disestablish Islam but established it in a different way. Despite these methodological differences, our analysis of secular state policies in Turkey is compatible, not mutually exclusive, with these two alternative perspectives. Our chapter's emphasis on the assertive secularist aim of pushing religion out of the public sphere in Turkey by means of a certain level of state control over religion is similar to the critical and hermeneutical approaches' emphasis on the Turkish state's goal of the "production" and "establishment" of a privatized version of Islam.

The authoritarian nature of secularism in Turkey is directly linked to its long-term "guardian"—the military. A leading expert on the Turkish military, Ümit Cizre, undertook a deeper public role in 2006 when she edited an authoritative and pioneering almanac on Turkey's security sector and the lack of democratic controls over it. She received strong public criticisms from Turkey's chief of the general staff. Here, in "A New Politics of Engagement," Cizre once again breaks new ground by documenting the recent transformation of the Turkish military's mode of relationship with society. She emphasizes that the Turkish armed forces have increasingly come to need active societal support against the AKP government. Therefore, instead of seeking to maintain people's tacit support based solely on respect and fear, the military has tried to create and mobilize supporters in voluntary associations, professional groups, and academia, who in unprecedented numbers have come out into the street.

Despite its new strategy to mobilize societal supporters, the Turkish military's political power has actually declined in some important respects, owing mainly to the information that has come into the public domain during the legal prosecutions of officers accused of planning coups. So far, about two hundred military officers, including some generals and admirals, have been detained and/or prosecuted for being involved with the "Ergenekon" terrorist organization or the "Cage" coup plot for destabilizing the AKP government. Fifteen different indictments (some of which are criticized for being cursorily constructed) have depicted these officers as perpetrators of assassinations of political figures and as planners of murders of Christians and Jews. The alleged aim of these provocations evidently was to create sufficient chaos and fear so the military would be asked by a frightened population to overthrow the government and to assume control of the state, as it did in 1980.

The main legacy of the 1980 coup in today's Turkey is the current constitution. In his second chapter, "The Turkish Constitutional Court and Political Crisis," Özbudun analyzes the constitutional crisis that began in 2007. He first documents the authoritarian spirit and articles of the 1982 Constitution and the historical background against which it was drafted. For

Özbudun, neither the 1982 Constitution nor Turkey's Constitutional Court was designed to protect citizens' rights and freedoms. Instead, they are meant to protect the ideological state against its citizens. As an example, Özbudun stresses the court's decisions to disband Kurdish nationalist and Islamist political parties. The essay also briefly examines the ruling AKP's recent attempt to lift the headscarf ban, by amending the constitution, and the judiciary's response, in which a closure case was opened against the party, a move that came within one vote of banning the AKP in July 2008.

The domestic dynamics of Turkish politics have obviously been influenced by several international factors, especially Turkey's application to the European Union. The chapter on this topic in our volume is written by one of the most informed and policy-relevant participant-observers of this process, Joost Lagendijk. From January 2002 until July 2009, Lagendijk was chair of the delegation to the EU–Turkey Joint Parliamentary Committee. Since then, he has lived in Istanbul and written about domestic struggles over EU accession as a columnist. In "Turkey's Accession to the European Union and the Role of the Justice and Development Party," Lagendijk analyzes Turkey's recent relationship with the EU, defining 2003 and 2004 as a golden era. More recently, however, he sees stagnation in Turkey–EU relations, especially from 2005 to 2008 but less in 2009, due to "enlargement fatigue" and the rise of right-wing parties in major EU countries, as well as declining popular support and government enthusiasm in Turkey for petitioning for EU membership. He concludes by examining some key continuing EU-related reform trends in Turkey and the tensions around them.

Given the increasing French and German opposition to its EU membership, Turkey has intensified its relations with Middle Eastern countries. This coincides with the recent anti-authoritarian mobilizations in the Arab world. As a result, debates about the "Turkish model" have once again become salient. We are lucky to have Stathis N. Kalyvas, a prominent political scientist and one of the leading experts on Christian Democratic parties, assess this issue. In "The 'Turkish Model' in the Matrix of Political Catholicism," Kalyvas brings together crucial insights from other pieces here to reveal how this volume contributes to the analysis of the "Turkish model." He summarizes the basic parameters of the Catholic mobilization in the second half of the nineteenth century in Europe and compares them with the characteristics of the contemporary AKP experience in Turkey. Bringing attention to the Catholic mobilization suggests that the Turkish model is not necessarily as idiosyncratic as it may otherwise appear. He discusses how the Turkish model can inspire the rest of the Middle East, in terms of allowing religious political activism in a democratizing context. His emphasis on the mutual transformations of Catholic parties and democratizing polities in European history is important for understanding the recent transformation in Turkey and provides indicators for the future of the Arab world.

In sum, this book's analysis of Turkey has multiple theoretical and policy-relevant aims: to expand our conceptual repertoire of the possible forms of toleration in pre-democratic settings by a close examination of the Ottoman Empire; to increase our capacity to understand and evaluate some of the strengths and weaknesses of different varieties of modernization theory by attention to the Kemalist ideology of the state and nation; to contribute to the emerging literatures on comparative constitutionalism by examining Turkey's attempt to transform an existing constitution with many authoritarian legacies without imposing a democratic but majoritarian constitution; to enrich our theories of the "multiple secularisms" of modern democratic and nondemocratic regimes via a comparative analysis of Turkish laïcité; to deepen our inquiry into a still undertheorized question of contemporary democratization theory and practice (how democratic incumbents can increase democratic control over a previously relatively autonomous and authoritarian coercive apparatus); to investigate, in a world of increasing globalization, whether, and how, states could simultaneously integrate into new international organizations like the EU while trying to build democratic, inclusionary, trusting, and participatory relations among the diverse constituencies in their own political communities; and, finally, to examine to what extent the AKP experience in Turkey has similarities with the European Catholic parties in the second half of the nineteenth century, asking what the "Turkish model" can inspire in the rest of the Middle East today.

We thank the Institute for Religion, Culture, and Public Life (IRCPL) and the Center for the Study of Democracy, Toleration, and Religion (CDTR) at Columbia University, in addition to the Henry R. Luce Initiative on Religion and International Affairs and the Institute of Turkish Studies, for sponsoring our various conferences on Turkey, and to Melissa Van and Emily Brennan for their help in organizing them. The essays of this book were improved greatly by the intellectually rich contributions of several other participants in the conferences to whom we want to give special thanks: Andrew Arato, Richard Bulliet, David Cuthell, Rashid Khalidi, Mirjam Künkler, and Nur Yalman.

Postscript

On September 12, 2010, the Turkish electorate voted by a landslide (58–42 percent) to approve a package that amended twenty-four articles of the constitution. The amendments, which were supported by EU representatives, deeply worried those at home and abroad who were already concerned about the declining Kemalist legacy in Turkish politics.[8] Those who actively campaigned against the amendments did not reject the entire package; instead, they opposed it for two major reasons. First, they regarded these reforms as the AKP's—especially Prime Minister Recep Tayyip Erdoğan's—single-handed initiative to overly dominate Turkish politics. Second, they mainly opposed the change of the balance of power in the judicial system. Other reforms realized by the amendments—such as recognition of affirmative action for women, the elderly, and the disabled; prohibition of the state's secret recording of individuals' private information; and authorizing the Constitutional Court as the supreme court of appeal for individuals in human rights violation cases—were appreciated by even the opponents, some of whom viewed the reforms as not being too much, but too little.

The amendments made it more difficult for the Constitutional Court to dissolve political parties. Since its foundation in 1963, the Constitutional Court has closed twenty-five parties while the rest of the long-standing democracies in Europe have closed four parties—one Nazi (1952) and one Communist party (1956) in Germany, a racist/xenophobic party in Belgium (2004), and one party linked to Basque Homeland and Liberty (ETA) in Spain (2003). Many democratic observers have urged that a constitutional amendment should be introduced to make this more difficult in Turkey. This now requires the approval of two-thirds of court members instead of the previous three-fifths voting. Following the amendments, Parliament elected two new members to the Constitutional Court, choosing one out of three candidates offered by the bar associations and another one from three candidates nominated by the Turkish Court of Accounts. The fact that both new judges are ideologically closer to the AKP has received criticism in the media and from other parties.

The level of criticism was much higher regarding the restructuring of the High Council of Judges and Prosecutors (HSYK), because it is the decision maker about the appointments to the High Court of Appeals and the Council of State, promotions and appointments of judges and prosecutors, and their disciplinary procedures. The amendments authorized the selection of fifteen additional new members of the HSYK, in addition to existing five members who were elected by the High Court of Appeals and the Council of State. President Abdullah Gül appointed four of the new members, and one was elected by the Justice Academy. The remaining ten new members were chosen via a nationwide election by Turkey's eleven thousand judges and prosecutors. Politically, the net result of this new process meant that the Kemalist control of the judiciary since the 1920s was weakened.

The amendments also weakened the second Kemalist stronghold, the military, by empowering civilian courts in prosecuting military officers and allowing military courts to review the military command's disciplinary expulsion decisions. Beyond the referendum, the military experienced a credibility crisis throughout 2010. More than eighty military officers, including on-duty generals and admirals, were detained for their alleged involvement in the "Sledge-hammer" coup plan. In a context where military legitimacy was somewhat declining and the government's legitimacy had been reinforced by a series of elections, President Gül and Prime Minister Erdoğan, for the first time, exercised their constitutional prerogative to play an active role in the annual review of military promotions concerning high-ranking officers.

The developments in the judiciary and military reveal that the Kemalist ideology is no longer preeminent in Turkey, although it still has powerful followers. Some pundits and even scholars exaggerate the tug-of-war between the Kemalists and their critics—mainly the coalition of conservatives and liberals. Turkey is not unique in terms of ideological polarization. Many other countries have faced sociopolitical cleavages over such issues as state–religion controversies. Historically, there was the "war of two Frances," and for decades there have been "culture wars" in the United States between pro-secular and pro-religious groups. Moreover, some scholars argue that beyond a severe polarization, the Kemalist state elite and conservative political (e.g., the AKP) and social (e.g., the Gülen movement) actors have reached a certain level of mutual understanding, or have at least developed a language of engagement.[9]

We hope this book will provide a historical, conceptual, and institutional framework within which to better understand the recent political changes in Turkey—crucial examples for worldwide debates on democracy, Islam, and secularism.

Notes

1. On the self-secularization and democratization of Christian Democratic parties in Western Europe as they engaged in competitive electoral politics, see the pioneering book by Stathis N. Kalyvas, *The Rise of Christian Democracy in Europe* (Ithaca, N.Y.: Cornell University Press, 1996).

2. On "multiple modernities" see S. N. Eisenstadt, "Multiple Modernities," *Daedalus* 129 (2000): 1–30, and the telling critique of classical modernization theory by Sudipta Kaviraj, "An Outline of a Revisionist Theory of Modernity," *European Journal of Sociology* 46 (2005): 497–526. For a conceptual and empirical argument that modern democratic theory needs the concept of "multiple secularisms," see Alfred Stepan, "The Multiple Secularisms of Modern Democracies and Autocracies," in Craig Calhoun, Mark Juergensmeyer, and Jonathan VanAntwerpen, eds., *Rethinking Secularism* (New York: Oxford University Press, 2011). For the conceptual and empirical distinction between "passive" and "assertive" secularisms, see Ahmet T. Kuru, "Passive and Assertive Secularism: Historical Conditions, Ideological Struggles, and State Policies Toward Religion," *World Politics* 59 (2007): 568–594, and *Secularism and State Policies Toward Religion: The United States, France, and Turkey* (New York: Cambridge University Press, 2009).

3. Note that none of the Kemalist six arrows refers to democratization.

4. Alfred Stepan, Juan J. Linz, and Yogendra Yadav, *Crafting State-Nations: India and Other Multinational Democracies* (Baltimore: Johns Hopkins University Press, 2011).

5. Talal Asad, *Formations of the Secular: Christianity, Islam, Modernity* (Stanford, Calif.: Stanford University Press, 2003).

6. Sinem Gürbey, "Islam, Nation-State, and the Military: A Discussion of Secularism in Turkey," *Comparative Studies of South Asia, Africa, and the Middle East* 29 (2009): 371–380.

7. Andrew Davison, *Secularism and Revivalism in Turkey: A Hermeneutic Reconsideration* (New Haven, Conn.: Yale University Press, 1998).

8. Aslı Ü. Bali, "Unpacking Turkey's 'Court-Packing' Referendum," *Middle East Report Online*, November 5, 2010, http://www.merip.org/mero/mero110510.

9. Berna Turam, *Between Islam and the State: The Politics of Engagement* (Stanford, Calif.: Stanford University Press, 2006).

[1]

Rethinking Ottoman Management of Diversity

What Can We Learn for Modern Turkey?

KAREN BARKEY

The conference organized at Columbia University around the themes of politics, religion, democracy, and the constitution in Turkey—as well as this book, which follows these themes more intensely—centered on contemporary Turkey. We might then ask what the point is of including a chapter on the legacy of the Ottoman Empire, a legacy that imbued the early centuries of the empire but was essentially completely discarded in the last hundred years or so of imperial existence. The legacy I refer to is clearly that of interreligious peace and coexistence, the spirit of toleration that enabled the Ottoman state and society to flourish for many centuries.

A discussion of contemporary Turkey cannot be conducted without serious attention to the themes of religion, politics, democracy, and nationalism; most significantly, the changing relationships between religion and politics and religion, democracy, and nationalism remain key to understanding modern Turkey. And to any even casual observer, it will be clear that contemporary Turkey is still unsettled in its understandings of accommodation, forbearance, and tolerance of religious difference or, more generally, diversity. Furthermore, in their attempt to represent the new Turkey as different from the early nationalist and immediate Kemalist past, politicians are reaching back into history to claim a history of toleration and coexistence without fully understanding the context of its emergence, deployment, and tragic undoing. Even more serious is the chopping up and freezing of history, claiming ancestry with Ottoman toleration while denying any relation to the final annihilation of diversity in the transition from empire to nation. It is therefore important to put the question of Ottoman toleration into historical and political context as well as to discuss how modern Turkey can benefit from its Ottoman past.

In this chapter, I intend to bring back the Ottoman past in the context of the empire's management of diversity over the centuries and the relationship between politics and religion as it unfolded over time, to elucidate both the mechanisms and the long-term processes of state–society relations in the Ottoman lands. I will show that the Ottomans forged early on a framework for capacious relations between state and religion, a dynamic and flexible system of rule over diversity as well as imperial features amenable to remaining an Islamic polity. I will then use these historical resources to examine the modern Turkish understandings of diversity.

The Ottoman organization of diversity is increasingly referred to as an excellent example of religious and ethnic cohabitation without serious violence over four centuries of rule. There seems to be a superficial agreement that the Ottoman formula for organizing diverse communities under a common religious umbrella and incorporating them into the state through their own religious hierarchy seemed to work. There is, however, little agreement with regard to what it actually was that produced interethnic and religious peace in the first centuries of Ottoman rule. Understanding the historical mechanisms and processes of toleration in this period will certainly help contribute to the debate on modern instances of religious and ethnic cohabitation in contemporary Turkey and elsewhere.

Ottoman Diversity: A Project of State Toleration

The Ottoman Empire is perhaps the best example of imperial accommodation of religion, in which a state carefully watches religious differences and shapes the role that religion should play in the imperial polity. Much of the contemporary literature on religious and ethnic diversity in the Ottoman Empire has adopted the term "toleration" to refer to the relatively persecution-free centuries of early Ottoman rule.[1] The "toleration" of the East is contrasted to the "persecuting society" of the medieval West. Especially regarding the Jews of Islam, historical analyses maintain that they suffered much less persecution than their brethren in medieval and Reformation Europe.[2] Most scholars provide an explanation that lies within Islam, a body of religious thought and practice that classifies non-Muslims, Jews, and Christians as protected people. According to Islam, they argue, as long as these groups remained cognizant and observant of their second-class status, they were protected. This emphasis on religious and cultural aspects leads us away from the political, economic, and especially organizational functions of "toleration" in multiethnic, multireligious empires.

In fact, there has been little attempt to study the Ottoman toleration of diversity in sociological terms. Rather, political clichés have filled the field. Over time, the pendulum has swung from a representation of the Ottomans as barbarians and terrible Turks, to a much more benign picture of a hybrid, multiconfessional society that the state protected and where everybody lived happily forever after. In the first image, multiplicity is rigidly separated and defined and restricted contact between groups is presumed. In the second, the hybridity of a class of travelers, scholars, sages, and merchants has been stretched to include all, extrapolating from the rather unusual experience of a few. The respective ends of this continuum posit two ideal types rather than more complex and nuanced versions of actual relations between the state and different communities.

Recently, more balanced arguments have surfaced. In Aron Rodrigue's analysis, we find that Ottoman Islam is not an essentialized version of intergroup relations, but rather a framework within which religion, language, and structure provide the milieu in which groups can interact. Focusing on "difference" came with the abandonment of efforts to force "sameness."[3] We also cannot underestimate the degree to which Islam was pervasive in Ottoman society, as "sameness" for the majority and rulers, and remained a litmus test of inclusion. Islam provided a clear political identity, and a state-sponsored version of Islam was institutionalized by members of the *ulema* (organized body of Muslim scholars), diffused top–down into the far reaches of Ottoman society.[4]

What were the perimeters of Ottoman tolerance? There is no doubt that the Ottoman resettlement and massacres of Armenians in the late nineteenth and early twentieth centuries have permanently sullied perceptions of Ottoman tolerance. Yet from 1300 to 1700 at least, if not longer, the Ottoman Empire was open and tolerant of the "other," while the Habsburg leaders consolidated with a policy of "confessional absolutism" that enforced Catholicism and persecuted the Protestant minorities, and the Russians wavered in their policies depending on the strength of the Orthodox Church. Russian state enforcement of religious conformity could be quite violent and assimilation-oriented.

I am attempting to understand both the construction and the limits of Ottoman "toleration." My interest is in building an organizational understanding of Ottoman "toleration," explaining the relative lack of persecution of non-Muslims in terms of state legibility, and the construction of an organizational, boundary-conscious, yet flexible system of interreligious interaction. I focus on the first centuries of Ottoman rule, when we can actually observe the construction of a state–community compact based on both boundaries imposed by an Islamic cultural framework and the organizational needs of the state and the communities. This model of "toleration," I argue, meant a specific form of relations between the state and religious communities that was altered after the eighteenth century. Its construction can be studied through the emergence of the Ottoman state, the relations between Islam and the state, and the establishment of an organizational form of indirect rule of diversity, the *millet* system. Even though Ottomans arrived at this model of toleration through ad hoc and strategic means not fully related to toleration, they understood its meaning and relevance to a well-managed diverse imperial society and reproduced it for a long time.

The Nature of an Emergent Imperial Society

The model of Ottoman toleration developed within an imperial, premodern society; its most important features were acceptance of diversity, inclusion of a plurality of traditions, and acknowledgment of the similarity of experiences across groups. Part the result of pragmatic decision making and part the result of the principle of homology, decisions of inclusiveness, and accommodation, brokerage across religions undergirded the building of the Ottoman state. As cliché as it sounds, empires—especially the old, traditional, contiguous, land-based examples—were quite varied in their understanding and acceptance of diversity. Before the rise of nationalism, early modern imperial states—in which loyalty and political cohesion could not be defined by ethnic/racial myths of unity—relied on religion as one of the major building blocks of state authority, social discipline, and cultural legitimacy. Religious traditions were accepted and included in the larger state–society compact that facilitated imperial rule. Unity was conceived from piecemeal diversity, rather than through its denial or its forced as-similation, as is often the case in the modern nation-state.

The nature of the relationship between different groups in such a polity was set on its trajectory by early encounters, within the constraints of geopolitical, demographic, and cultural circumstances of contact. In the case of the Ottoman dynasty, circumstances provided the context for the early development of tolerance and flexibility toward the "other," mostly the Christian populations of the growing imperial polity. Many factors influenced the accommodation toward conquered populations. Among those, certainly the location of the embryonic Ottoman territory and the unresolved Islamic identity of the conquerors worked in tandem with the extended geopolitical frontier contact and the probable demographic differences between these two groups. These were also fierce warriors, and despite attempts at accommodation it cannot be denied that they left havoc in many of the areas they encountered. Yet, on balance, early Ottoman rulers seem to have triumphed by a combination of warfare and accommodation.

The Osmanlı dynasty—named after the first leader, Osman—had arisen from among many small states, emirates, and principalities that occupied the plains from the frontier edges of Byzantium and the foothills of Anatolia. They expanded to southeastern Europe and the Anatolian plateau, and from there to the heartlands of the Arabs, dominating Mecca and Medina. By the mid-sixteenth century, from the Danube to the Nile, from the Anatolian lands to the holy cities of Islam, the Ottomans had acquired a multi-ethnic, multireligious empire. At first, when the Ottomans conquered land in the Balkans, they acquired a predominantly Christian population, and it was only with the expansion of the empire into Arab lands in the sixteenth century that a balance between Christian and Muslim populations was reached. The 1478 census illustrated the differences in the religious make-up of the population quite clearly; in the European parts of the empire, the Christians were in a clear majority: 80.7 percent were Christian households, as opposed to a mere 18.8 percent for the Muslim households.[5] The non-Muslim population estimate for the 1490s was about 4 million in the Balkans and about 32,000 in Anatolia. By the 1520s and 1530s, study of the population in the major cities of the Balkans and Anatolia had started showing the effects of the expansion toward the east, with 62.4 percent of the population being Muslims and 37.4 percent non-Muslims.[6] Especially at their very origins, the Ottomans had to be flexible in the face of diversity and Christian predominance. As the Ottoman conquerors incorporated vast territories and an extraordinary medley of peoples into the empire, they—as many other large imperial states had done over the course of history—worked to understand and manage difference.

There is no doubt that rule over diversity necessitated classification of some sort, and that Ottoman rulers articulated a boundary that operated at different levels, separating Muslims from non-Muslims and further dividing the latter according to ethnicity and religion. Accordingly, Ottomans tended to accept the ascribed status of the different groups while shaping it according to their understanding of their own origins and religious beliefs. Thus the compact that defined boundaries between the populations of the empire was heavily influenced by what it meant to run an Islamic state that had to incorporate non-Muslim populations that were ensconced in their own particular religious and ecological niches. Yet this Islamic framework was there to be manipulated; it was flexible. Early Ottoman rulers were especially prone to subordinating the requirements of Islam to the running of an empire.

Alongside Islam, the Turkish-Mongolian origins of the conquerors, as well as their experience in the vast space from China to the Pontic steppes, with its various religions and different ethnicities, also shaped their view of intergroup relations. The patterns of intermarriage and the commonplace appropriation of religious symbols and imagery point toward fluid boundaries in multicultural settings that would be branded open-minded even by modern standards.[7]

The particular nexus of emergence and the early encounters with the "other" remain indispensable to understanding the precise brand of Ottoman "toleration." As the Turkic tribal forces under the leadership of Osman pushed at the eastern frontiers of the Byzantine Empire, the encounter between these two frontier peoples turned out to be more familiar then expected. A similar frontier organization, comparable interests, and related methods of survival made it possible for these Turcoman leaders to expand by association and brokerage across religious lines. Linking men of different religions, bringing them under the same warrior-and-booty mentality, they spread their local networks. In a sense, the conjuncture happened at the edge of both cosmopolitanism and decay, of frontier culture and revivalism, where the locals were ready for new opportunities and the innovators among the wave of new immigrants had the initiative to deliver this change.

That early Ottomans were not boundary conscious—in fact, they exhibited a strong syncretic religious understanding favored by a heterodox form of Islam—was crucial to the structure of opportunities present in that moment. At the same time, there is no doubt that they strategized, since conquering tribes practiced a policy of *istimalet*—that is, an attempt to make the indigenous population look on them favorably by offering incentives and promising generosity and concessions, such as permission to retain lands and resources.[8] It is also now questionable whether they had a military or demographic advantage over the Christian forces. Heath Lowry argues that part of the syncretism of these Muslim fighters was due to their rather small numbers, their clear demographic weakness. Had there been large-scale Turkish movements into this territory, he surmises, there would have been a much less accommodating state, with less Byzantine input and less toleration of others.[9] Fikret Adanır also stresses the similarity of occupations, the resemblance between the Turkic *yürüks* (nomads) and the Vlach and Albanian nomadic elements in the Balkans. Such similarity could facilitate exchange and cooperation, but also conquest.[10]

Moreover, the frontier between Orthodox Christianity and Islam had become permeable and fluid, allowing for alliances and cultural interchange. This fluidity and tolerance regarding interreligious exchange was reinforced by the antagonism between Greek Orthodoxy and Western Catholicism. The schism within Christianity, especially the memory of the Latin sacking of Constantinople in 1204, would bring Orthodox Christians and Muslims closer together and provide the conquering Ottoman state with room to maneuver and exploit divisions outside its realm.[11] Within Asia Minor, the struggle for predominance among the diverse Turkish groups and the Mongol invasions pitted Muslims against one another, pushing Muslims closer to the Christian frontiers. In this fluid, syncretic, militaristic, competitive, but innovative world of Asia Minor, Muslim *ghazis* (warriors on behalf of Islam) sometimes relied on their Christian counterparts to help in the struggle against fellow Muslims.[12]

Also, much of the movement back and forth at the frontiers occurred during the period the Turkish tribes did not have a strong institutionalized Islamic identity, and when religion had not become atrophied into one formal tradition. The openness of the time is demonstrated clearly in the shift in the demographic balance of the region, as Byzantine peasants chose to migrate to Ottoman zones of control.[13] Given such obvious absence of deep-seated religious identity, incorporation of and negotiation with Christian elements occurred at diverse locations under the aegis of various actors. *Ghazis*, beys, and dervish colonizers as well as Greek Orthodox theologians were all active participants in the early definition of the relational structures of the empire. For example, many followed the teachings of the dervish leader Bektashi, whose *tekke* (monastery) in the thirteenth century became the refuge for those of Christian and Sunni background, but also for the heretical orders from the Christian and Islamic sides: Nestorians, Bogomils, and Shi'i believers.

The Ottoman State and Islam

The second feature of the Ottoman Empire that helps us in the comparison between empire and nation-state comprises the relations between politics and religion. The Ottoman Empire distinguished itself by creating a strong Islamic religious identity, yet taming it through state-dominated and state-guided administrative structures. The acceptance of diversity—of manifold religions and traditions coexisting—could happen only as long as a strong state retained control in cases of religious dogmatism and extremism.

Within Islam, traditionally, the relation between politics and religion has often been characterized by a subordination of religion to the state, and the Ottomans exemplified this pattern. The relationship between the state and Islam that furthered diversity within and across religions lasted until the era of reforms in the early nineteenth century, when religious leaders emerged as strong opponents of the Ottoman state and its attempts at Westernization. We need to understand, however, the initial set of relations forged between the state and Islam to see how these relations advanced the cause of a diverse empire.

For centuries the Ottomans were a strong imperial polity that claimed Islam as their main source of legitimacy and gave Islam pride of place in the empire. The rulers of the empire were also the caliphs—that is, the leaders of the Sunni Islamic community. Vis-à-vis the world, this claim remained a potent source of Islamic unity and strength, but within the empire, Islam played a more constrained role. And despite displays of loyalty and devotion to the religious world of Orthodox Sunni Islam, Ottoman society for centuries remained free of large-scale religious conflict.

The particular construction of the Ottoman state was such that it maintained and nurtured an important separation between religion as an institution and religion as a system of meanings and relations that connected a community of faith. Religion as an institution would help administer the empire. Religion as a system of beliefs would provide the tools for everyday practice. Şerif Mardin argues that religion mediated between the local social forces and the more macro institutions and political structure and therefore also linked the different aspects of religion with the different levels of society.[14] The institutional and meaning-generating aspects of religion were not entirely separate in that they were connected in the person of the judge.[15]

The state also facilitated a pattern of negotiating between alternative legal and institutional frames, between the various dualities that provided a basis for coexistence and conflict. Islam in the Ottoman Empire was subordinated to a strong yet flexible and integrationist state; the state was able to both segment and integrate religion along multiple dimensions, making religious institutions compliant to its interests. Among the differences that were built into Ottoman state and society were those related to orthodox and heterodox Islamic faith and practice, religious and secular law, and the construction of an organization of religious difference, the *millet* system. In the cultural repertoire of society, many dimensions of religious pluralism were both allowed and persecuted at the same time—allowed when variations did not threaten the state, persecuted when heterodoxies became amorphous, unstructured, or allied with enemies of the state. The in-built pluralism within the legal system, with sultanic and religious law in tension and in coexistence, was also maintained from the very top of the patrimonial household down to the levels of the magistrate. The sultan himself, a master juggler of all forms of dualities negotiated between religious and sultanic law, maintained both heterodox and orthodox religious leaders at the palace, often playing them against one another. There is no doubt that the Ottoman state benefited from tensions between Sunni and Sufi and Sunni and Shi'a practices, from the division of secular and religious law, and especially from the embodiment of such tensions in the person of the magistrate, the religious official versed in both religious and secular law. In everyday practice, the workings of the *şeriat* courts show clearly that magistrates were equally adept at interpreting religious and sultanic law, pressing for local custom and precedent when necessary and allowing each source of legal wisdom to function independently from the other.[16]

Many choreographies of everyday life were executed between formal Orthodox Sunni, imperial Islam, and the informal heterodox Sufi popular Islam that remained the backbone of Ottoman cultural life. Again the early history of the relationship between sultans and brotherhoods partly explains the plurality of religious configurations that were accepted in the empire, even as persecution of some forms reflected state intransigence. Early in the thirteenth and fourteenth centuries, the rising Ottomans, who needed foot soldiers both for faith and for army, deliberately exploited the zeal of the Sufi brotherhoods for conquest and settlement. The resulting alliance between the colonizing dervishes who supported the Turcoman armies and the incipient state remained sealed in the emergence of the empire. In the fifteenth century, the tendency of Sufi brotherhoods for rebellious activity, their quarrel with the tenets of Orthodox Sunni Islam, and their association with the lawlessness that followed the Mongol invasion of Anatolia pushed Ottoman sultans to attempt to control Sufi institutions while also trying to integrate them into the mainstream. This noteworthy realignment—from open support of the Sufi brotherhoods to conservative and well-ordered Sunni orthodoxy—was meant to reign in the rebellious potential of mystic brotherhoods and dervish orders.[17] It would have been dangerous, without a doubt, for the state to eradicate this popular aspect of Islamic faith, maintained in local and powerful mystical practices and larger networks of solidarity carried by charismatic leaders. In many ways, then, Orthodox Sunni Islam and heterodox popular Sufi Islam competed and shared the space of the Ottoman Empire in respect to influence and practice among the faithful. The range of phenomena that this orthodoxy–heterodoxy duality was applied to is much broader and thicker in its complexity.[18]

Once again, the conclusion that we can gather from this is that the Ottoman space offered manifold alternatives while maintaining the essence of a broader Islam—in regard to the degree to which the variety of experiences, the multiplicity of local styles of believing and worship, and the pluralism inherent in various systems of law were understood and legitimized within the framework of Ottoman Islam, both administrative and local, experiential and meaningful.

Millet: Indirect Rule of Diversity

The third aspect of Ottoman diversity has been much discussed and contested, yet is only very superficially understood. The Ottoman version of indirect rule vis-à-vis different confessional communities was known as the *millet* system. The *millet* system, a loose administrative set of central–local arrangements systematized only in the nineteenth century, was a script for multireligious rule, though it was never fully codified, nor was it ever equivalent across communities. Yet, with the simultaneous division and integration of communities into the state, it became a normative as well as practical instrument of rule, one based on the notion of social boundaries between religious communities, regulating the transactions between categories. Moreover, as the state arranged communities into organizational units administered by intermediaries with a real stake in the maintenance of the status quo, it ensured that top–down and bottom–up interests in ethnic and religious peace were maintained.

Initially, the intention of the system was for the state to get a handle on the diversity within its realm, to increase legibility and order, enabling the administration to run smoothly and taxes to flow unhindered.[19] The aftermath of the conquest of Constantinople was the most plausible moment for the emergence of new, fluid, and still somewhat opaque organizational forms that would grow into the three large-scale identity vessels that organized diversity in the empire. As such, these were separate from one another, contained within their institutional forms, and internally administered by religious or lay leaders who acted as intermediaries between the state and the community. In addition to the Muslim *millet*, three non-Muslim *millets*—a Greek Orthodox, an Armenian, and a Jewish—were organized around their dominant religious institutions, with the understanding that religious institutions would define and delimit collective life. The Orthodox *millet* was recognized in 1454 and the Armenian in 1461, while the Jewish *millet* remained without a declared definite status for a while, though it was unofficially recognized around the same time as the other two. In 1477, there were 3,151 Greek Orthodox households; 3,095 combined Armenian, Latin, and Gypsy households; and 1,647 Jewish households in Istanbul. The number of Muslim households had reached 8,951.[20]

As such, this administrative format provided for a capacious understanding of the boundary between Muslims and non-Muslims, providing as well room for variation in the boundary, whereby groups with distinct organizational structures produced varying state–society arrangements. Sultans, and Mehmed II in particular, forged the early arrangements that were consequently periodically renewed by diverse communities. These arrangements folded into their practice the existing authority structures of each community and thereby provided them with significant legal autonomy and authority. Attention was paid to maintaining the internal religious and cultural composition of communities. Where there was strong community organization and/or a strong ecclesiastical hierarchy, the central state adopted these institutions as the representative structures of the community. For the Greeks, the Conqueror recognized the Greek Orthodox Patriarchate in Constantinople as the most powerful force among the Christian population. Jews, who had no overarching rabbinical authority but rather an assembly of religious and lay leaders, were recognized as a series of communities with their own leaders.

Having now established the parameters of the interreligious boundaries and the administrative ecology of the *millet*, we can once more ask the question: How did the Ottoman Empire manage to maintain interreligious and interethnic peace and preserve a relatively tolerant imperial space until the eighteenth century?

Institutional reproduction and continuity was based on three premises. First, the acceptance and internalization of existing native organizational forms and their adaptation to an Ottoman model of rule made the different groups more willing to accept Ottoman rule. Second, the creation of intermediary personnel for each community with a vested interest in the reproduction of institutional arrangements empowered some to work hard to maintain the boundaries as the Ottomans had set them up. Third, the creation of competing alternative organizational forms that behaved as checks and balances to the accumulation of power by intermediaries ensured that they would not ally to organize against the state. Probably the most important mechanism of rule was reliance on intermediaries. Once these *millet* arrangements were agreed on, they were maintained by religious or secular intermediaries from each community, enforced by incentives and punishments.

As the key brokers between the state and the *millets*, these intermediaries strategically behaved as boundary managers, maintaining peace and order through the active and efficient monitoring of relations across religious and community lines. James Fearon and David Laitin discuss such behavior as "institutionalized in-group policing," by which leaders successfully watch over their own members within the community and in transactions across communities.[21] To prevent such incidents from blowing up into large-scale ethnic conflict, the intermediaries, be they religious or secular leaders, were empowered by the state to monitor their internal affairs in return for continued benefits and autonomy. Community leaders who maintained peace and paid their dues on time would be rewarded with continued appointment and increased opportunity for wealth. Community leaders who became embroiled in violence or were unable to collect taxes lost their livelihoods and, more often, their heads. This intense monitoring was especially successful in respect to the ecclesiastical leadership, which was interested in maintaining boundaries for religious reasons as much as political ones and also because they had invested much time learning the legal and religious systems of the others, especially the ruling Islamic ones, in order to predict, prevent, and manage possibly detrimental breaches of intercommunal relational space.

Thus the components of the Ottoman style of management of diversity were based on the particular historical circumstances of emergence, the establishment of a robust yet flexible relationship between politics and religion, and a system of organizing diversity that was adaptable yet specialized to the needs of various communities and the state. It is from the sum of all these components that we see the emergence of toleration. The character of Ottoman toleration was therefore not entirely a political and administrative product of state policy, nor was it the result of an internal, organic, ideological germination by Ottoman humanists who thought that toleration should be normative in society. Within this mixture of cultural blueprints, past experiences, diversity on the ground, and the nature of imperial negotiated rule, an imperial toleration was shaped to structure intergroup relations in the least contentious manner possible. Toleration was rather an organizational by-product of top–down interests in legibility and interreligious peace and order and bottom–up concern for maintaining an interference-free and coercion-free imperial space. As such, over time it became normative to Ottoman society and was reproduced as a successful practice of managing diversity.

To sum up, Ottoman relations between politics and religion grew out of a strong central authority, control over religious institutions, powerful linkages to everyday religious practice, and the integration and acceptance of diversity. The Ottomans utilized these methods to maintain four hundred years of flexibility around religious and political identities, ethnic and religious pluralism, and forms of legal and institutional pluralism.

Is There a "Usable Past" in Ottoman History?

If we think of the concept of "usable past" as comprising acquired knowledge and a set of practices that make up successful repertoires of action,

then we need to ask—especially when we employ the trope of Ottoman toleration—whether parts of the Ottoman heritage can be extracted to refashion a renewed understanding of diversity in contemporary Turkish politics
and society. Since there is some indication that Turkish society is just now
poised to move toward both a form of liberalization and more plural and
multivocal repertoires of political culture, we need to highlight the best of
the Ottoman tradition for all to reflect on. To carry out such a task will require a study of the continuities and discontinuities between the Ottoman
past and the Turkish present. First we have to consider the degree to which
the multiplicity, the multivocality, and the pluralism of the Ottoman project
was eroded in the nineteenth century and then was even more diluted as
the republican nation-state was constructed in the first half of the twentieth century. And second, we have to trace the institutional continuities
between past and present. Only then will we be able to recognize the similarities and differences between imperial and national political formations
and identify what can be brought into the contemporary political discourse.

The Ottomans in the late eighteenth century still demonstrated a condition of compound diversity, the slow materialization of "multiple modernities,"[22] and a pluralism of state–society relations and arrangements,
all accompanied by a rise in interethnic, interreligious identity debates.
The modern Turkish Republic constructed out of this transition period—
through the Young Turk period and the early Kemalist years—a project of
national unity, a fairly homogeneous nation, and a single modernity as
well as a single political culture with a dominant national identity.[23] Part
of this transformation has to do with the fact that nation-states are built
on principles of national self-determination, on exclusionary or strongly
assimilationist premises, and on homogenization and standardization of
state–society relations. The project of the nation-state is an ideological,
demographic, and socioeconomic one in which state- and nation-build-
ers will employ both symbolic and physical means of violence to enforce
their aims.[24]

Turkey was no exception. It exemplified the most fervent of construc-
tions of a national unitary state, exercising state action to remove diversity
and conducting a campaign of homogenization that was the direct opposite of the formation of its imperial ancestors. It was the Young Turks who
most dramatically initiated the reversal of Ottoman toleration, directing the
massacres of at least a million Armenians and inciting interethnic strife
in the eastern Anatolian lands. The early republic continued these policies

through the removal, relocation, and extermination of Kurdish rebels in Dersim and other regions.[25] Throughout the era of reforms in the Ottoman Empire, such changes in diversity were rationalized as the necessities of modernity and of the marriage between modernity, secularism, and Westernization. In the continuity between the Young Turk reforms and the modern republic, we see these become intertwined and resolved as the various pieces of a new national ideology. As Erik-Jan Zürcher maintains: "Clearly, Kemalist secularism was anchored in the mainstream of Young Turk ideas on the subject. The Kemalist reforms of 1924 (abolition of the caliphate and Şeyhulislamate, closing of religious courts, the unification of education under a secular ministry and the institution of directorates for religious affairs and for charitable foundations) can all be seen as the logical conclusions to the Ottoman secularization process."[26] Moreover, republican state-makers completed the task when they abolished religious courts, dissolved the dervish orders, and closed the local shrines. They instituted European family law, latinized the alphabet, reformed the calendar, and "Turkified" the call to prayer while they simultaneously closed religious schools, centralizing educational institutions under one ministry of education. In making all these changes, "the secularizers saw themselves as bringing into Turkish society the principles of toleration and religious freedom which prevailed in the West."[27] Yet in truth they were abandoning the best practices of the Ottomans.

The decision to build a "Turkish nation" as a counterweight to the old Ottoman imperial society meant the construction of a mono-lingual, mono-ethnic, and (as much as possible) mono-religious society characterized by loyalty to the Turkish state. The assimilationist policies that resulted from this state-driven project were not accepted by all, though many small ethnic groups chose to belong and to participate in the politics of Turkish citizenship. Religion remained a major point of consideration, discussion, contention, and rethinking as the parameters of nationhood were redrawn. In this reconceptualization of the role of religion, we also see that certain groups remained beyond the purview of social administration, which never would have occurred under the Ottomans. That is, through both the new religious administrative project and the constitutional arrangements, Jews, Christians, Alevis, and others were left outside the official realm.[28] As Ergun Özbudun powerfully demonstrates, the 1982 Constitution added to the already existing Turkish national project, by the inclusion of articles that define Turkish nationhood in exclusive and unitary terms.[29]

An alternative to a national ethnic reconceptualization of Turkish nationhood was also the religious rethinking of Islam and Turkishness in a
new light within an old institutional framework. The most obvious sites of
Ottoman–Turkish continuity were to remain in the omnipotent role of the
state, the continuing ability of the state leaders to forge nearly every aspect
of state–society relations, especially shaping the new compact between religion and politics. With the establishment of the Directorate of Religious
Affairs (Diyanet), which was subordinated to the office of the prime minister, the new republic attempted to emulate the institutional control of
religion that the Ottomans had always maintained. Although the Ottoman
control of religious institutions was reenacted, religion was to become a
private matter, which meant that the Diyanet was instructed to issue religious thoughts on private matters. The counterpart Ottoman institution,
though, had addressed its discourse to issues of state and law.[30] Moreover,
beyond the private, the role of the Diyanet—as an institution closely associated with and carefully controlled by an authoritarian state—became
one of promoting national Turkish identity and unity, and representing the
state and its accomplishments in a positive light. The Diyanet became a
national institution, with a forceful message of nation-building as well as
a homogenizing function that privileged Sunni Islam to the detriment of
non-Sunni forms of Islam as well as non-Muslims.[31] Even though the religious administration in the Ottoman Empire was also strongly based on
Sunni orthodoxy, and often fought various forms of heterodoxies, religion
did not and could not destroy diversity. For the Ottomans, religion was certainly a way to build unity—"a cement of society"—but they understood it
as a way to unite elites and people, and worked to encompass the varieties
and forms of worship that different peoples might exhibit.[32] Religion was
more an organizing principle than a unifying standard to build homogeneity in Ottoman society.

Even though the institutions have historical continuity, the goal of the
modern directorate has been to move away from diversity and to build unity. In the context of early republican Turkey and still in contemporary Turkey, religion is also "a cement of society," but in national terms. It served
and continues to serve a state-directed national project of furthering the
Turkish nation as defined by the state. It functions to further the goals and
the needs of the Sunni majority, in education and in civic and national
terms. Furthermore, in contemporary Turkey the role of the Diyanet is not
decreasing, but on the contrary is steadily growing, with a bloated budget,

"2.4 billion Turkish liras, more than the amount allocated for institutions of social policy and even more than some ministries."[33] It has furthermore not demonstrated any willingness to deal with issues concerning the needs of non-Sunni Muslims, such as Alevis, who have been able to mobilize around some demands of political and religious freedom.[34] The Diyanet has provided the language to claim a larger umbrella to Islam, and the Justice and Development Party (AKP) has not been open to responding to the demands made by the Alevi leadership.[35]

Assessments of the contemporary debates on pluralism and democracy in Turkey are not fully encouraging. Murat Akan argues that the AKP policies toward Alevis and the response to the political discourse after the murder in Istanbul in 2007 of Hrant Dink, an Armenian journalist, engendered "serious doubts about how dedicated the party was to challenging the 'nation-state policy' oriented organic state tradition in Turkey."[36] Similarly, Henri Barkey argues that both on the issue of Kurdish reforms and in respect to more general appeals for constitutional reform, the AKP has not shown enough initiative to significantly move in the direction of cultural tolerance and political freedoms. He argues that they have been more careful to respond to the rights of observant Muslims, to the detriment of other, similarly disenfranchised populations.[37] A good case in point is the work to dismantle the headscarf ban at universities, without any other more general programs for constitutional change. This tendency is only growing as the AKP gets more comfortable in its projected electoral victory.

These questions remind us that the Ottoman legacy of pluralism, toleration, and an inclusive state agenda has not yet been attained in contemporary Turkey. The Ottoman past is certainly important and remains viable as a conversational trope, yet it has to be more than that. It has to be understood in terms of state–society relations, negotiations of inclusion and participation, and freedom for religious diversity and observance with an acknowledgment of the strength of plurality of traditions. In many ways what toleration meant in Ottoman society was the acceptance and inclusion of diversity. In modern Turkey, toleration has to work in tandem with extended democratic principles and must translate into equal rights for all Turkish citizens. These are crucial tests for the continued development and liberalization of Turkey, not only for its own sake, but for the tremendous object lessons it carries for the rest of the Islamic world vis-à-vis questions of Islam and democracy.

Notes

1. Benjamin Braude and Bernard Lewis, eds., *Christians and Jews in the Ottoman Empire: The Functioning of a Plural Society*, 2 vols. (New York: Holmes and Meier, 1982).

2. Mark R. Cohen, *Under Crescent and Cross: The Jews in the Middle Ages* (Princeton, N.J.: Princeton University Press, 1994), and "Persecution, Response, and Collective Memory: The Jews of Islam in the Classical Period," in Daniel Frank, ed., *The Jews of Medieval Islam: Community, Society, and Identity* (Leiden: Brill, 1995), 145–164.

3. Aron Rodrigue, "Difference and Tolerance in the Ottoman Empire," interview by Nancy Reynolds, *Stanford Humanities Review* 5 (1995): 81–92.

4. Bruce Masters, *Christians and Jews in the Ottoman Arab World: The Roots of Sectarianism* (Cambridge: Cambridge University Press, 2001).

5. Peter Sugar, *Southeastern Europe Under Ottoman Rule, 1354–1804* (Seattle: University of Washington Press, 1977), 50; Ömer Lütfi Barkan, "Essai sur les données statistiques des registres de recencement dans l'Empire ottoman aux XVe et XVIe siècles," *Journal of the Economic and Social History of the Orient* 1 (1957): 7–36.

6. Halil İnalcik, "The Ottoman State: Economy and Society, 1300–1600," in Halil İnalcik and Donald Quataert, eds., *An Economic and Social History of the Ottoman Empire, 1300–1914* (Cambridge: Cambridge University Press, 1994), 257.

7. Claude Cahen, *Pre-Ottoman Turkey: A General Survey of the Material and Spiritual Culture and History, c. 1071–1330*, trans. J. Jones-Williams (London: Sidgwick and Jackson, 1968), 203.

8. Halil İnalcık, "Ottoman Methods of Conquest," *Studia Islamica* 3 (1954): 103–129, and "The Status of the Greek Orthodox Patriarch Under the Ottomans," *Turcica* 21–23 (1991): 407–437.

9. Heath W. Lowry, *The Nature of the Early Ottoman State* (Albany: State University of New York Press, 2003), 139.

10. Fikret Adanır, "The Ottoman Peasantries, c. 1360–c. 1860," in Tom Scott, ed., *The Peasantries of Europe: From the Fourteenth to the Eighteenth Centuries* (London: Longman, 1998), 277.

11. Charles A. Frazee, *Catholics and Sultans: The Church and the Ottoman Empire, 1453–1923* (Cambridge: Cambridge University Press, 1983).

12. Metin Kunt, "State and Sultan up to the Age of Süleyman: Frontier Principality to World Empire," in Metin Kunt and Christine Woodhead, eds., *Süleyman the Magnificent and His Age: The Ottoman Empire in the Early Modern World* (London: Addison-Wesley, 1995), 11.

13. Elizabeth Zachariadou, "Notes sur la population de l'Asie Mineure turque au XIVe siècle," *Byzantinische Forschungen* 12 (1987): 228–231.

14. Şerif Mardin, "The Just and the Unjust," *Daedalus: Journal of the American Academy of Arts and Sciences* 120 (1991): 113–129; "Religion and Secularism in Turkey," in Ali Kazancıgil and Ergun Özbudun, eds., *Atatürk: Founder of a Modern State* (Hamden, Conn.: Archon Books, 1981), 192–195; and "Power, Civil Society, and Culture in the Ottoman Empire," *Comparative Studies in Society and History* 11 (1969): 258–281.

15. Karen Barkey, *Empire of Difference: The Ottomans in Comparative Perspective* (Cambridge: Cambridge University Press, 2008).

16. Haim Gerber, *State, Society, and Law in Islam: Ottoman Law in Comparative Perspective* (Albany: State University of New York Press, 1994).

17. Mardin, "Just and the Unjust," 128.

18. For more details, see Barkey, *Empire of Difference*.

19. James C. Scott, *Seeing Like a State: How Certain Schemes to Improve the Human Condition Have Failed* (New Haven, Conn.: Yale University Press, 1998).

20. Halil İnalcık, "The Policy of Mehmed II Toward the Greek Population of Istanbul and the Byzantine Buildings of the City," *Dumbarton Oaks Papers* 23–24 (1969–1970): 247.

21. James D. Fearon and David D. Laitin, "Explaining Interethnic Cooperation," *American Political Science Review* 90 (1996): 715–735.

22. I take the term from S. N. Eisenstadt, "Multiple Modernities," *Daedalus* 129 (2000): 1–29. For a discussion of the multiple ways in which the eighteenth century displayed various and different pockets of modernity in the Ottoman Empire, see Barkey, *Empire of Difference*.

23. Since the point of this chapter is not to give a historical analysis of the periods of reform, Young Turks, and the modern Turkish Republic, I am concerned only with an analytical summary of the major transformations. For serious analyses of the period, see Şerif Mardin, *The Genesis of Young Ottoman Thought: A Study in the Modernization of Turkish Political Ideas* (Princeton, N.J.: Princeton University Press, 1962); Şükrü Hanioğlu, *The Young Turks in Opposition* (New York: Oxford University Press, 1995), and *Preparation for a Revolution: The Young Turks, 1902–1908* (Oxford: Oxford University Press, 2001); Erik-Jan Zürcher, "Kemalist Düşüncenin Osmanlı Kaynakları," in Tanıl Bora, ed., *Modern Türkiye'de Siyasal Düşünce* (Istanbul: İletişim Yayınları, 2002): 44–55, and *Turkey: A Modern History* (London: Tauris, 1993); Bernard Lewis, *The Emergence of Modern Turkey*, 2nd ed. (Oxford: Oxford University Press, 1961); Stanford J. Shaw and Ezel Kural Shaw, *History of the Ottoman Empire and Modern Turkey*, 2 vols. (Cambridge: Cambridge University Press, 1977); and Roderic H. Davison, *Reform in the Ottoman Empire, 1856–1876* (Princeton, N.J.: Princeton University Press, 1963).

24. The literature on nation-state formation is vast and informative. See the classical works of Charles Tilly, *The Formation of National States in Western Europe*

(Princeton, N.J.: Princeton University Press, 1975), and *Coercion and Capital and European States, A.D. 990–1992* (Oxford: Blackwell, 1990); Pierre Bourdieu, Loic J. D. Wacquant, and Samar Farage, "Rethinking the State: Genesis and Structure of the Bureaucratic Field," *Sociological Theory* 12 (1994): 1–18; Michael Mann, *The Dark Side of Democracy: Explaining Ethnic Cleansing* (Cambridge: Cambridge University Press, 2004); and Anthony W. Marx, *Faith in Nation: Exclusionary Origins of Nationalism* (Oxford: Oxford University Press, 2003).

25. Murat Yüksel, "Taming the Nation: Forced Migration and Politics of Internal Displacement in the Making of Modern Turkey, 1923–1950" (Ph.D. diss., Columbia University, 2006).

26. Zürcher, "Kemalist Düşüncenin Osmanlı Kaynakları" (translation at http://www.leiden.edu).

27. Mardin, "Just and the Unjust," 127.

28. David Shankland, *Islam and Society in Turkey* (Walkington: Eothen Press, 1999), 22.

29. Ergun Özbudun, "The Turkish Constitutional Court and Political Crisis" (chap. 6, this volume).

30. Haldun Gülalp, "Enlightenment by Fiat: Secularization and Democracy in Turkey," *Middle Eastern Studies* 41 (2005): 351–372.

31. Murat Akan, "Twin Tolerations or Siamese Twins? Kemalist Laicism and Political Islam in Turkey," in Douglas Chalmers and Scott Mainwaring, eds., *Institutions and Democracy: Essay in Honor of Alfred Stepan* (Notre Dame, Ind.: University of Notre Dame Press, 2011). See also Ergun Özbudun, "Turkey—Plural Society and Monolithic State" (chap. 3, this volume).

32. The term "religion as a cement of society" was used by Atatürk and many early Republican politicians as well as members of the AKP today. See Akan, "Twin Tolerations or Siamese Twins?"; and M. Şükrü Hanioğlu, "The Historical Roots of Kemalism" (chap. 2, this volume).

33. Akan, "Twin Tolerations or Siamese Twins?" 13.

34. For a discussion of this point, see ibid.

35. Joost Lagendijk, "Turkey's Accession to the European Union and the Role of the Justice and Development Party" (chap. 7, this volume).

36. Akan, "Twin Tolerations or Siamese Twins?" 35.

37. Henri J. Barkey, "Turkey's Moment of Inflection," *Survival* 52 (2010): 39–50.

2

The Historical Roots of Kemalism

M. ŞÜKRÜ HANİOĞLU

What Is Kemalism?

In order to trace the historical roots of Kemalism, one must first conceptualize what it is—a difficult task made more so by the fact that Mustafa Kemal Atatürk, the founder of the Turkish Republic, did not actually attempt to produce an ideology. It was his followers who strove to craft a creed called Kemalism (or "Kamalism," as it was known in the 1930s) based on his main ideas and practices. The intellectuals and statesmen who attempted to produce a Kemalist ideology knew well that this was an exacting undertaking. In fact, two major Kemalisms, a right-wing and a left-wing version, emerged during Mustafa Kemal's lifetime. The major difficulty was the lack of a coherent philosophy, ideological tenets, or a major book explaining the ideology.

Atatürk was no Marx or Lenin. He was not a thinker who produced a major philosophy or theory attempting to encompass all aspects of life and society. He was not even a devout disciple of an ideology. Likewise, he did not try to reinterpret and implement a philosophy within a society, as Brazilian leaders did when they made positivism the official ideology of their state. Indeed, a scholar of political theory might find Atatürk's ideas extremely pragmatic and on shaky theoretical ground. This should not, however, make us underestimate the transformation that he brought about as a down-to-earth leader who strove to materialize a vision not by depending on an ideology, but by utilizing a range of different sources without paying much attention to contradictions among them. Interestingly enough, Mustafa Kemal was not even the initiator of this vision. The Westernizers of the Second Constitutional Period had envisioned a Mannheimian utopia consisting of a scientist society; they categorically rejected tradition and wholeheartedly embraced a modernity described with the parameters of an "international (European) civilization." Mustafa Kemal, as an "authoritarian savior," brought this utopia into being. Thus his role was that of interpreter and implementer; more precisely, he was the individual who transformed an intellectual utopia envisaged by a marginal group into a political program, and then proceeded to implement it vigorously as head of state.

The lack of an ideological basis for policy naturally meant an absence of clear ideological tenets as well. Only later did those intellectuals and statesmen who attempted to produce a Kemalist ideology present the so-called six arrows of Mustafa Kemal's Republican People's Party as the tenets of this creed. Yet these arrows—symbolizing the principles of republicanism, nationalism, populism, étatism, laïcité, and revolutionary character—were too vague and remained open to different kinds of interpretation.

Additionally, there was no major treatise to serve as the basis of an ideology. Mustafa Kemal's followers attempted to turn his magnum opus, The Speech, into such a text, albeit unsuccessfully. It was nothing other than a long description of the Turkish War of Independence and major events occurring in its wake, from the vantage point of the new leader of Turkey. Supplemented with hundreds of documents reproduced to support Mustafa Kemal's narrative, The Speech looks like a hybrid of a historical monograph and a memoir. Thus, with the exception of Mustafa Kemal's advice to the Turkish youth to "safeguard Turkish independence and the Republic under all circumstances," given at end of the text, its use as the guiding book of an ideology was difficult, if not impossible.

While the lack of guiding text was an obvious obstacle standing before the intellectuals and statesmen who attempted to mold a Kemalist ideology, another problem that exacerbated their difficulties stemmed from Mustafa Kemal's own political career. Between 1919 and 1922, Mustafa Kemal was compelled to adopt both socialist and Islamist rhetoric.[1] As the leader of a movement ostensibly fighting a war of independence to save the caliph but receiving financial and military aid from the Bolsheviks and Muslims in the Soviet Union and India, respectively, he adopted a unique combination of Pan-Islamist and socialist rhetoric. For instance, when he invited the Muslims to extend a helping hand to the Turkish War of Independence he asked them to "hear this voice of *sharī'a*."[2] Similarly, he stated that the group of people that he and his comrades were trying to save was composed not only of Turks, but also of many Muslim ethnic groups, such as Turks, Kurds, and Circassians, who formed an "Islamic community."[3]

Meanwhile, during the war he had used rhetoric similar to that of the Muslim Communist leader Mirsäyet Soltangäliev to promote "a special form of communism" for Turkey.[4] Likewise, as a pragmatic politician, he limited his criticism of Communism during the early years of the new regime and especially during his election campaign in 1923, until the obliteration of opposition in 1925. Obviously he had merely pretended to be an Islamist, Pan-Islamist, Bolshevik, and internationalist, but during the first four years of his political leadership he made a host of statements that contradicted his later policies. Similarly, his actions and rhetoric as a political leader before and after the consolidation of the single-party regime differed considerably. The conflicting rhetoric advanced by Mustafa Kemal made the molding of a Kemalist ideology extremely difficult, a challenge captured succinctly by the title of a recent book by a prominent journalist: *But Which Atatürk?*[5]

Against all these odds, however, Turkish intellectuals and statesmen attempted to construct an ideology out of Mustafa Kemal's ideas and the reforms of what they called "the Turkish revolution." Initial attempts toward this goal took place during the 1930s, while Mustafa Kemal was still alive. In 1932, a group of left-wing intellectuals began publishing a journal called *Kadro* (Cadre) and strove to interpret the Turkish revolution using a loosely Marxist, historical materialist theoretical approach. In the words of Şevket Süreyya Aydemir, one of the group's leading intellectuals, their aim was "to transform our revolution . . . into one based on a chain of thought [and] . . . by turning [this] chain of thought into an ideology, have it serve as the foundation of the revolution."[6] They conceded that the Turkish revolution had not been produced by an ideology, but claimed that it was nonetheless an innate response to the expansion of capitalism (as well as its natural consequence, colonialism) and that it represented a decisive victory against these evils.[7] Thus the Turkish revolutionary state could not be a bourgeois state as produced by the French Revolution or a proletarian state as generated by the Communist revolution, but was the first example of the liberation of a technologically backward "semi-colony."[8]

They further maintained that all national liberation movements resembled one another and that the Turkish example led by Mustafa Kemal should serve as a model for the colonized peoples of Asia and Africa. To achieve this goal, the Turkish experience should be turned into an ideology that would serve all oppressed people. According to these intellectuals, unlike societies in the West divided by class, Turkey was on its way to becoming a classless society; thus intellectuals, together with Mustafa Kemal as their brain, should serve as the engine of the revolution and change, and the state should be their main agent.[9] They were also quite positive about the transformation that the revolution had brought about. Mustafa Kemal initially allowed these intellectuals to publish their journal, but he disliked their attempt to produce an ideology out of his work or the Turkish experience. He was also particularly dismayed by their application of Marxist analyses, even though these intellectuals distorted Marxist theory to an extreme and adopted quite an idealistic approach. The regime forced the intellectuals to abandon their attempts and shut down *Kadro* in 1935.

During the same period, another journal, published as the organ of the People's Houses, represented the attempt to forge a right-wing Kemalist ideology. The statesmen and intellectuals who began publishing the journal *Ülkü* (Ideal) in 1933 wished to produce an ideology resembling German National Socialism and Italian Fascism. Yet despite the visceral hatred that they harbored toward Bolshevism, they also benefited from Soviet methods of ideology diffusion. This movement's main ideologue, Mehmet Recep (Peker), a former officer and the general secretary of the country's sole political party, was deeply impressed by the Partito Nazionale Fascista and the Nazionalsozialistiche Deutsche Arbeiterpartei. He wished to elevate the Republican People's Party to a status similar to that of these organizations while underscoring the differences of the Turkish case and repeating Mustafa Kemal's maxim that "we can only be likened to ourselves."[10] In 1934 Mehmet Recep started lecturing on the "Turkish revolution" at the first Turkish Revolution Institute and prepared a textbook to serve as the basis of Kemalism. While he wished to have Mustafa Kemal as the leading guide, he also desired to become a party secretary similar to Stalin in the All-Union Communist Party. In 1935 his plan expressing this desire and a fully fledged corporatism was rejected by Atatürk, who dismissed him from his post the following year.[11] He and his friends, however, continued their work to forge a scientist, corporatist, étatist, and solidarist Kemalist ideology expressed as a personality cult.

Aside from the single-party ideologies promoting corporatism and the strong scientism prevailing in early republican intellectual circles, right-wing intellectuals and statesmen were also deeply influenced by Alfred Fouillée and Léon Bourgeois in advancing solidarism. According to one of the leaders of this right-wing Kemalism, "one of the greatest duties of the Turkish intellectual [was] to invent the science of Kemalism . . . through scientific methods and to turn it into a societal engineering."[12] In the words of Şevket Kansu, the leading pyhsical anthropologist of the period, "this pure, masculine, and robust ideology that can be called National Kemalism" should use bio-sociology and even eugenics to form the new society.[13] According to the right-wing Kemalists, the greatest characteristic of the Turkish revolution was "its expression in a real genius and not . . . in a prophet created by hidden psychological illnesses."[14] Mustafa Kemal was "the first great guide to find cures to the social ills."[15] Thus the ideology inspired by "the first genius who manifests both the soul of a societal guide and the mind of an intellectual"[16] should be solidarist and corporatist while rejecting individualism, liberalism, and socialism.

This right-wing Kemalism promoting a totalitarianism akin to analogous ideologies prevailing in the Europe of the 1930s enjoyed better success and continuity, although Mustafa Kemal himself remained aloof toward this initiative. When the founder of the Turkish Republic passed away in 1938, right-wing Kemalism had established a virtual monopoly over the concept. Despite Atatürk's successor İsmet İnönü's more accommodating attitude toward the left-wing Kemalists, the right-wing Kemalism formed the backbone of the official version strenuously promoted between 1938 and 1950. In general, this Kemalism advocated social transformation and authoritarian developmentalism under a single-party regime. It depended on a scientist Weltanschauung, a new interpretation of Turkish nationalism based mainly on racial anthropology, and a robust personality cult.

Although Mustafa Kemal appeared as the revered leader of two different ideologies, the two branches did share significant ideological characteristics. Both promoted a strong étatism, a concept favored by many after the Great Depression. They also endorsed a single-party regime to transform Turkish society and viewed multiparty politics as a threat to "progress." Interestingly enough, one of Atatürk's confidants, Falih Rıfkı (Atay), recommended the adoption of Soviet and fascist practices in the early 1930s.[17]

For many Turkish intellectuals and statesmen authoritarianism seemed to be the only alternative for implementing the transformation program; thus they wished to benefit from the fascist and Bolshevik practices despite the substantial differences between them.

Surprisingly, the switch to a multiparty system after World War II did not alter Kemalism's role in the system despite its original authoritarian character. Rather, the new system prompted the multiplication of Kemalism alongside the reproduction of political parties and opened a new period in which the maxim "More Kemalist than thou" reigned supreme. Transplanting an authoritarian ideology into a semi-democratic system brought about numerous problems, however. The establishment responded to this uncontrolled "Kemalisticization" of politics and the relatively free discussion taking place under the shield of Kemalism by redefining the ideology's "official version" and constraining all politics within its boundaries. This does not mean that official Kemalism remained an unchanged dogma. Rather, the Turkish establishment could use this "official Kemalism"—that is, a flexible interpretation of Atatürk's various sayings and acts—as a tool to guide and interpret contemporary politics. Thus it could be étatist or liberal and elitist or populist, depending on the interpretations and sayings referenced. Similarly, it could promote either an active foreign policy by referring to Atatürk's policy during the Alexandretta crisis or inactivity by referring to his utterance, "Peace at home, peace in the world."

Especially since 1960, there have been several Kemalisms competing acrimoniously against one another. It should be remembered that even Celâl Bayar, the third president of the Turkish Republic—who had asserted that "to love Atatürk is a national cult"[18]—was tried after a coup d'état for deviating from the path of Atatürk.

The aim of this chapter is not to trace the roots of all Kemalisms, but to uncover the roots of the early Kemalism that emerged in the 1930s by relating it to Mustafa Kemal's own work. Likewise, I will dwell on this early Kemalism's main ideological precepts rather than its political aspects, since its founders based it on the late Ottoman authoritarianism led by the Committee of Union and Progress with adaptations from the totalitarian regimes of the post–Great War era.[19] In addition to a strong personality cult, the early Kemalism of the 1930s was based on three major tenets: scientism, Westernization, and Turkish nationalism. Although the founder of the republic and his disciples who produced the Kemalist ideology redefined these concepts, they did not coin them, but rather based their interpretations on existing theories. Here I will discuss these elements in turn.

The Roots of Kemalist Scientism and Its Approach to Religion

Mustafa Kemal himself belonged to the second generation of the Young Turk movement, composed primarily of college students, low-ranking bureaucrats, and officers. An overwhelming number of these young men were disciples of a peculiar mid-nineteenth-century German philosophy called *Vulgärmaterialismus*. This was a vulgarized version of the doctrine of materialism that mixed ideas on materialism, scientism, and social Darwinism. Although they took an extremely hostile view of religion, many Young Turks saw no irony in the fact that they themselves worshiped prominent German materialists like gods and treated their works, above all Ludwig Büchner's *Kraft und Stoff* (Force and Matter), as Bibles. Their attitude seems taken straight out of Dostoyevsky's novel *Besy* (The Possessed), in which the protagonist assaults the Christian icons of his landowner with an ax, only to replace them with candle-adorned lecterns bearing the books of Ernst Haeckel, Jacob Moleschott, Karl Vogt, and Büchner.[20] The Ottoman materialists were not troubled by the tensions between nineteenth-century German vulgar materialism, with its exclusive emphasis on the empirical, and the materialism of eighteenth-century French philosophers such as Voltaire and Baron d'Holbach. Late Ottoman materialism was not only a further vulgarization of the German original but also a medley of highly disparate ideas, the common denominator of which was the rejection of religion. Although an extremely marginal group at the time, the Young Turks were destined to rule the Islamic caliphate for almost a decade and then go on to craft a secular nation-state out of its remains. It was by a bizarre twist of fate indeed that the German doctrine of *Vulgärmaterialismus* came to bear its most meaningful fruits in a context wholly alien to its original environment, and that a further vulgarized version of its central tenets would in time form one of the ideological pillars of the Turkish nation-state.

Mustafa Kemal and his fellow founders of the Turkish state belonged to the educated class of a generation that embraced a crude conception of science as a panacea for the ills of the empire, and saw in the doctrine of vulgar materialism a handbook for constructing a prosperous, rational, and irreligious modern society. They avidly read such Ottoman journals as *Musavver Cihan*, which offered "Chemistry Lessons for Everybody,"[21] provided scientific explanations for "supernatural" events, and conveyed the essence of Darwinism by means of simple illustrations depicting the extinction of species through evolution.[22] But unlike their popular counterparts in Europe, such as *Die Gegenwart*, *Die Natur*, and *Science pour tous*, Ottoman materialist publications were treated as serious scientific journals; and their most important message—"science reigns supreme"—became the motto of a generation. Consequently, a huge proportion of that generation's educated class espoused a view of human history that revolved around the notion of a perpetual struggle between science and religion, which would inevitably end with the triumph of science and its coronation as the new and final religion. Like most millenarians, they tended to the belief that the victory of science would take place in their own lifetime. Not surprisingly, when John W. Draper's *Conflict Between Religion and Science* was translated into Turkish in 1897, it became a best seller in the Ottoman Empire.[23]

The grip on the Young Turk movement by a group of individuals of scientist orientation gained force after 1889, when a society named the Ottoman Union Committee was established at the Imperial Medical Academy. One of its early members, Dr. Şerafeddin Mağmumî, gained notoriety for his suggestion to abandon poetry, since it was "not scientific."[24] In 1895, upon the insistence of a devout positivist who assumed the leadership in the movement, the name of the organization was changed to the Ottoman Committee of Union and Progress (CUP).[25] The transformation of the CUP from a materialist student club into an activist committee seeking and planning revolution in a polyethnic empire was to result in the obfuscation of its scientist agenda in later years, particularly after the Young Turk Revolution of 1908. The pillar of scientism was never abandoned, however, and the founders of modern Turkey could again be more open in stressing the importance of science its conflict with religion.

As stated earlier, Mustafa Kemal belonged to the second generation of Young Turks, born in the early 1880s. His upbringing in Salonica and education at secular institutions undoubtedly made him more receptive to criticisms of the religious establishment. The Royal Military Academy was not a hotbed of Ottoman materialist activism (although one of its prominent graduates, Beşir Fu'ad, committed suicide in 1887 just to prove that life was a mere "scientific" phenomenon).[26] Like many of his peers, Mustafa

Kemal gained his first exposure to the movement through journals and pamphlets. He read selections from Büchner's *Kraft und Stoff*, and seemed particularly struck by the suggestion that human thinking had a material basis.[27] Like many others in his generation, Mustafa Kemal confused the vulgar materialism popularized by the likes of Büchner with the materialist tradition of Baron d'Holbach and Voltaire.[28] A similar pattern of oversimplification plagued his vigorous espousal of evolutionary theory, derived primarily from Herbert George Wells. He once wrote that "since humans came from seas like all other reptiles, our forefathers were fish. . . . We are monkeys but our mental senses are human."[29] His frequent references to life as a "natural struggle for survival" reveal strong Huxleyian social Darwinist convictions.[30] Mustafa Kemal and his fellow nation-state founders adopted Thomas Henry Huxley's interpretations of Darwinism through H. G. Wells's *Outline of History*. An attempt to explain history from the creation of cosmos to modern times, this work also served as the basis for history taught at Turkish high schools between 1931 and 1941.

Although he read through the major works of popular materialism and was deeply influenced by them, Mustafa Kemal never became a scientist thinker in his own right. The simple insight he derived from what he read was that science promoted progress, while religion undermined it. One of his best-known aphorisms, "The most truthful guide in life is science," reveals a simplistic worldview that ascribed an overarching role to science in every aspect of human life. "Seeking any guide other than science," he continued, making a veiled allusion to religion, "is thoughtlessness, prevarication, and ignorance."[31] The notes he scribbled in books about religion bear the unmistakable imprint of scientism. He wrote, for instance, that religions were man-made phenomena, produced by their respective prophets in concrete historical circumstances: "Moses was a person who strove towards the emancipation of Jews whimpering under the lashes of Egyptians"[32] or "Jesus was a person who comprehended the unlimited poverty of his time and turned the reaction to the pains of his age into a religion of love."[33] As for Islam, he agreed with the comment maintaining that it had not "arisen as a result of the national evolution of the Arabs, but as a consequence of the emergence of Muḥammad."[34]

Such criticisms went as far as the espousal of the Dutch Orientalist Reinhart Dozy's claim that the emergence of Islam resulted from the Prophet Muḥammad's alleged muscular hysteria, a claim originally put forward by Aloys Sprenger. A Young Turk journal published initially in Geneva and

Cairo later propagated such theses in the Ottoman capital.[35] This journal, ironically named *İctihad* (Ijtihād), attempted to recast Islam as a materialist philosophy, maintaining that it could be used only as a cultural resource to build the new irreligious society of the future. The idea of a new religion free of dogma, myth, supranatural command, and rites and rituals was taken from the French philosopher-poet Jean-Marie Guyau and became a tenet of the late Ottoman scientist vision.[36] The journal naturally aroused strong reactions from all actors. While Sharif Ḥusayn of Mecca listed the attacks on Islam published in the pages of this journal as one of the leading causes of the Arab Revolt of 1916,[37] Mustafa Kemal is said to have remarked to the editor of *İctihad*, up for an open seat in the Turkish chamber in 1925: "Doctor, until now you have written about many things. Now we can make them reality."[38] Furthermore, the founder of the republic made Celâl Nuri (İleri) and Kılıçzâde Hakkı (Kılıçoğlu)—two leading intellectuals who advanced the most extreme theses on issues of religion, modernity, and Westernization in the pages of this journal—deputies in the Turkish Grand National Assembly.

Although he was later idealized as a mythic harbinger of change, it is important to realize that Mustafa Kemal emerged from within a specific social context, which limited the range of options open to any prospective revolutionary leader. The important point to understand here is that many of the radical ideas destined to become central planks in Mustafa Kemal's reform program were widely held in intellectual circles at the turn of the twentieth century and were expressed with increasing explicitness after the Young Turk Revolution. For instance, key elements of the Turkish Republic's program to promote superstition at the expense of religion as a tool to bring about modernity in the 1920s could be found in the pages of *İctihad* twenty years before. Indeed, many former Young Turks of scientist orientation later described Mustafa Kemal as a "savior authority" who had brought their ideas to fruition.[39]

Like many Ottoman literati, Mustafa Kemal realized that Islam was so deeply embedded in Ottoman culture that it could not be eliminated with the wave of a wand. Accordingly, he adopted a much softer approach to religion than his contemporaries in the Soviet Union. His attitude can be summed up in the famous maxim of the Westernizers of the Second Constitutional Period: "Religion is the science of the masses, whereas science is the religion of the elite."[40] According to this line of thought, an all-out attack on Islam in a predominately Muslim society would be unwise. Instead, a redefined version of Islam could be co-opted to serve as a vehicle for progress.

The establishment of the Directorate of Religious Affairs on the very same day as the abolition of the caliphate in March 1924 expressed the new regime's and its leader's strong desire for an ambitious religious reform program to redefine and control Islam. This institution, under the strict guidance of the new administration, would end the relatively free hand in interpreting Islam that the old religious establishment had enjoyed. Musta-fa Kemal did not wish to launch a campaign to ridicule religion in the eyes of the masses, as Soviet leaders had. In fact, he self-censored his strongly critical views on Islam that had been drafted for an official book of civics, and left stronger criticisms to other ideologues.[41] Like the Westernizers of the pre-1914 period, he instead wanted to reform Islam for the masses by rendering religion as an easy-to-understand guide for better morals. In ad-dition, he wished to include the Turkification of Islam in the reform pro-gram, as described by Ziya Gökalp in his *Yeni Hayat* (New Life, 1918) and *Türkçülüğün Esasları* (The Principles of Turkism, 1923). Thus while a pleth-ora of anti-religious publications, such as Holbach's *Le bon sens*, appeared as state-sponsored publications and extreme anti-religious journals, such as *İctihad* and *Hür Fikir* (Libre Pensée), enjoyed full liberty, the state also launched a major religious reform program.

The main idea behind this initiative was that a reform program similar to that of the Protestant Reformation of the sixteenth century would prompt a twentieth-century Turkish renaissance. Thus unlike the puritanist Muslim movements such as Wahhabism and Salafism, which proposed a return to the original sources of Islam for the sake of creating a new orthodoxy, Mus-tafa Kemal and his Kemalist followers wished to do the same to inspire a Turkish renaissance. In this regard, he also wished to bring about chang-es similar to those that Lutheran or Calvinist movements had achieved in Christendom; indeed, Charles H. Sherrill, the American ambassador to Turkey, compared him with Luther and Wycliffe for his efforts.[42]

In 1923, Mustafa Kemal declared that a new library of books drawn from three continents would become a source for "contemporary *mujtahids*" to reform the religion. In 1925 the Grand National Assembly commissioned a Turkish translation of the Qur'ān and a multivolume Turkish Qur'ān commentary and *ḥadīth* compilation.[43] The assumption was that the avail-ability of such sources in the vernacular would have an impact similar to that of Luther's Bible of 1534. It was not that the Qur'ān had never before been translated into Turkish: early renderings into Turkic languages went back many centuries, just as did translations of the Bible into Germanic languages. In addition, a number of contemporary versions in a more contemporary Turkish had appeared after 1841. But the hope was that a new translation would pave the way for a purification of the religion, a Turkish *Ralliement*, and a renaissance among the masses. In a similar vein, starting in 1927 the Directorate of Religious Affairs not only decided the topics of *khuṭba*s to be delivered at Friday prayers, but also required that prayers and direct quotations from the Qur'ān and *ḥadīth*s have Turkish translations. Any admonitions or interpretations were henceforth to be given only in Turkish. However, attempts at a full switch to Turkish met with little enthusiasm, and were abandoned after 1928. A similar fate befell Mustafa Kemal's stipulation in 1932 that *khuṭba*s be given in frock-coats and no headgear.[44] Legal changes made in the same year nevertheless required the use of Turkish at three stages of the ritual prayer: the call to prayer (*adhān*), the invitation to prayer at the mosque (*qad qāmat al-ṣalāt*), and the recitation of the phrase "God is Great (*Allāhu Akbar*)."[45]

Mustafa Kemal and the republican leaders assumed that the original sources, now available in Turkish, would render the religious establishment, the *'ulamā'*, and the *Sufi tarīqa*s obsolete and help them privatize religion in addition to promoting a "Turkish Islam." Thus while launching an ambitious reform project, the republican authorities closed down the *madrasah*s in 1924 and outlawed all the *tarīqa*s and dervish lodges (*tekye*s and *zāwiya*s) in 1925.[46] In Mustafa Kemal's words: "The most truthful *tarīqa* is the *tarīqa* of civilization," and "Primitive individuals seeking moral and material prosperity through the guidance of such and such a sheikh despite the enlightenment of science, technology, and civilization as a whole should not exist in Turkish society."[47] It was thought that the elimination of the orthodox and *Sufi* religious establishments and traditional religious education and their replacement with the original sources available to all in the vernacular language would pave the road to producing a new vision of Islam open to progress, modern life, and a society ruled by a scientist and Turkish nationalist ideology.

Obviously, the republican leaders grossly overestimated the potential of the genre of Qur'ānic interpretation and pinned too much hope on the Turkish translation of the Muslim holy text and the *ḥadīth* collection. Efforts toward the Turkification of Islam made only limited headway among the masses. Despite the elite's glorification, pious Muslims in general adopted a critical stand vis-à-vis these attempts, and thus the republican leaders never implemented the final phase of the reform program, aimed at shifting to Turkish in all rites. In fact, despite its noteworthy impact on Muslim thinking, the unfinished *al-Manār* commentary had also affected the masses quite insignificantly, and a return to the original sources thesis, an idea championed by the Salafis, had demonstrated a negligible influence even on the Arab public who could comprehend those texts in Arabic. The downfall of the single party in the first free Turkish elections held in 1950 also marked the end of the religious reforms, and call to prayer returned to Arabic at once. Finally, the early republican leaders undervalued Islamic social networks and falsely assumed, like many fin-de-siècle Western intellectuals, that religion would soon become a memory of the past.

In addition to such secularizing legislation, Mustafa Kemal promoted reforms aimed at introducing new secular mores. Many of these changes entailed abolishing symbols associated with Islam and replacing them with equivalents associated with Christianity. The adoption of the Gregorian calendar in 1925 (including the concepts "b.c." and "a.d."), the replacement of the fez with the European hat in 1926, the switch from the Arabo-Persian Ottoman script to a modified Latin alphabet in 1928, and the acceptance of Sunday as the weekly holiday instead of Friday in 1935—all these further sidelined Islam in Turkish society and strengthened a secular way of life.

Like many Young Turks deeply influenced by the 1905 victory of the secularists in the "war of two Frances," Mustafa Kemal viewed French *laïcité* as the authentic form of secularism and sought to apply it to the letter—and even surpass it—in Turkey. Like its French counterpart, Turkish *laïcité* was aimed at controlling religion and reducing it to a private affair instead of merely creating a separation between the state and the mosque. Early Kemalism adopted an antagonistic stance vis-à-vis religion and internalized this version of secularism as not only the authentic but also the only form of secularism. In addition, as a result of its scientistic interpretation of religion, early Kemalism viewed religiosity as the antithesis of secularism. Unlike Mustafa Kemal, the early Kemalist ideologues found little value in reforming Islam and wished to transform Kemalism based on such a secularism into a religion. In fact, a deputy, Şeref Aykut, called it "a religion promoting a faith of living" in 1936 in a book on "Kamâlism."[48] As late as 1945, the Turkish lexicon prepared by the Turkish Language Association provided the following example in its entry for religion as the metaphorical meaning of the gloss: "An idea or ideal to which one fervently adheres.

Kemalism is the religion of the Turk."⁴⁹ Likewise, Behçet Kemal Çağlar's *Mevlid* eulogized Mustafa Kemal as a prophet, imitating the famous example of this genre composed by Süleyman Çelebi (d. 1422) in honor of the Prophet Muḥammad.⁵⁰ A poem by the Republican People's Party deputy Kemalettin Kamu ran:

> Çankaya [Mustafa Kemal's presidential residence]—here Moses
>   reached spiritual perfection
> Here Jesus ascended
> . . .
> Neither miracle nor sorcery
> Let the Arab possess the Ka'ba
> Çankaya is sufficient for us.⁵¹

While Kemalism has continued to make strong claims on the "sacred" by creating a parallel sacrosanct sphere through its peculiar interpretation of *laïcité*, it has gradually blunted its stance against religion and abandoned its insistence on being a fully fledged belief system. Official Kemalism attempted to accomplish a peace with Islam in the aftermath of the 1980 coup d'état and has supported the "Turkish-Islamic synthesis" thesis. This was obviously a major deviation not only from early Kemalism's approach to Islam, but also from the Turkish nationalism redefined and reproduced by this ideology. Not surprisingly, this repositioning on the part of the establishment prompted the orthodox Kemalists to reemphasize the original theses of the 1930s and to mold the "Ulusalcı" version sixty years later. Despite being a major example of anachronism, in many regards this version represents original Kemalism better than its rivals, and helps us better comprehend the strained relations between a strictly scientist, anti-clerical ideology and the masses that it dubbed as backward crowds.

The Roots of Kemalist Westernization

The roots of Kemalist Westernization may be found in the Westernist movement of the Second Constitutional Period. In fact, the famous Westernization plan published in two installments in the scientist journal *İctihad* in 1913 looks like a blueprint of both the early republican reforms and the later Kemalist vision of modernity. This plan, presented as a report of a dream revealed to the author to avoid legal charges by public prosecutors, proposed a thorough Westernization through changes such as the abolition of the fez, the emancipation of women, the closure of dervish lodges, and a reformation of Islam.

The most important characteristic of the Westernization movement of the Second Constitutional Period was its interpretation of modernity.[52] This movement denied the existence of different modernities and envisioned a single (Western) modernity. Furthermore, it viewed modern scientific advances as the driving force of this single modernity. Likewise, Westernists perceived this way of life not as a result of the socioeconomic dynamics prevalent in certain societies, but as in and of itself a determinant of those dynamics. According to this thesis, adopting Western ways would bring about a transformation in social and cultural life going far beyond cosmetic visual changes. It was thus not a coincidence that the scientist Westernizers of the Second Constitutional Period produced the most important works on European good manners and pushed for their acceptance by Ottoman-Turkish society.

Mustafa Kemal was deeply influenced by the Westernizers of the Second Constitutional Period, and, like many of them, he rejected the separation of culture and civilization, a thesis made popular by Ziya Gökalp in late Ottoman intellectual circles. Consequently, unlike many contemporary Muslim Asian leaders—such as Mahathir bin Muhammad of Malaysia—who have defended "Asian Values" (a strongly anti-Western, authoritarian industrial developmentalism promoting an authentic superior culture and despising universal civilization), Mustafa Kemal considered civilization a concept that included all cultures but was shaped by the most advanced European ones.[53] Mustafa Kemal's new Turkish nationalism glorified the Turkish culture as a major source of the modern European civilization and not as something clashing with it. He agreed with those late Ottoman Westernists promoting a wholesale Westernization on the grounds that "there is no other civilization. Civilization is the European civilization."[54] Logically, he thought, those aspects of a non-Western local culture that clashed with the universal civilization should be eliminated. As a natural consequence of this train of thought, Mustafa Kemal also rejected the concept of a non-Western modernity, despite having lived in one of the major examples of such an environment, the late Ottoman Empire. Adopting the "unique and universal civilization" of Europe meant redefining what modernity meant for the country and eradicating local cultural elements (including many traditions genuinely or erroneously associated with Islam).

As a result of this description of modernity and the West, Mustafa Kemal launched one of the most astounding social, cultural, and aesthetic transformation projects of the twentieth century. This project aimed at the elimination of everything that made Turkey look non-Western. Yet Mustafa Kemal did not find these changes enough to transform Turkey into a modern, Western society. He wished the Turks to internalize the "international" culture and values in every aspect of their lives. If we use a concept originally coined by Jürgen Habermas, he wished to have "aesthetic modernity" as well as social modernity, and furthermore imagined a causal relationship between these concepts. This view prompted new approaches to architecture and the arts, resulting, for instance, in the promotion of polyphonic music at the expense of the traditional.

According to Kemalism, adopting Western ways would bring about a transformation in social and cultural life going far beyond cosmetic visual changes. Mushrooming etiquette books, such as the leading wholesale Westernist Abdullah Cevdet's 1927 Turkish rendition of Gaston Jollivet and Marie-Anne L'Heureux's *Pour bien connaître les usages mondains* taught Turks how to kiss the hand of a lady, make home visits, celebrate the New Year, serve Médoc after second courses, and keep fit with exercise (for women).[55] As described by the illustrated Turkish propaganda journal *La Turquie kémaliste (kamâliste)*, which began publication in 1934 and continued after Atatürk's death, Turkish women or villages actually began to resemble their western European role models. But many women had experiences different from those of Mihri İffet Pektaş, one of the first women deputies, who depicted this period of change from her vantage point as a process of enlightenment;[56] for many villages the "progressive village" pictured in this propaganda journal—which resembled so many other single-party publications in Europe—was in many ways foreign.

In the Muslim world, Mustafa Kemal was not unaccompanied in his attempts aimed at making his country look Western through social changes, adoption of civilization, and purging local values believed to be in contradiction to modern civilization. But he had significant advantages in carrying out his grand mission as compared with other contemporary Muslim leaders, such as the Iranian shah Reza Pahlavi and the Afghan ruler Amanullah Khan, who also attempted noteworthy cultural transformations in their societies. The Ottoman Empire had implemented a major reform program for almost one and a half centuries and fashioned its own Ottoman modernity by the turn of the twentieth century (although this could not penetrate to the deeper social strata, especially outside big cities). Serious codification attempts resulted in a hybrid legal system depending on both Western legal principles and Islam. It was an empire with a sizable socialist movement, trade unions, materialist journals, suffragettes, a school of fine arts, lotteries, cinemas, theaters, and newspapers featuring advertisements for women's corsets. The last caliph of the empire was known to paint nude women and compose concertos. Many of these changes, to be sure, affected only the elite—and the Ottoman elite was much smaller than its counterparts in the West—but they were real enough.

In order to absorb the "civilization," as he described it, and make Turkey a part of the West through this process, Mustafa Kemal launched an ambitious transformation program that changed the world around individuals. These were by no means cosmetic changes to render facility and to provide help in keeping up with fashion. They stemmed from an ideological concern and had deep, far-reaching intentions. The reforms encompassed the entire life from speaking to writing, from dressing to producing art, from understanding the past to locating oneself in time, and from developing a sense of belonging to forming identity. Thus it would be too simplistic to comment that these were mere technical alterations that could not penetrate the deeper social strata. Despite their shortcoming in reaching the masses, the reforms boldly launched by Mustafa Kemal changed Turkish society drastically and molded a new elite with a new Weltanschauung. A European would find Ankara of 1938 much more Western than the cosmopolitan Ottoman capital of 1918. The new, modern section of Ankara with its functional cubic pieces of official architecture resembled a medium-size European town; its mostly bureaucrat population dressed, lived, and entertained like Europeans, and Nevzat Tandoğan, who had become the governor of the province in 1929, did not allow people poorly dressed or in traditional garb to enter the new, sanitized section of the city.[57] Furthermore, the visiting European could decipher some signs, such as "telefon" written in a modified Latin alphabet, could do business on Friday, and had no problem in understanding the month or day.

Although it monopolized the tools of propaganda, the Turkish republican regime could not transform the society as a whole. Its weak agents, such as the People's Houses and People's Chambers, could not indoctrinate a predominantly rural population, a good portion of which was still illiterate despite all campaigns as well as deeply attached to tradition. Adherents to tradition did not present a paper tiger, but adopted a defensive stand against radical changes. But Mustafa Kemal's reforms went beyond "cosmetic" measures such as Shah Reza Pahlavi's ban on picturing non-Western depictions of Iran.[58] The difference between the two cases was that, while the Turkish regime did not succeed in transforming Turkish society as a whole, its influence went far beyond creating secluded green zones. A large section of the elite internalized the new modernism and considered it the only form of modernity. The segment of the population we might call "elite" was naturally more secluded from "traditional" elements of society, but they were still quite numerous compared with their counterparts in Iran or Afghanistan. Tradition and its proponents have themselves gradually responded to the challenges of the new modernity brought about by the regime. Thus the importance of the emergence of an elite and urban upper and middle classes enthusiastically embracing the new ideology should not be underestimated. This class and its ideology have ruled modern Turkey since the inception of the republic.

Kemalism's basis in Westernization, particularly in its early stage, was related to the pillar of scientism. To be modern, Kemalism avowed, is not only better but also more scientific; in fact, it is a result of scientific advances. Kemalism also maintained that tradition could not respond to the challenges of modernity that involved a "universal civilization." Thus for Kemalism, dress type, headgear, and music style are major determinants of the level of modernity. The reforms aimed at making Turkey a part of the West also rendered a service of de-Islamization, but did not render a completely non-Islamic society. The reforms affected the Islamists and conservatives along with the classes wholeheartedly embracing the changes. A very different Turkish Islam emerged after the implementation of Mustafa Kemal's reform program. During the early republican reforms, Egyptian Sheikh Muḥammad al-Ghunaymī al-Taftāzānī commented in trepidation that in the near future the Qur'ān could be seen only in museums in Turkey.[59] Events proved him wrong, and a Turkish Islam that had redefined its relationship with the new modernity emerged in the wake of Mustafa Kemal's reforms. During the early republican transformation, very few people could have envisaged an Islamist party leading Turkey on the path to European Union membership.

The scholarship generally views Mustafa Kemal Atatürk's own attempts at Westernization and the later Kemalist approach in this regard as a continuation of the elongated Ottoman Europeanization movement that can be traced back to the late eighteenth century. This kind of historicization of the early republican and Kemalist visions of Westernization, however, obscures their major differences from Ottoman Westernization. The initial Ottoman responses to modernity could be broadly categorized under the heading of "Europeanization" (often termed "Westernization"); by the late nineteenth century, however, the forging of an Ottoman modernity through a process of acculturation was almost complete. The Westernization of the Kemalists and of the young republic, however, differed substantially from this vision. In fact, it was nothing other than a revamped version of the vision of the Westernists of the Second Constitutional Period, and can thus be traced back only to 1908. Highlighting, like its predecessor, "a single civilization," it rejected the possible existence of modernities. Kemalist Westernization did not aim to create a Turkish modernity, but wished to absorb the *only* modernity, terming it the "universal civilization."

The Roots of Kemalist Turkish Nationalism

Kemalist Turkish nationalism was very original and mainly reflected Mustafa Kemal's own interpretation. Mustafa Kemal had closely watched the blossoming of Hamidian-era Turkism after 1904. Early Turkism had placed a low priority on race because Turks, along with other Asiatic peoples, lay at the bottom of the racial pyramids common at that time. But race became a central theme of Turkism after the Russo-Japanese war of 1904/1905 (which Mustafa Kemal followed closely). Japan's victories gave impetus to a renewed interest in racial theory and the Turkic past among the Young Turks and Ottoman intellectuals. Two Young Turk journals, the Committee of Union and Progress's official organ *Şûra-yı Ümmet* and the intellectual periodical *Türk*, promoted a new Turkism attributing a centripetal role to the Turks in running the empire,[60] and Yusuf Akçura avowed that one of the alternatives before the Ottoman state was to "pursue a Turkish nationalism based on race."[61] It is in this context that we find reports of an argument in 1906 between an Albanian captain, a Turkish sergeant, and Mustafa Kemal, in which the last rejected the traditional nobility of the Arabs and touted instead the "noble qualities of the Turkish race."[62] Later in his career, in the course of constructing the "Turkish History Thesis,"

Mustafa Kemal denounced Eurocentric claims that the Turks belonged to the secondary (*secondaire*), yellow race.[63]

The third tenet of Kemalism, the redefined Turkish nationalism, took its cues from the aforementioned Turkism, but carried this nascent intellectual current to new horizons. As a Young Turk who subscribed to this proto-nationalist ideology, Mustafa Kemal wished to have a Turkish nationalism supported by scientism, fashionable racial models based on phrenology, and popular Darwinian theories of evolution. Such a nationalism would be used to supersede religion in forming identity. As expressed by the official history thesis, Turks should "rectify their thoughts by abandoning superstitions," mainly based on "Jewish myths," to understand that their evolution stemmed from "deep racial roots."[64] In fact, the title of a manuscript penned exclusively for Mustafa Kemal's perusal, "There Is No Religion but Nationalism: My Turkishness Is My Religion," expressed this desire in the most passionate terms (the manuscript received high praise from its reader).[65] While the high school textbooks prepared under Mustafa Kemal's guidance to educate the new generations discarded religion as an obsolete concept in modern times by stating that it "had been established by humans like other institutions,"[66] they praised the Turkish race and nation as great producers of civilization. Actually, these judgments on religion were plagiarized from Wells's *Outline of History*, which itself reiterated the main theses of Herbert Spencer and Edward B. Taylor regarding the emergence of religions and their evolution.[67]

Historical studies played a very important role in advancing the new Turkish nationalism. Mustafa Kemal charged the Turkish History Section of the Turkish Hearths (a Turkish society that had helped the CUP advance Turkism during the last years of the empire) with producing a new, nationalist, and scientist interpretation of Turkish history. Like the famous Egyptian archaeologist Jacques Jean-Marie de Morgan, the founder of the republic wished to find the origins of human life, the cradle of civilization, and the evolution of human life—with the hope of discovering major Turkish involvement at all stages. The result, *The Outlines of Turkish History*, a Wellsian scientific oeuvre reconciling scientism, racial theories, and the past of the Turkic peoples and explaining world history from the emergence of cosmos to the establishment of the Turkish Republic under "Mustafa Kemal's flag," appeared in 1930.[68] It was also a Turkish summary of the volumes of Henri Barr's ambitious *L'évolution de l'humanité* series that had a strong focus on Turks. This 606-page study—only a hundred copies of which were published for state historians and statesmen—served as the basis of further studies, including a fourth volume, published the following year, that set history to be taught at high schools. Under Mustafa Kemal's personal guidance, a further and more elaborated Turkish history thesis was advanced and vigorously promoted, especially after the establishment of the Society for the Examination of Turkish History in 1931 (the name was changed to Turkish Historical Association in 1935) and the first Turkish History Congress held in 1932. In 1938, the absolute victory of the thesis was declared and criticisms (called "incongruous nonsense" in the official language) were denounced as dependent on foreign works" and judged "incontestably unscientific."[69]

Like Wells's study, which profoundly impressed Mustafa Kemal, early Turkish textbooks attempted to situate the human in "space and time" by using theories advanced by Huxley and Haeckel but provided a different explanation of the last phases of human evolution and history. Early Turkish textbooks also proposed that the history of human life should not be reduced to the known history of the humans but rather should go as far back as the cosmic changes that had produced the solar system (an idea that Wells took from Haeckel's disciple and private secretary, Heinrich Schmidt),[70] but their chronological table moves from the emergence of mammals and the start of tool-making by humans to the emergence of civilized life in the Turkish homeland in 9,000 B.C.E. These studies further maintained that "the real evolution of the humankind will be well enlightened when the pickaxe of science starts working in Central Asia . . . the Turkish homeland."[71] Hence Turkish nationalism produced under Mustafa Kemal's guidance was far from being a simple political ideology; backed by Darwinian evolutionary theories, it claimed to be a key to understanding and reinterpreting the entire human history of thousands of years. Situated in such a turgid context, the Turks with their "brachycephalic skulls" should be proud of being members of "such a great historical race evolved into a nation," and this was "a great power and honor not enjoyed by many human groups."[72] Henceforth, accordingly, Turkish identity was to be founded not on the alien import of Islam but on this "scientific" theory of Turkish peoplehood.

According to the Turkish history thesis, the cradle of human civilization had been Central Asia, the Turkish homeland, and the Turks who migrated to all old continents from this base established major civilizations, such as the Sumerian and Hittite empires, or helped backward human groups such as the Chinese and Indians establish impressive civilizations. Similarly, ancient Greek and later Mediterranean civilizations including Rome were products of Turkic peoples who migrated to Crete and Italy. Not all of the peoples in these regions were racially Turkic, but they owed their civilization to the Turkish immigration prompted by environmental changes. This thesis, resembling the *Kulturkreise* (culture circles) hypothesis of the German diffusionist school of anthropology, further maintained that "Turks lived clothed during the stone (Neolithic) age in 12,000 B.C., and Europeans reached that stage 5,000 years later."[73] The Turks were not merely the founders of "world civilization" but also the people who diffused it to the world. Had there been no Turkish migration, the other parts of the world would still have been living in the conditions of thousands of years ago.

A glorious history bypassing the Ottoman past—which Mustafa Kemal wished to erase in toto—would provide many advantages to the new regime. First, it would reduce the Ottoman history, especially its later phases, to an inglorious detail in the elongated history of a civilization-founder race. Second, it would be used in claiming a more magnificent past for this race in periods when it had not been affiliated with Islam, thereby underscoring Islam's determining role in the later decadence. Third, it would render rival nationalist claims recounting Turks as latecomers, as Mustafa Kemal had personally observed during the last decades of the empire, untenable. And finally, by advancing a thesis of a Turkish *mission civilisatrice* that occurred in the Neolithic age, Turkey could be made an integral part of the West and replace Greece as the founder of Western civilization. It was quite telling that the new republic based its claims on the *sanjak* (subprovince) of Alexandretta—awarded to Syria under French mandate—upon the fact that it had been an integral part of the old Hittite Empire, and later that a Turkic people, the Hurris, had migrated there long before the Semite Arabs.[74] In Mustafa Kemal's own words, "the Turkish homeland of four thousand years [Alexandretta] could not be remained as a prisoner in the hands of enemy."[75] Similarly, when the regime desired to establish an understanding between Turkey and Greece, it would make claims that Turks were the founders of the so-called Greek civilization and that Greeks and Turks are racially similar; and when it wished to underscore problems between the two countries, it would trace the conflict back to the Trojan War, with the claim that horse-taming Trojans were of Turkish origin.

Although after Mustafa Kemal's death, early Kemalism gradually revamped the Turkish history and language theses and finally abandoned them, a nationalism based on these concepts flourished in modern Turkey and was embraced as the main component of identity by a substantial portion of the population. Today, very few people invoke the passionate debates on the Hittites, brachycephalic skull formations, common Turkish blood types, the Turkic origins of the Tlaskaltek dialects, and the time in which proto-Turks had lived the Neolithic age. The major problem with the major theses advanced mainly in the 1930s was the difficulty in relating them to the average person. Naming major institutions after Sumerians and Hittites (the Turkish banks Sümerbank and Etibank were established in 1933 and 1935, respectively) was not sufficient to create a meaningful relationship with these ancient civilizations. Like the proto-Turks, who allegedly spoke the first language of the humankind, these civilizations were too remote compared with the Ottomans, whom Kemalists wished to expunge from history.

Less than a year after Mustafa Kemal's death, the regime decided to commemorate the centennial of the Tanzimat, the announcement of the Gülhane Hatt-ı Hümayûnu (Rose Chamber Edict) of November 3, 1839, which had promised sweeping reforms; this was already a clear signal of a desire to re-include the Ottoman past in Turkish history. A major volume appeared out of this project in 1940.[76] Despite its criticism of Tanzimat's dualism, and the judgment that Tanzimat did not achieve the goals later accomplished by the republic, it regarded the late Ottoman reforms as a precursor of the republican transformation, and thus marked a drastic change in the historiography that had been accentuating change and rejecting continuity since 1922. Likewise, at the Third Turkish History Congress held in 1943, a good number of the presentations dealt with subjects in Ottoman history.[77] Gradually, the regime incorporated early Ottoman history into the glorious past of the Turks and accepted the late Ottoman reforms as antecedent to the republican reforms. This was a different vision of history and nationalism than what characterized Mustafa Kemal's original project and early Kemalism; however, thanks to these efforts, the idea that Turks were a leading people in bringing civilization to others has been deeply entrenched in society, and Turkishness plays a much greater role in forming identity in Turkey than any ties felt to the late Ottoman period.

The Kemalist pillar of Turkish nationalism also began to ease its antagonism toward Islam. By 1944, Kemalism had further distanced itself from extreme racial Turkish nationalism by bringing the leaders of this intellectual movement before a tribunal, and the multiparty era witnessed an expeditious reconciliation between Islam and Turkish nationalism in official circles. The final blow occurred in 1986 after the military coup, when a new official institution—merging the Turkish Language and Historical associations under the umbrella of the Turkish Atatürk Council of Culture, Language, and History—accepted a new policy of culture that had been advocated by a conservative organization named Hearth of Intellectuals since the 1970s. According this new policy, Turkishness and Islam should be considered the two main pillars of the national culture, and efforts should be exerted toward achieving an evocative synthesis of Turkish nationalism and Islam. One might consider this new policy to be a serious deviation from the original republican project of Mustafa Kemal and the early Kemalists, and indeed a considerable intellectual and political movement, Ulusalcılık, emerged in the 1990s to redeem the Kemalist nationalism of the 1930s and place it into a republicanism based on Régis Debray's ideas. This represents the minority opinion, however, despite its strong acceptance in official circles.

Concluding Remarks

The roots of Kemalism can be traced back to mid-nineteenth-century Ottoman scientism, the Westernization movement of the Second Constitutional Period, and the Turkism of the early twentieth century. Thus, despite its strong claims of originality and of manifesting a rupture with the past, early Kemalist ideology was also a product of the late Ottoman intellectual debates. Interestingly, all tenets of the Kemalist ideology had been avant-garde but marginal currents in the Ottoman context. The nineteenth-century scientism and early-twentieth-century Westernization movement had gained much ground by 1922, but they were not dominant currents even within the elites in the empire. Likewise, while Turkism had overshadowed any other tenet shaping the ideology of the Committee of Union and Progress, the version embraced by Mustafa Kemal Atatürk and later promoted by Kemalism was an extremely avant-garde type among many others.

Because its adherence to a transformative mission based on intellectual theses attracted marginal interest, early Kemalism felt a need to adopt authoritarian stances and methods. To that end, Kemalism and its main political agent, the Republican People's Party, did not need any example other than the CUP, in which almost all early republican leaders, including the father of the republic, had served in different capacities. Unlike the CUP ideology, which also promoted a self-imposed mission of transformation and created a major institutional cult, Kemalism based itself on a personality cult molded around Mustafa Kemal Atatürk. These characteristics render the original Kemalism of the 1930s and 1940s an anachronism today, like many aspects of its three major tenets. Attempts aimed at revamping and reinterpreting Kemalism have made limited headway, but they have always faced the conundrum of converting an authoritarian ideology of transformation based on hero-worship and contrived religious connotations into a political ideology promoted within a democratic system.

Notes

1. Taha Akyol, *Ama Hangi Atatürk* (Istanbul: Doğan Yayıncılık, 2008), 214–298.
2. "Büyük Millet Meclisinin Bütün İslâm Âlemine Beyannamesi, 9.V.1920," in *Atatürk'ün Tamim Telgraf ve Beyannameleri*, vol. 4, *1917–1938*, ed. Nimet Arsan (Ankara: Türk İnkılâp Tarihi Enstitüsü Yayımları, 1964), 323–326.
3. "Türk Milletini Teşkil Eden Müslüman Öğeler Hakkında, May 1, 1920," in *Atatürk'ün Söylev ve Demeçleri*, vol. 1, *T.B.M. Meclisinde ve C.H.P. Kurultaylarında, 1919–1938* (Istanbul: Türk İnkılâp Tarihi Enstitüsü Yayımları, 1945), 70–71.
4. Mehmet Perinçek, *Atatürk'ün Sovyetler'le Görüşmeleri: Sovyet Arşiv Belgeleriyle* (Istanbul: Kaynak Yayınları, 2005), 272ff.
5. Akyol, *Ama Hangi Atatürk*.
6. Şevket Süreyya [Aydemir], *İnkılâp ve Kadro: İnkılâbın İdeolojisi* (Ankara: Muallim Ahmet Halit Kitaphanesi, 1932), 46.
7. Ahmet Hamdi, "Kapitalizm (Emperyalizm) ile Millet İktisat Rejimi ve Ferdiyetçilik ile Devletçiliğin Manaları," *Kadro*, June 1933, 45.
8. Vedat Nedim, "Devletin Yapıcılık ve İdarecilik Kudretine İnanmak Gerekir," *Kadro*, March 1933, 13.
9. Vedat Nedim, "Sınıflaşmamak ve İktisat Siyaseti," *Kadro*, November 1932, 17–21, and "Mefhum Teşkilâtı Değil Madde Teşkilâtı," *Kadro*, August 1932, 13–17.
10. "Bakanlar Kurulu'nun Görev ve Yetkisini Belirten Kanun Teklifi Münasebetiyle, December 1, 1921," in *Atatürk'ün Söylev ve Demeçleri*, 1:191.
11. Hasan Rıza Soyak, *Atatürk'ten Hatıralar* (Ankara: Yapı ve Kredi Bankası Yayınları [1973]), 1:58.
12. Nusret Köymen, "Kemalizm ve Politika Bilgisi," *Ülkü*, July 1936, 323–324.
13. Şevket Aziz, "Biyososyoloji," *Ülkü*, June 1934, 253–262.

14.. "İnkılâp Ülkülerini Yayma Yolunda," *Ülkü*, August 1933, 25.

15. Şevket Aziz, "Türk Topraklarının Adamı," *Ülkü*, October 1934, 81–82.

16. Nusret Köymen, "Kemalizmin Hususiyetleri," *Ülkü*, August 1936, 417.

17. Mete Tunçay, *Türkiye Cumhuriyeti'nde Tek-Parti Yönetiminin Kurulması, 1923–1931* (Istanbul: Cem Yayınevi, 1989), 313.

18. *Celâl Bayar'ın Söylev ve Demeçleri*, vol. 1, *1921–1938, Ekonomik Konulara Dair*, ed. Özel Şahingiray (Ankara: Doğuş Ltd. Ortaklığı, 1955), 241.

19. For more information on the political aspects of early Kemalism and the impact of European totalitarianism on this ideology, see Fikret Adanır, "Kemalist Authoritarianism and Fascist Trends in Turkey During the Interwar Period," in Stein Ugelvik Larsen, ed., *Fascism Outside Europe* (Boulder, Colo.: Social Science Monographs, 2001), 313–361.

20. F. M. Dostoyevsky, *Besy: Roman v trekh chastiakh* (Leningrad: Khudozhestvennaia literatura, Leningradskoeotdelenie, 1989), 327–328.

21. A[bdullah] Cevdet, "Herkes İçün Kimya," *Musavver Cihan*, no. 4 [September 23, 1891]: 30–31; no. 34 [April 27, 1892]: 266–268.

22. See, for example, *Musavver Cihan*, no. 43 [August 30, 1892]: 344.

23. J. W. Draper, *Niza'-i İlm ü Din*, trans. Ahmed Midhat, 4 vols. (Istanbul: Tercüman-ı Hakikat Matbaası, 1313 [1895]–1318 [1900]).

24. M. Şükrü Hanioğlu, "Blueprints for a Future Society: Late Ottoman Materialists on Science, Religion, and Art," in Elisabeth Özdalga, ed., *Late Ottoman Society: The Intellectual Legacy* (London: RoutledgeCurzon, 2005), 32, 90.

25. "İlk Meclis-i Mebusan Reisi Ahmed Rıza Bey'in Hatıraları (1)," *Cumhuriyet*, January 26, 1950.

26. Orhan Okay, *Beşir Fuad: İlk Türk Pozitivist ve Natüralisti* (Istanbul: Dergâh Yayınları, 2008), 68–71.

27. *Atatürk'ün Okuduğu Kitaplar*, ed. Recep Cengiz (Ankara: Anıtkabir Derneği Yayınları, 2001), 8:439–440; *Kraft und Stoff oder Grundzüge der natürlichen Weltordnung*, 16th ed. (Leipzig: Verlag von Theodor Thomas, 1888), 267–269.

28. *Atatürk'ün Okuduğu Kitaplar*, ed. Cengiz, 8:396–407; [Paul-Henri Dietrich d'Holbach], *Le bon sens du curé Meslier, suivi de son testament* (Paris: Au Palais des Thermes de Julien, 1802), 175, 178, 181–183, 287–289, 291, 300–302.

29. Ruşen Eşref Ünaydın, *Atatürk: Tarih ve Dil Kurumları Hâtıralar*, vol. 7, *Türk Dil Kurultayında Söylenmiştir* (Ankara: T.D.K, 1954), 53; H. G. Wells, *The Outline of History: Being a Plain History of Life and Mankind* (New York: Review of Reviews, 1924), 1:23ff.

30. See, for example, "Tarsus'da Gençlerle Konuşma, 21.III.1923," in *Atatürk'ün Söylev ve Demeçleri*, vol. 2, *1906–1938*, ed. Nimet Unan (Ankara: Türk İnkılâp Tarihi Enstitüsü Yayımları, 1952), 133.

31. "Samsun Öğretmenleriyle Konuşma, 22.XI.1924," in ibid., 197.

32. "Subay ve Kumandan ile Konuşmalar," in *Atatürk'ün Bütün Eserleri*, vol. 1, *1903–1915* (Istanbul: Kaynak Yayınları, 1998), 168.

33. Ibid.

34. Şerafettin Turan, *Atatürk'ün Düşünce Yapısını Etkileyen Olaylar, Düşünürler, Kitaplar* (Ankara: Türk Tarih Kurumu Yayınları, 1982), 23.

35. M. Şükrü Hanioğlu, *Bir Siyasal Düşünür Olarak Doktor Abdullah Cevdet ve Dönemi* (Istanbul: Üçdal Neşriyat, 1981), 32ff.

36. Hanioğlu, "Blueprints for a Future Society," 62–66.

37. Sulaymān Mūsā, *al-Ḥusayn ibn 'Alī wa'l-thawra al-'Arabīya al-kubrā* (Amman: Lajnat Tārīkh al-Urdunn, 1992), 134.

38. M. Şükrü Hanioğlu, "Garbcılar: Their Attitudes Toward Religion and Their Impact on the Official Ideology of the Turkish Republic," *Studia Islamica* 86 (1997): 147.

39. Ibrahim Temo, *Atatürkü N'için Severim?* ([Medgidia], 1937), 8.

40. Abdullah Cevdet, "Şehzâde Mecid Efendi Hazretleri'yle Mülâkat," *İctihad*, no. 57 [March 20, 1913]: 1257.

41. Afet [Âfet İnan], *Vatandaş İçin Medenî Bilgiler* (Istanbul: Devlet Matbaası, 1931), 1:12.

42. Charles H. Sherrill, *A Year's Embassy to Mustafa Kemal* (New York: Scribner, 1934), 193–196.

43. A nine-volume *tafsīr* entitled *Hak Dini Kur'an Dili* [The religion of God and the language of Islam] by Elmalılı Muhammed Hamdi (Yazır) appeared between 1935 and 1938, and a twelve-volume translation of *Tajrīd al-ṣarīḥ li-aḥādīth al-Jāmiḥ 'al-sa'ḥīḥ* between 1928 and 1948.

44. Dücane Cündioğlu, *Türkçe Kur'an ve Cumhuriyet İdeolojisi* (Istanbul: Kitabevi, 1998), 239–240.

45. Dücane Cündioğlu, *Bir Siyasî Proje Olarak Türkçe İbadet*, vol. 1, *Türkçe Namaz, 1923–1950* (Istanbul: Kitabevi, 1999), 92–93.

46. "Tekye ve Zâviyelerle Türbelerin Seddine ve Türbedârlıklar ile Bir Takım Ünvanların Men' ve İlgasına Dair Kanun" (law no. 677, November 30, 1925), in Karakoç Sarkiz, ed., *Türkiye Cumhuriyeti Sicill-i Kavanini* (Istanbul: Cihan Matbaası, 1926), 2:18.

47. "Kastamonu'da İkinci Bir Konuşma, 30.VIII.1925," in *Atatürk'ün Söylev ve De-meçleri*, vol. 2, *1906–1938*, ed. Unan, 218.

48. Şeref Aykut, *Kamâlizm: C.H. Partisi Programının İzahı* (Istanbul: Muallim Ahmet Halit Litap Evi, 1936), 3.

49. *T.D.K. Türkçe Sözlük: Türk Dil Kurumu Lûgat Kolu Çalışmalariyle Hazırlanmıştır* (Istanbul: Cumhuriyet Basımevi, 1945), 153.

50. Osman Ergin, *Türkiye Maarif Tarihi* (Istanbul: Osmanbey Matbaası, 1943), 5:1532–1534.

51. *Kemâlettin Kâmi Kamu: Hayatı, San'atı ve Şiirleri*, ed. Gültekin Sâmanoğlu (Ankara: Kültür ve Turizm Bakanlığı Yayıları, 1986), 77.

52. [Kılıçzâde Hakkı], "Pek Uyanık Bir Uyku," *İctihad*, no. 55 [March 6, 1913]: 1226–1228; no. 57 [March 20, 1913]: 1261–1264.

53. "Kültür Hakkında, 29.X.1923," in *Atatürk'ün Söylev ve Demeçleri*, vol. 3, *1918–1937*, ed. Nimet Unan (Ankara: Türk İnkilâp Tarihi Enstitüsü Yayımları, 1954), 67.

54. Abdullah Cevdet, "Şime-i Muhabbet," *İctihad*, no. 89 [January 29, 1914]: 1979–1984.

55. Gaston Jollivet and Marie-Anne L'Heureux, *Mükemmel ve Resimli Âdâb-ı Mu'aşeret Rehberi*, trans. Abdullah Cevdet (Istanbul: Yeni Matbaa, 1928), 115–116, 147–195, 316–318, 341, 367.

56. Mihri Pektaş, "Turkish Woman," *La Turquie kémaliste*, nos. 32–40 (1939–1940): 10–14.

57. Funda Şenol Cantek, *"Yaban"lar ve Yerliler: Başkent Olma Sürecinde Ankara* (Istanbul: İletişim Yayınları, 2003), 218–224.

58. Vincent Monteil, *Iran: "Petite planète"* (Paris: Éditions du Seul, 1957), 13.

59. Gotthard Jäschke, "Der Islam in der neuen Türkei: Eine Rechtsgeschichtliche Untersuchung," *Die Welt des Islams* 1, nos. 1–2 (1951):168–169.

60. M. Şükrü Hanioğlu, *Preparation for a Revolution: The Young Turks, 1902–1908* (New York: Oxford University Press, 2001), 62–73, 175ff.

61. Yusuf Akçura, *Üç Tarz-ı Siyaset* (Cairo: Matbaa-i İctihad, 1907), 4, 12.

62. Ali Fuat Cebesoy, *Sınıf Arkadaşım Atatürk: Okul ve Genç Subaylık Hâtıraları* (Istanbul: İnkılâp ve Aka, 1967), 99–100.

63. Afet İnan, "Atatürk ve Tarih Tezi," *Belleten*, April 1, 1939, 244.

64. *Türk Tarihinin Ana Hatları*, ed. Afet et al. (Istanbul: Devlet Matbaası, 1930), 1–3.

65. *Atatürk'ün Okuduğu Kitaplar*, ed. Cengiz, 8:466.

66. *Tarih*, vol. 1, *Tarihtenevvelki Zamanlar ve Eski Zamanlar* (Istanbul: Devlet Matbaası, 1931), 23–24.

67. Wells, *Outline of History*, 1:121–136.

68. *Türk Tarihinin Ana Hatları*, ed. Afet et al.

69. Şemsettin Günaltay, "Türk Tarih Tezi Hakkındaki İntikatların Mahiyeti ve Tezin Kat'î Zaferi," *Belleten*, October 1938, 337–365.

70. *Tarih*, 1:6.

71. Ibid., 35–36.

72. Ibid., 20.

73. "Maarif Vekili Esat Beyefendinin Açma Nutku," in *Birinci Türk Tarih Kongresi: Konferanslar Müzakere Zabıtları* ([Ankara]: Maarif Vekâleti, 1932), 6.

74. Nureddin Ardıç, *Antakya-İskenderun Etrafındaki Türk Davasının Tarihî Esasları* (Istanbul: Tecelli Matbaası, 1937), 7ff.

75. Tayfur Sökmen, *Hatay'ın Kurtuluşu İçin Harcanan Çabalar* (Ankara: Türk Tarih Kurumu Yayınları, Ankara 1978), 70.

76. *Tanzimat*, vol. 1 (Istanbul: Maarif Vekâleti, 1940).

77. *III. Türk Tarih Kongresi, Ankara 15–20 Kasım 1943: Kongreye Sunulan Tebliğler* (Ankara: Türk Tarih Kurumu Yayınları, 1948), 124–130, 229–268, 367–379, 441–518, 556–562, 590–598, 648–688, 700–703.

3

Turkey—Plural Society and Monolithic State

ERGUN ÖZBUDUN

The main argument of this chapter is that although Turkish society is reasonably pluralistic, this is not sufficiently recognized by or reflected in the political structure of the country, paradoxically despite more than sixty years of experience in competitive, multiparty politics. The principal reason for this, it will be argued, is the "founding philosophy" of the Turkish Republic, some features of which are incompatible with the development of a truly pluralistic political system. In the first section, I will try to identify the meanings of the terms "pluralistic democracy" and "plural society." In the second section, the pluralistic characteristics of Turkish society will be discussed. In the third section, I will analyze the relevant characteristics of the founding republican philosophy. The fourth section will be devoted to an analysis of the developments concerning the autonomy and political influence of civil society organizations.

Pluralistic Democracy and Plural Societies

It is a commonplace to state that contemporary democracy is pluralist democracy. Briefly, this term refers to "organizational pluralism, that is, to the existence of a plurality of relatively autonomous (independent) organizations (subsystems) within the domain of a state," although "relatively autonomous organizations also exist under some nondemocratic regimes."[1] Indeed, there is a strong correlation between a democratic political system and organizational pluralism; organizational pluralism is a necessary but not sufficient condition of democracy "both as a prerequisite for its operation and as an inevitable consequence of its institutions. The rights acquired for democracy on a large scale make relatively autonomous organizations simultaneously possible and necessary. . . . Because organizations are possible and advantageous, they are also inevitable."[2] Autonomous organizations provide a mechanism of control over the exercise of governmental power and thus serve the cause of individual freedom, as Tocqueville among others observed a long time ago. Contemporary democratic theorists also emphasize the importance of autonomous civil society organizations for the consolidation of democracy. Thus Juan Linz and Alfred Stepan argue that one of the conditions for democratic consolidation is "the development of a free and lively civil society"—that is, a "polity where self-organizing groups, movements, and individuals, relatively autonomous from the state, attempt to articulate values, create associations and solidarities, and advance their interests."[3]

While some form of organizational pluralism is an indispensable condition for democracy, there are considerable national variations among democratic countries as to how such organizations operate and interact with government authorities. Different patterns of interest representation may be due, among other things, to the cleavage structure in society, political institutions, and the inclusiveness and concentration of organizations.[4] Thus Philippe Schmitter distinguishes between two modes of interest representation, pluralism and corporatism, a distinction significant for the Turkish case, as it will be spelled out later:

> Pluralism can be defined as a system of interest representation in which the constituent units are organized into an unspecified number of multiple, voluntary, competitive, nonhierarchically ordered and self-determined (as to type or scope of interest) categories which are not specially licensed, recognized, subsidized, created or otherwise controlled in leadership selection or interest articulation by the state and which do not exercise a monopoly of representational activity within their respective categories.

Alternatively:

Corporatism can be defined as a system of interest representation in which the constituent units are organized into a limited number of singular, compulsory, noncompetitive, hierarchically ordered and functionally differentiated categories, recognized or licensed (if not created) by the state and granted a deliberate representational monopoly within their respective categories in exchange for observing certain controls on their selection of leaders and articulation of demands and supports.[5]

Probably the most extreme examples of societal corporatism, or "corporate pluralism" as Stein Rokkan called it, can be found in such Scandinavian countries as Norway, Sweden, and Denmark. In this system, major economic policy decisions are not made in parliament or by the government, but through the negotiations, bargainings, and compromises among major economic interest organizations. As Rokkan wrote of Norway,

> the crucial decisions on economic policy are rarely taken in the parties or in Parliament: the central area is the bargaining table where the government authorities meet directly with the trade union leaders, the representatives of the farmers, the smallholders, and the fishermen, and the delegates of the Employers' Association. These yearly rounds of negotiations have in fact come to mean more in the lives of rank-and-file citizens than the formal elections. In these processes of intensive interaction, the parliamentary notions of one member, one vote and majority rule make little sense.[6]

Surely the compatibility of such a system with the classical notions of parliamentary democracy may be questioned, but it seems to be working satisfactorily in highly homogeneous and consensual societies.[7]

The experience of a number of smaller European democracies suggests that similar processes may not be limited to a purely economic policy field and to highly homogeneous and consensual societies. On the contrary, in some plural or segmented European societies, stable democracy was achieved through a system named "consociational democracy" by Arend Lijphart.[8] A "plural society" is one deeply divided by segmental cleavages "of a religious, ideological, linguistic, regional, cultural, racial, or ethnic nature," each tending to create a subculture of its own.[9] In such societies, democratic stability can be maintained only through the accommodation of rival elites representing their segments using such techniques as grand coalition, mutual veto or "concurrent majority" rule, proportional representation, and "a high degree of autonomy for each segment to run its own internal affairs."[10] In Europe, the Netherlands, Switzerland, Belgium, and Austria (between 1945 and 1966) are examples of such a consociational system. Lijphart observes that "under the unfavorable circumstances of segmental cleavages, consociational democracy, through far from the abstract ideal, is the best kind of democracy that can realistically be expected."[11]

These reasonably successful European democracies should not, however, hide the serious problems confronted by segmented societies. As Robert Dahl rightly observes,

> any dispute in which a large section of the population of a country feels that its way of life or its highest values are severely menaced by another segment of the population creates a crisis in a competitive political system. . . . Because an ethnic or religious subculture is incorporated so early into one's personality, conflicts among groups divided along lines of religion, race, or language are specially fraught with danger, particularly if they are also tied to region. . . . The junction of race, language or religion with regional subcultures creates an incipient nation, demands for autonomy, even independence. That subcultural pluralism often places a dangerous strain on the tolerance and mutual security required for a system of public contestation seems hardly open to doubt.[12]

A Plural Society

The Ottoman Empire was a textbook example of plural or segmented societies divided along religious, sectarian, ethnic, and linguistic cleavages. In the words of Benjamin Braude and Bernard Lewis,

> For nearly half a millennium the Ottomans ruled an empire as diverse as any in history. Remarkably, this polyethnic and multireligious society worked. Muslims, Christians, and Jews worshipped and studied side by side, enriching their distinct cultures. The legal traditions and practices of each community, particularly in matters of personal status—that is, death, marriage, and inheritance—were respected and enforced through the empire. Scores of languages and literatures employing a bewildering

variety of scripts flourished. Opportunities for advancement and prosperity were open in varying degrees to all the empire's subjects. During their heyday the Ottomans created a society which allowed a great degree of communal autonomy while maintaining a fiscally sound and militarily strong central government. The Ottoman Empire was a classic example of the plural society.[13]

What made the maintenance of such unity in diversity was the Ottoman *millet* system, which can perhaps be described as an early and primitive example of "nonterritorial" or "corporate" federalism.[14] The *millet* system consisted of recognizing a substantial degree of autonomy to non-Muslim communities in matters of religion, personal status, culture, and all kinds of community services. According to Braude and Lewis, "rather than a uniformly adopted system, it may be more accurately described as a series of *ad hoc* arrangements made over the years, which gave each of the major religious communities a degree of legal autonomy and authority with the acquiescence of the Ottoman state."[15]

The population data pertaining to the nineteenth-century Ottoman Empire show the religious diversity of its population. Kemal Karpat's figures on the religious structure of the Ottoman population in Europe in the nineteenth century are as follows:

1820s	Total non-Muslims: 68.0 percent; total Muslims: 32.0 percent
1840s	Total non-Muslims: 63.9 percent; total Muslims: 36.1 percent
1870s	Total non-Muslims: 57.0 percent; total Muslims: 43.0 percent
1890s	Total non-Muslims: 52.5 percent; total Muslims: 47.5 percent[16]

The steady decline in the percentage of non-Muslim population in Europe was obviously the result of the successive loss of the empire's European territories. However, even after the humiliating defeat in the Balkan Wars—which resulted in the almost complete loss of the European territories—the empire still contained substantial non-Muslim minorities. Thus according to the official 1914 Ottoman population statistics, the figures for the major religious groups were as follows: Muslims, 15,044,846; Greeks, 1,729,738; Armenians, 1,161,169; Jews, 187,073; Greek Catholics, 62,468; Armenian Catholics, 67,838; Protestants, 24,845; Syriacs, 54,750; and Maronites, 47,406.[17]

Obviously, autonomy granted to the non-Muslim communities or tolerance shown to non-Muslims in general does not mean fully equality with

Muslims or a right to take part in governmental affairs. Such were achieved only with the Tanzimat reforms of the nineteenth century, particularly with the Reform (Islahat) edict of 1856 and the first Ottoman Constitution of 1876. The number of non-Muslim officials in the Ottoman bureaucracy rose rapidly after 1856.[18] In the first Ottoman parliament, Christians and Jews were proportionately better represented than were the Muslims. According to Robert Devereux's figures, in the first session of the Chamber of Deputies, there were seventy-one Muslim, forty-four Christian, and four Jewish members, and in the second session the numbers were sixty-four, forty-three, and six, respectively. Devereux observes that "although the Empire's Muslims as a whole enjoyed a rightful majority in the Chamber, the Turks as an ethnic group, while comprising a majority of the Muslim deputies, were a minority of the deputies as a whole since they had to share the Muslim seats with Arabs, Kurds, Albanians, Bosnians, etc."[19]

This was the time when the Young Ottoman intellectuals tried to introduce the concept of Ottoman citizenship, based on the loyalty to a common state and common homeland, regardless of religious, ethnic, and linguistic differences.[20] This concept may be considered the early precursor of the contemporary concept of constitutional citizenship or constitutional patriotism. Indeed, the reforms seem to have been received warmly by the non-Muslim communities. Enver Ziya Karal quotes a number of patriotic statements by non-Muslim deputies in the Ottoman Chamber of Deputies, particularly in the face of interventions by foreign states.[21] It is also well known that the restoration of the constitution in 1908 was jubilantly greeted by Muslim, Christians, and Jews in joint public demonstrations. No matter how well intentioned, however, the cause of Ottomanism was not a realistic one in an age of growing ethnic nationalism, with the frequent interventions of the great European powers in favor of their protected Christian communities. As Feroz Ahmad says, "by the end of the nineteenth century all the non-Muslim *millets*, save the Jews, had found a *de facto* protector." He also observes that, after a brief honeymoon period, relations between the Committee of Union and Progress (CUP) and the Greek and Armenian communities quickly deteriorated,[22] parallel to the rise of Turkish nationalism effectively promoted by the CUP leadership.

The Ottoman population statistics, based on religious affiliations, obviously say nothing about the diversity within the Muslim community. The Muslim community, besides the Turkish population, included many ethnically and linguistically diverse groups, such as Arabs, Kurds, Circassians,

Bosnians, Albanians, Pomaks, and Laz. Thus Karal notes that the members of the First Ottoman Chamber of Deputies "spoke some fourteen different languages, but all, as was required by law, knew some Turkish."[23] The rise of ethnic nationalism also affected the Arabs in particular and resulted in the secession of the Arabic-speaking provinces at the end of World War I.

The tragic deportation of the Armenians in 1915 and the exchange of populations with Greece in 1924 made the territory of the new Turkish Republic much more homogeneous, at least as far as the Christian population of the empire was concerned. Thus the non-Muslim population, which had constituted roughly 20 percent of the Ottoman population before World War I, dwindled to 2.78 percent (378,664) in the 1927 census, and continues to decline up to the present day.[24] This group consisted of Armenians and Greeks of Istanbul who were spared from deportation and the population exchange, respectively, and a fairly large Jewish community (81,872 persons, according to the 1927 census) who had no problems with the Ottoman-Turkish state and were considered loyal subjects.[25] The exodus of the non-Muslim population continued during the republican period. Today, the percentage of the non-Muslim population is much less than 1 percent: about 55,000 to 60,000 Armenians; fewer than 2,000 Greeks; about 25,000 Jews, most of whom live in Istanbul; and an estimated 25,000 Syriacs (Süryani), who live in the southeast, Istanbul, and elsewhere.[26] In addition to the discriminatory practices against minorities to be alluded to below, major historical events played a role in this exodus. The Jewish pogroms in Thrace in 1934 resulted in the migration of several thousand Jews to Istanbul to seek security.[27] The discriminatory and scandalous poll tax (Varlık Vergisi) of 1942/1943 that taxed non-Muslims up to ten times as heavily as their Muslim counterparts resulted in a very significant transfer of wealth and property from non-Muslims to Muslims.[28] The establishment of the State of Israel in 1948 led about 30,000 Jews to migrate to Israel.[29] The tragic pogrom and destruction of September 6–7, 1955, in Istanbul destroyed about five thousand shops and houses belonging mostly to Greeks but also to Armenians and Jews, and caused a large-scale emigration of Istanbul Greeks.[30] Finally, the unilateral abrogation by Turkey of the 1930 Turkish–Greek treaty in 1964 as a result of the Cyprus crisis forced Greek citizens living in Turkey to emigrate. Since many of them were married to Greeks of Turkish citizenship, emigration involved entire families, and thus the exodus involved about 30,000 people.[31] The Syriacs, an autochthonous Christian community living in southeastern Turkey, were caught between the fires of the Kurdistan Workers' Party (PKK) and the state in the 1980s and emigrated in large numbers to Western countries. The result is a 99.5 percent Muslim-majority country, a complete opposite of the multi-religious Ottoman Empire.

In addition to these catastrophic events, official policies and de facto practices of Turkish governments made life difficult and insecure for non-Muslim minorities. It is beyond the scope of this study to give a full account of such discriminatory policies and practices. But to under-line just a few main points, Turkish governments have complied with those provisions of the Lausanne Treaty recognizing a number of positive rights for "non-Muslim" minorities only with respect to the three major non-Muslim communities, Greeks, Armenians, and Jews, but not with respect to other smaller non-Muslim communities such as the Syriacs. Second, implementation even with regard to the three major communi-ties has been deficient. Third, Lausanne's provisions concerning linguis-tic rights (art. 39/4, 5) have largely been ignored or violated in connection with Muslim linguistic minorities such as the Kurds. Fourth, despite the official claims of nondiscrimination on the basis of religion, race, and ethnicity, there have been a number of legislative and court decisions that defined Turkishness in terms of ethnic origin. Fifth, at the level of popu-lar culture, there is a strong tendency to consider non-Muslim Turkish citizens not as equal citizens but as aliens whose loyalty to the Turkish state is dubious.[32]

The exodus of the non-Muslim communities, however, did not mean the creation of a homogeneous society united in "language, culture, and ideal" as dreamed of by the founders of the nation-state. For there remained important ethnic, linguistic, and sectarian cleavages among the Muslim population, so that the Turkish society can still be considered a "plural" or "segmented" society as defined above. Kurds constitute the largest eth-nic and linguistic minority, estimated between 12 million and 15 million (roughly 15–20 percent of the population, about 75 percent of whom are Sunnis and the rest are Alevis). They are followed by Arabic speakers, esti-mated about 1 million, again divided between the Sunnis and Alevis. Alevis are a heterodox Islamic sect, although some Alevis consider their creed as an independent religion or as "a philosophy and a way of life specific to the Anatolian people."[33] Probably because of the differences in defin-ing Alevism, there are huge differences in their estimated numbers, which range between 6 and 17 million.[34] Baskın Oran estimates their numbers at

12 million; Alevis are also divided among Turkish, Kurdish (mainly Zaza), Arabic, and Azeri Turkish speakers, although a great majority of them are Turkish speakers.[35]

Of course, neither Kurds nor Alevis enjoy an officially recognized minority status and the positive rights that go along with it. In fact, both refuse to demand such a status, arguing that they themselves are the essential or founding components of the republic. Nevertheless, they both conform to the generally accepted sociological definition of a minority. Sociologically speaking, a group of people who are different from the dominant majority of the population on the basis of such objective differences as language, race, ethnicity, religion, or sect, and are conscious of their differences, constitute a minority. This is clearly the case for the Kurds and the Alevis, and after a long period of forced silence, they both have begun to assert claims for the recognition of their separate cultural identities. Actually, such claims are among the most hotly debated issues in Turkish politics today.[36]

Obviously, social pluralism in contemporary Turkey is not limited to Kurds and the Alevis. Being the heir to the multiethnic, multilinguistic Ottoman Empire, the Turkish Republic naturally includes a number of different ethnic/linguistic groups, such as Arabs, Circassians, Georgians, Abhaz, Laz, Albanians, Bosnians, and Pomaks. Most of them, however, are immigrants from neighboring Transcaucasian or Balkan countries who found a refuge in the Ottoman Empire. Therefore, they had no difficulty in adopting a Turkish/Muslim identity and saw themselves as essential and equal components of the population, even though they may have preserved some of their original cultural characteristics.[37]

To this ethnic and linguistic pluralism was added another line of cleavage, beginning in the 1970s. Long-suppressed Islamist or Islamic tendencies started to find political expression with the establishment of the National Order Party (MNP) of Necmeddin Erbakan. The MNP, closed down after the military intervention of 1971, was followed by a series of successor Islamist parties: National Salvation Party, Welfare Party, Virtue Party (all closed down either during the periods of military rule or by decisions of the Constitutional Court), and Felicity Party. The present governing party of Turkey, the Justice and Development Party (AKP) can no longer be considered an Islamist party, even though its top leadership came from Islamist roots. It can more correctly be described as a conservative democratic party inspired by faith-based values in social and cultural matters. The 1990s witnessed the rapid rise of political Islam. Thus the Welfare Party (RP) emerged as the strongest party from the 1995 elections, with 21.4 percent of the vote, and became the major partner in the short-lived coalition government of the RP and the center-right True Path Party in 1996 and 1997. The turbulent period of this coalition government ended with the "soft" or "postmodern" military intervention known as "the February 28 process," which forced the government to resign, closed down the RP, and put a five-year political ban on Erbakan and a number of leading party figures.

The rise of Islamist parties was paralleled by the growth of a huge number of Islamist or Islamic civil society organizations, such as an Islamic business association (MÜSİAD); an Islamic trade union (HAK-İŞ); a large number of Islamic newspapers, television and radio networks, publishing houses, business enterprises, schools, dormitories, and cultural and charitable associations; and the like. To these one should add a number of officially unrecognized but actually very active Islamic orders (tarikats) and communities (cemaats). Thus one can speak of the emergence of a distinct Islamic subculture side-by-side with strictly secular state institutions and civil society organizations, a distinguishing mark of a "segmented society." Just as in the case of the growing demands of recognition by the Kurds and the Alevis, the statist and tutelary mentality inherited from the single-party period was ill-prepared to meet this new challenge. At present, the cleavage between the ultra-secularists and the religiously inspired conservatives is the main dividing line in Turkish politics.

Thus Turkey, despite the systematic assimilationist and homogenizing policies of its republican founders, still retains many of the characteristics of a plural society. The most fundamental problem facing the present-day Turkish democracy is to reconcile this social pluralism with an authoritarian state tradition that seeks to impose an artificial homogeneity, even uniformity, on the society. Although some elements of this state tradition derive from Ottoman times, others were added to it during the nation-building process of the republican era. Our next task is to analyze the political culture of the early republican (single-party) period in terms of its compatibility with the development of a pluralist democracy.

The Kemalist Legacy

It is debatable whether Turkey today has a "dominant official ideology."[38] A related matter of debate is whether the founding philosophy of the republic

(Kemalism) can more appropriately be termed a "mentality" or an "ideology."[39] If the word "ideology" is not confined to excessively rigid, comprehensive, and systematic bodies of ideas, then Kemalism can be defined as a soft or "middle-range" ideology.[40] Without proceeding further with this semantic discussion, it can safely be argued that the founding ideology of Kemalism, after almost sixty years of multiparty politics, is still a very important component of Turkish political culture. In the words of Taha Parla, "in contemporary Turkish political life there is hardly any instance of expressions of ideas, sentiments, and judgments without reference to Kemalism, of producing of political proposals and projects without depending on it, of debating and acting on the political history or the future of the country without relating them to Kemalism, at both cognitive and affective-normative levels."[41] Indeed, the influence of the Kemalist ideology is keenly felt in the discourses and actions of the military; the high judicial bodies, including the Constitutional Court; the current main opposition party (Republican People's Party [CHP]); much of the mainstream media; and many of the institutions of higher learning. Particularly strong traces of the Kemalist ideology can be found in the 1982 Constitution, and to a lesser extent in the 1961 Constitution. Examples of this will be presented in the following sections.

Officially, the Kemalist ideology consists of six principles ("six arrows") adopted at the 1931 Party Congress and incorporated into the constitution in 1937. These are republicanism, nationalism, populism, statism, secularism (laïcisme), and revolutionism (more correctly, transformationism [inkılâpçılık]). Of these, republicanism has never been really challenged since the proclamation of the Turkish Republic in 1923, and the terms "statism" and "revolutionism," at least in their original senses, started to fall into disuse with the transition to a competitive political system in 1945 to 1950. "Populism" as such is rarely used as a political term nowadays, but its traces and connotations are found in the 1961 and especially in the 1982 Constitutions. Nationalism and secularism, or rather their proper meanings, are subjects of heated political debate today.

However, the Kemalist ideology cannot be reduced to these six official principles. There are other components of it that are less often officially pronounced but probably as important as the six arrows. Among those one can mention a strongly elitist outlook, insistence on the absolute unity of the nation, rejection of liberal democracy and a competitive party system, rejection of class struggle, rationalism and scienticism, corporatism, solidarism, authoritarianism, tutelarism, radicalism, and developmentalism.

During the years of the War of Independence (1919–1922) the term "populism" was used both as an anti-imperialist and anti-capitalist slogan, and as a synonym for popular sovereignty and popular government (i.e., political democracy). An example of the first use can be found in an Assembly speech delivered by Atatürk on December 1, 1921:

> When we think in terms of social doctrines, we are a working people, a poor people, striving to save our lives and independence. Let us know ourselves. We have to work to live and to achieve our liberation. Therefore, all of us have rights. . . . But we acquire such rights only through working. In our society there is no place or rights for a person who wants to lie down and does not want to work. . . . Populism is a social doctrine which aims to base its social order on work. . . . To protect this right and to keep our independence secure, all of us pursue a doctrine which justifies nationwide struggle against imperialism that wants to destroy us and against capitalism that wants to devour us.[42]

However, these anti-imperialist and anti-capitalist overtones, probably designed to secure and maintain the support of the Soviet Union during the crucial years of the War of Independence, were dropped soon after the military victory over the Greek armies in 1922, when Turkey started to turn its face to western European powers.[43] Similarly, references to popular sovereignty and popular government were gradually replaced by a new solidaristic notion of populism. Thus the CHP Program adopted in May 1931 defined populism as follows:

> The source of will and sovereignty is the nation. The Party considers it an important principle that this will and sovereignty be used to regulate the proper fulfillment of the mutual duties of the citizen to the State and of the State to the citizen. We consider the individuals who accept an absolute equality before law, and who recognize no privileges for any individual, family, class, or community to be of the people and populist. . . . It is one of our main principles to consider the people of the Turkish Republic, not as composed of different classes, but as a community divided into various professions according to the requirements of the division of labor for the individual and social life of the Turkish people. A) Small farmers, B) Small industrialists and small traders, C) Workers and laborers, Ç) Free professionals, D) Industrialists, large landowners, business-

men, and merchants are the main groups of work composing Turkish society. The work of each of them is essential for the life and happiness of
the others and of the community at large. The aim of our Party pursued
by this principle is to secure social order and solidarity instead of class
conflict, and to establish harmony of interests in a way that none will ne-
gate the others. The benefits are to be proportionate to the aptitude and
to the amount of work.[44]

This notion of populism is clearly solidarist and corporatist. In the words
of Taha Parla, "it is both anti-liberal and anti-socialist. . . . There can be no
more succinct and recipe-like definition of the Durkheimist and Gökalpist
solidarist corporatism both as a sociological theory and a political theory-
ideology."[45] Populism in this sense was the backbone of the single party's
ideology, and as such frequently was emphasized in the speeches of Atatürk
and other party subleaders. Thus Atatürk argued in 1922 that Turkey in the
past had "suffered greatly from political parties. . . . In other countries parties are formed in all cases on the basis of economic aims, because in those
countries there are different classes." When a party is formed to defend
the interests of one class, another party is formed to defend the interests of
another class: "This is very natural. The results we have witnessed because
of political parties formed as if there are different classes in our country are
well-known. Whereas when we speak of the People's Party, the whole nation is included in it, not one part. . . . Consequently, since the interests of
the members of different professions are harmonious with each other, it is
impossible to divide them into classes; all of them consist of the people."[46]
Parla characterizes this notion as "a corporatist model of society that re-
jects the existence of classes (or rather of class conflict), and an above-class,
above-party Bonapartist conception of politics and government."[47]

This solidarist and corporatist concept of populism requires the state
to play an active role in economic life in order to reconcile and harmonize
diverse interests. Hence, it leads to one aspect of another arrow, statism
(étatisme). In its other aspect, statism refers to state entrepreneurship to
achieve rapid industrialization, especially in areas where private capital
is either unwilling or unable to take the lead. In this "developmentalist"
sense, statism has been a rather flexible and conjunctural principle of economic policy that does not interest us here. But statism in the sense of mediation and reconciliation of diverse interests is an important complemen-
tary of the populist principle. Atatürk pointed out in 1931 that "our people,

by their very nature, are statist; they see it as their right to demand all their needs from the state. Therefore, there is a complete correspondence with the nature of our country and the program of our party. . . . Our party is an organization that aims to satisfy the interests of all classes of the people in an equal way and without letting them harm each other."[48] Similarly, Recep Peker, the secretary general of the party, explaining the Party Program in 1935, repudiated class conflict and the notions of privilege and domination. He stated that the CHP was against both the domination of the working class (interestingly, often referred to as the "nationalist" working class, a clear repudiation of the internationalism of socialist doctrines) and their exploitation by big businessmen. Therefore, the state should play an active role of arbitration to reconcile and harmonize their interests; strikes and lockouts as well as trusts and cartels would be prohibited.[49] Thus the CHP's corporation populism was presented as a "third way," different from both liberal capitalism and socialism.[50]

Even more important for our purposes, statism as a complement of populism was conceived not only as a matter of economic policy, but also as a much broader political/administrative principle including the fields of education and culture. Thus, it was stated in the 1931 to 1935 Party Programs that "at all levels of education a necessary point of attention is to raise strongly republican, nationalist, populist, statist, secular, and revolutionary citizens. It will be inculcated [in them] as a sense of duty to respect and make others to respect the Turkish Nation, the Turkish Grand National Assembly, and the State of Turkey. . . . Education should be free of all kinds of superstitions and foreign ideas, superior, national, and patriotic."[51] In the words of Parla, CHP's "statism may be moderate in the economic field, but statism, state guidance, and control will also include culture and education. Kemalist statism in this sense is not limited to 'moderate economic statism.' It is at the same time an administrative political statism with integrationist and totalitarian dimensions as well."[52]

Populism as the backbone of the Kemalist ideology is also associated and fused with another important arrow, nationalism. Both principles conceive of the people as a united and harmonious whole, sharing the same culture and ideals, and without deep cleavages or conflicts. National unity, or even uniformity, is one of the most frequently used concepts in the speeches of Atatürk and other leading party figures. For example, according to Peker, the emergence of classes "leads to a merciless, fanatic, and bigoted class struggle, and thereby to constant conflict among citizens. Such conflict slowly destroys national unity and nationalist ideas that are the greatest forces for the survival of the state and its protection from dangers. Such frictions cause the useless waste of national forces. Therefore, we reject [the emergence of] classes, and defend instead the massification of the nation."[53] The fusion of the populist and nationalist principles in the CHP's discourse also gave the party a convenient way to claim sovereignty for the nation while excluding the people from political participation, since the nation was conceived, under the influence the French political thought, not as a body of people living in a certain territory at a particular point in time, but as a moral personality embracing the past and the future of the society.

Clearly, the CHP's notion of populism leaves little room for a pluralist and competitive party system or even for the expressions of a genuine social pluralism. Starting from the early days of Kemalist rule, Atatürk and his close colleagues rejected the idea of a competitive party system. As quoted earlier, political parties were seen as the natural outgrowths of a class-based society and, therefore, completely unnecessary, even harmful, in the classless Turkish society. Thus in the days preceding the formation of the CHP, Atatürk announced his intention to establish a party "to ensure the common and general interests and the happiness of our people." "But," he added, "there can be no greater sin than pushing the nation who is still suffering from political organizations that were based on personal rather than national aims, and from the practices caused by their seductions and fights, to engage in activities of a similar nature."[54] Similarly, he said in 1925 that the "CHP is not a party engaged in common street politics as in other countries. . . . People's Party has the duty of enlightening and guiding the entire nation. Those who attribute common politicking to our Party are ungrateful people. The country needs a solidary unity. To break up the nation by way of ordinary politics is treason."[55] Atatürk's Great Speech of 1927 and some of his other speeches are full of strong accusations against his political opponents, some of whom were his former comrades-in-arms, ranging from being "bewildered and ignorant brains" to being traitors.[56] These statements show the "passion for unanimity"[57] and the strong dislike for opposition and criticism prevalent in Turkish political culture, certain traces of which can still be found in contemporary Turkish politics.

It may well be argued, though, that the roots of this attitude can be found in Ottoman political culture. Şerif Mardin maintains that "there is an element in Turkish political culture to which the notion of opposition

is deeply repugnant. . . . [E]ven the slightest deviation from political orthodoxy was considered to be treachery (*fitne*), and an ever-present suspicion about the possibility of such treachery was a characteristic of Ottoman
statesmanship." Mardin also observes that this characteristic is not specific
to the elite culture, but also shared by the mass culture, or the "little tradition" as he puts it: "Thus at the level of the 'little society' and of its culture,
we encounter the *gemeinschaftlich* view of society and a lack of tolerance for
variations from the norm." Mardin gives examples of this attitude from the
Ottoman as well as modern (essentially the 1950s) times. He observes that

> at the moment of writing, headlines in Turkish newspapers are contrib-
> uting in their own inimitable way to this pattern of behavior by proclaim-
> ing that politicians with evil designs are trying to "divide" the Turkish na-
> tion. But fifty years ago, the Party of Union and Progress hurled the same
> accusations at its opponents. In Republican times when the Progressive
> Party was accused of treasonable practices the indictment was worded in
> a similar fashion. The Free Party established at the request of Atatürk in
> 1930 disappeared from the political horizon when it was made the butt
> of similar attacks.[58]

Against this picture one can, of course, point out the Free Republican
Party, established in 1930 with the active encouragement of Atatürk as a
loyal opposition party. Atatürk, in his letter to Fethi Okyar, who was his personal choice for the opposition party's leadership, said that "I am glad to
observe once again that we are united on the principle of secular Republic.
In fact, this is the principle which I have always sought, and will continue
to seek, resolutely in political life. . . . Rest assured, sir, that within the principle of secular Republic, any kind of political activity by your party will not
be obstructed."[59] However, Atatürk's perception of the relations between the
CHP and the Free Party, as well as his own perceived rule, does not give one
the impression that what was intended was a full-fledged, truly autonomous
opposition party. Thus he said to Okyar: "I expect to see much struggle between the two parties and their leaders, but I welcome it with great pleasure.
It will strengthen the foundations of the Republic. I can now say to you that
even during your bitterest fights, I will gather you together at my table, and
ask each of you 'What did you say and why did you say it?', 'What was your
answer and how do you justify it?' I admit that this will be a great pleasure
for me."[60] These statements clearly indicate the hegemonic or controlled

nature of the arrangement. In any case, the experiment ended after about three months, when it appeared that the new party was attracting significant popular support. This alarmed the CHP leadership, and when Atatürk withdrew his moral support, the party decided to dissolve itself. Most observers agree that after the dissolution of the Free Party, the CHP further strengthened its authoritarian control over society.[61]

The 1930s were the years when the principles of economic and political liberalism were most clearly and explicitly repudiated by the CHP. Perhaps the best example of this mood is the 1935 speech by Peker explaining CHP's program. In his view, under the liberal order, the abuse of rights and liberties led to a period of anarchy that destroyed human beings. While everyone exercised his or her unlimited liberty, they overlooked the need to protect the state authority. Consequently, masses of people lived in an endless fight: "All kinds of evil, disorder, and fight found a favorable environment in the bosom of the liberal state." He concluded by saying that "the liberal state was moribund . . . and was collapsing everywhere in the world as a result of corruption from within."[62]

It is a matter of debate whether the Turkish single party had the potential or the ultimate aim of eventually transforming itself into a democratic pluralist party. Those who answer in the affirmative present as their main proof its peaceful and orderly transition to competitive politics in the late 1940s on the initiative of its own leadership.[63] Other scholars argue, however, that the single-party arrangement was intended to be a permanent one, pointing to certain statements in party documents and the speeches of its leaders. For example, in the introduction of the 1931, 1935, and 1943 Party Programs, it was stated that the party's ideas concerned "not only the next few years, but were also valid for the future."[64] Similarly, in an important party document dated 1943, it was claimed that "in the twentieth century, the Turkish conception of the state and the regime will be seen as an example by many nations of the world, admittedly or implicitly."[65] In Parla's view, such statements indicate a permanent, not a transitory, conception of the regime, worthy to be emulated by other nations.[66] A fuller analysis of this question is beyond the scope of this chapter. Suffice it to say that the CHP's ideology, at least as it was in the 1930s and the early 1940s, did not provide a fertile ground for the development of a genuine social and political pluralism. The most interesting question for our purposes is whether the traces of this ideology can still be found in present-day Turkish politics and political culture.

The CHP's single-party ideology fits within the "exclusionary" rather than the "revolutionary" single-party type in Samuel Huntington's classification. In his view, both the exclusionary and the revolutionary (totalitarian) types of single parties have their origins in a sharp social bifurcation, but they differ in the ways in which they react to the original bifurcation and to the subordinated social force. The exclusionary systems "accept the bifurcation of the society and use the party as a means of mobilizing support from their constituency while at the same time suppressing or restricting political activity by the subordinate social force." The revolutionary single-party systems, however, "attempt to eradicate the bifurcation of society by shrinking society to correspond to its constituency through liquidation of the subordinate social force or by expanding its constituency to correspond to society by the assimilation of the subordinate social force." Thus Huntington argues that during the CHP rule "political participation was effectively limited to the Westernized urban classes and the mass of the traditional peasantry were excluded from power."[67] Frederick Frey argues in the same vein that the Kemalist revolution exploited the basic bifurcation between the educated elite and the uneducated masses, rather than deploring it or immediately attacking it. The essence of the Turkish revolution is that it concentrated on the extension and consolidation of the precarious beachhead won by the Westernized intellectuals, "to make it secure beyond all possible challenge. . . . It was not . . . a revolution 'from the bottom up'—an attempt to remold the society by starting with the peasant masses. Such an attempt was not in keeping with the movement's history nor with the attitudes of its leaders. Moreover, the task was simply too immense for such an approach. As in most emerging nations, a smaller handle was necessary, a lever more easily grasped."[68]

The exclusionary nature of the Turkish single-party regime also explains its deeply elitist, tutelary traits. The party was conceived neither as an ordinary party involved in "common street politics" nor as a mass-mobilizational party,[69] but as an instrument of educating, enlightening, and guiding the people. Thus Atatürk said that "the duty that falls upon the intellectuals and scholars is to go into the people to enlighten and to exalt them and to be their leaders in progress and civilization. . . . People's Party will be a school to give people political education. . . . Let us all work in such a way that what we shall create will be a national institution. This will only be possible by giving the nation a political education." "People's Party has the duty of enlightening the entire nation and guiding the entire nation."[70]

The CHP's understanding of nationalism and secularism (two of the most important components of the party ideology) also makes difficult the growth of a genuine organizational pluralism. Nation was defined in the 1931 Party Program as "a political and social body composed of citizens tied to each other by the unity of language, culture, and ideal." With regard to nationalism, it is stated that "the Party considers it its principle to preserve the special character and the independent identity of Turkish social body, while walking parallel to and in harmony with all contemporary nations in international contacts and relations on the way of progress and development."[71] The definition of nationalism shows the nonchauvinistic and nonirredentist character of Kemalist nationalism, while the definition of the nation conforms essentially to the "subjective" understanding of the nation, free from religious, racist, or ethnic overtones. However, the emphasis on linguistic and cultural unity does not leave much room for the recognition of cultural and linguistic diversity. Thus Recep Peker stated in a 1931 speech that the party considers those citizens to whom the ideas of being Kurd, Circassian, even Laz and Pomak were to be "propagated" as our own people: "It is our duty to correct with good will and sincerity these wrong ideas that are the legacy of the dark despotic periods of the past and the products of long historical aggressions."[72] Clearly, these differences are not seen as legitimate realities, but as "wrong ideas" propagated from the outside. In Parla's words,

> the national culture is defined in such a way that there is no room for multiculturalism based on ethnic origins. No space is left to other cultural characteristics that can live side by side or inside a dominant national culture. The notion of the monolithic nation-people and cultural unity amounts to the rejection of ethnic pluralism. Cultural Turkish nationalism turns into an exclusionary-singularist ethnic Turkish nationalism. In other words, an understanding of the unconditional superiority of the dominant ethnic culture, an absolute unity and singleness instead of diversity in unity, predominates.[73]

A natural extension of this strong emphasis on the unity of the nation is the rigid notion of a unitary and highly centralized state, as will be spelled out below.

Indeed, it is interesting to trace the changes in the concepts of nation and nationalism through the CHP's history. It has been pointed out that

Atatürk's notion of nationalism was far from racism, chauvinism, and ir-redentism. During the years of the War of Independence, the terms "Turk-ishness" and "Turkish nation" were hardly ever pronounced. On the con-trary, in the declarations of the Erzurum and Sivas Congresses as well as in the National Pact, the "national community" was defined in more tradi-tional criteria, such as Ottomanism and Islam: "Ottoman lands" (*Memalik-i Osmaniye*), "all Muslim elements" (*bilcümle anasır-ı İslamiye*), "Muslim majority" (*ekseriyet-i İslamiye*), and "Ottoman Muslim majority" (*Osmanlı İslam ekseriyeti*), for example. Even more interestingly, this community was conceived not as a monolithic body, but as one composed of different Muslim elements (components) tied to one another by sentiments of "real brotherhood" (*öz kardeşlik*), "reciprocal respect and sacrifice," "full partner-ship in happiness and disaster," and a desire to "share the same fate." Fur-thermore, it was stated in all three important documents that "full respect" would be shown to the "ethnic and social rights" (*hukuk-u ırkîye ve içtimaiye*) of these elements and to their "environmental conditions" (*şerait-i muhiti-yelerine*). Even though the meanings of these terms were not clarified, they can be interpreted as a promise of cultural pluralism and a high degree of administrative decentralization. It is no accident that the 1921 Constitution adopted a system of broad decentralization never seen in Turkey either be-fore or after that date.[74]

The interesting question of how and why these highly pluralistic notions of state and society were abandoned in favor of a strict emphasis on cul-tural unity may be the subject of another study. One possible explanation is that the promises of cultural pluralism and administrative decentraliza-tion were due to the exigencies of the War of Independence period—that is, the need to maintain the loyalty of non-Turkish Muslim ethnic groups. Atatürk's Assembly speech on May 1, 1920, is a good illustration of this sen-sitivity: "The persons who compose your sublime Assembly are not only Turks, only Circassians, only Kurds, only Laz, but a sincere community composed of all Muslim elements. Therefore, the aims of your sublime body are not limited only to one Muslim element. They belong to a mass composed of Muslim elements. Certainly, the nation whose preservation and defense we are occupied with is not limited to a single element. Each Muslim element that composes this body is our brother and our citizen whose interests are entirely common."[75]

It is generally agreed, however, that after the consolidation of the single-party regime this pluralistic approach was gradually abandoned and replaced by Turkish nationalism, which, while essentially preserving its culture-based characteristic, from time to time developed traits that were ethnicist, even racist. Nevertheless, in foreign relations, nonchauvinistic, nonirredentist, peace-promoting policies were carefully maintained, and the discriminatory practices in domestic politics never reached the heights of the racist ideologies prevalent in much of Europe in those days.[76]

Finally, another area of conflict between the founding philosophy of the republic and the development of a genuine pluralistic social and political system concerns the principle of secularism, or the relations between the state and religion. As it is commonly accepted, the Kemalist notion of secularism differed significantly from its counterparts in most Western democracies. Kemalist secularism did not limit itself to the separation of state and religious affairs, but conceived of it as a way of life guided by rational and scientific thought in a manner reminiscent of Comteian positivism. Thus, according to the 1931 and 1935 Party Programs, "the Party sees it as its principle that all laws and regulations shall be made and implemented in accordance with the latest scientific and technical principles and worldly requirements. Since religion is a matter of conscience, the Party considers the separation of religion from the world and state affairs and politics as one of the main conditions for our nation's progress on the road to contemporary civilization."[77] Kemalist secularism fits in the "assertive secularism" type of Ahmet Kuru, who has distinguished between passive and assertive types of secularism. Passive secularism requires that the state play a passive role in avoiding the establishment of any religion, but "allows for the public visibility of religion. Assertive secularism, by contrast, means that the state excludes religion from the public sphere and plays an 'assertive' role as the agent of a social engineering project that confines religion to the private domain. Thus, passive secularism is a pragmatic political principle that tries to maintain state neutrality toward various religions, whereas 'assertive' secularism is a 'comprehensive doctrine' that aims to eliminate religion from the public sphere."[78] Admittedly, such a notion does not allow the emergence of religious political parties and interest associations.

Whether the Kemalist regime had to follow this authoritarian, solidarist, and corporatist road under the circumstances prevailing at that time is beyond the scope of this study. Besides, such a retrospective analysis is bound to be essentially speculative. What is more important for our purposes is to examine whether the traces of this legacy are still present in contemporary

Turkish politics and, if so, how they interact with pressures toward greater pluralism. That will be the task of the last section.

The Structure and Development of Organizational Pluralism

As expected, the state of organized pluralism in Turkey is closely tied to the important cycles of change in Turkish politics. Although the Ottoman Empire displayed a relatively high degree of traditional, or de facto, pluralism composed of non-Muslim *millet* organizations, Muslim religious orders (*tarikats*), sects, tribes, clans, craft guilds, charitable foundations (*vakıf*), and the like, the strict separation between the rulers and the ruled and the absence of a representative system even in a rudimentary form did not permit this traditional pluralism to evolve into the organized pluralistic infrastructure of a modern state.[79] The Ottoman-Turkish political culture always exalted the state as an entity autonomous from and superior to society with a tutelary and paternalistic role. Consequently, the always-dominant state elites, considering themselves the guardians of the state and protectors of the permanent public interest, viewed with suspicion all pluralistic interests and the political parties or interest groups that represent them.[80] Even the term "interest group" still has a negative connotation in Turkish, as expressing narrow and selfish particularistic interests that are incompatible with "public interest." As Robert Bianchi has observed, such attitudes persisted in the multiparty period. "Throughout the multi-party era," he says, "much of the political elite has continued to share a lingering fear that unless partitive interests are repressed, closely regulated, or prudently harmonized, divisions along such lines as class, religion, and region will threaten both the unity of the nation and the authority of the state."[81]

Consequently, the first interest associations in the modern sense appeared only in the late nineteenth century. For example, the first chamber of commerce was established in Istanbul in 1882 based on a regulation issued in 1880. Similarly, the first bar association was established in Istanbul in 1878 based on a regulation dated 1876.[82] The Second Constitutional Period, beginning with the restoration of the constitution in 1908, provided a promising start. In the extensive revision of the constitution in 1909, the right of association was recognized, as long as groups did not pursue such aims as violating the territorial integrity and the constitutional regime of the state, acting against the provisions of the constitution, and politically dividing the Ottoman elements, and did not violate public morals (art. 120). The following period (1908–1924) is described as "incipient pluralism" by Bianchi; this "was characterized by intense organizational and ideological competition between a wide variety of political parties and groups proposing conflicting solutions to such fundamental issues as the definition of the political community and the nature of the regime."[83]

The following period (1925–1946) was that of the consolidation of the single-party regime; during this era, policies toward interest groups were highly restrictive and authoritarian. Such policies were further intensified after the self-imposed dissolution of the Free Party in 1930. The popularity gained by this party during its very brief lifetime must have alarmed the CHP leadership and convinced them of the need to pursue a more sustained and authoritarian policy of mobilization. Atatürk's statement in 1931 heralded the beginnings of the new policy: "There are certain periods in nations' history that necessitate bringing together and leading to the same direction all material and moral forces in order to achieve certain objectives. All nationalist and republican forces must come together for the protection of the country and the revolution from dangers that may come from the inside or the outside. Forces of the same kind must unite in the service of the common aim."[84] The new policy led the major voluntary associations such as the Turkish Hearths, Women's Union, and Masonic lodges, all sympathetic to the regime, to dissolve themselves "voluntarily."[85] This was followed by the draconian Law on Associations, passed in 1938, which prohibited all class-based associations, including trade unions. It will be recalled that this period corresponds to a phase in the CHP's life when authoritarian, solidarist, and corporatist ideas were most enthusiastically and systematically pronounced. Thus between 1938 and 1946, the total number of associations grew very slowly from 205 to 820, and these consisted "mainly of local sporting clubs that were concentrated in the metropolitan centers of Istanbul, Ankara, and Izmir."[86]

The transition to a multiparty system, aided by the relaxation of the Law on Associations in 1946, witnessed a rapid rise in the number of associations, to over 2,000 in 1950 and over 17,000 by 1960: "This was a period of rapid growth and extensive geographic diffusion for a wide variety of associations. It signals the emergence of associability as a nationwide phenomenon, extending broadly though still unevenly over several aspects of social and economic life in nearly every region."[87]

The development of associational life received a further boost with the adoption of the liberal constitution of 1961, which recognized the right of association, stating that "everyone possesses the right to establish associations without prior permission. This right can be limited by law only in order to protect public order and public morals." The constitution also gave trade unions the rights to free unionization, to strike, and of collective bargaining. Between 1960 and 1971, the number of associations again multiplied two and a half times: "By 1970 the total number of associations reached an estimated 42,000. Though the vast majority of these were still small and politically insignificant local community organizations, several of the largest occupational associations had become active and influential participants in Turkey's expanding network of interest group politics."[88]

Associational life underwent a serious setback with the military intervention of 1980 and its product, the 1982 Constitution. The leaders of the military regime thought that one of the main maladies of the regime was the excessive politicization of associations and other civil society institutions. Therefore, one of their chief objectives was to depoliticize the associational activities and to cut all ties between political parties and all kinds of civil society organizations. Perhaps the plainest expression of this philosophy can be found in the following words of General Kenan Evren, the leader of the coup:

> The new Constitution lays down a principle valid for all institutions. Each institution, whether a party, a school, or a professional organization, should remain in its own functionally specified area. In other words, a party will function as a party, an association as an association, a foundation as a foundation, and a trade union as a trade union. Political activity is reserved for political parties. No institution which is not organized as a political party may engage in political activity. On the other hand, political parties should not interfere in areas reserved for trade unions, associations, professional organizations, and foundations. Every institution will function within its own framework.[89]

Thus the 1982 Constitution banned all interest groups from pursuing political aims, engaging in political activities, receiving support from or giving support to political parties, and taking joint action with those parties or with each other (articles 33, 52, 69, 135, 171). Union rights and the right to strike were restricted (articles 51, 53, 54). Freedom of association was severely limited (art. 33). Bans on the political activities of civil society institutions were repealed by the constitutional amendment of 1995, and the articles on the freedom of association and the right to form trade unions (articles 33 and 51, respectively) were somewhat liberalized by the constitutional amendment of 2001.

More recently, the legal regime of voluntary associations was further liberalized by Law no. 5231, dated July 17, 2004. This law has been characterized by a leading Turkish NGO (Third Sector Foundation of Turkey [TÜSEV]) as "the most progressive Law on Associations in over 20 years." Thus associations are no longer required to obtain prior authorization for foreign founding, partnership, or activities. They are no longer required to inform local government officials of the day, time, and location of their general assembly meetings and to invite a government official to such meetings. Audit officials must give twenty-four-hour notice and just cause for random audits. They are permitted to open representative offices for federations and confederations internationally. Security forces are no longer allowed on the premises of associations without a court order. Specific restrictions for student associations have been entirely removed. Children from the age of fifteen can form associations. Internal audit standards have been raised to ensure the accountability of members and the management. They will be able to form temporary platforms and initiatives to pursue common objectives. Government funding for up to 50 percent of their projects will be possible. They will be allowed to buy and sell necessary immovable assets.[90]

Ironically, the social prestige and political influence of civil society organizations increased most meaningfully in the post-1983 period, despite the intentions of the military founders of the 1982 Constitution and its highly restrictive clauses. Several reasons may be suggested for this. First, the liberalizing economic reforms of the Motherland Party (ANAP) governments under the leadership of Turgut Özal (1983–1991) integrated the inward-looking, import substitution–based Turkish economy much more strongly with the world economy. Worldwide processes of globalization also greatly helped this integration. Second, at the level of popular political culture the state (described as "sacred" in the Preamble to the 1982 Constitution) is no longer perceived as a sacred or sublime entity over and above the society, but is conceived as an organization at the service of the people. Discourses of political parties have become less ideological and more service oriented. Third, cultural globalization in general and the proliferation of private television and radio networks following the abolition of the state monopoly in 1993, in particular, made the people more keenly aware of the experiences of democratic foreign countries. Commitment to democratic institutions and procedures seems to be appreciably stronger as compared to earlier periods. As a result of all these factors, the prestige and trustworthiness of civil society institutions improved in the public image.

Structurally, the Turkish associational universe has long been divided between two major legal types of organizations: voluntary associations (*dernekler*) and public professional organizations (*kamu kurumu niteliğindeki meslek kuruluşları*), with trade unions representing a third, sui generis, intermediate type. Each of the two major types corresponds to a particular mode of interest representation—pluralism and corporatism, respectively, as defined earlier.

Under Turkish law, voluntary (private) associations approximate the pluralist model, whereas public professional organizations approximate the corporatist model. Trade unions, subject to separate legislation since the early 1960, are closer to the pluralist model while maintaining their own specific characteristics. Public professional organizations have a hybrid nature. On the one hand, they bring together members of certain professions to promote their professional interests; their members do not normally work for the government, and their functions are essentially nongovernmental; and they elect their own executive bodies from among their members without interference by any governmental authority. On the other hand, they are created by law; membership in them is obligatory in the sense that nobody may practice his or her profession without becoming a member of the relevant professional organization; they exercise certain regulatory and disciplinary powers that are derived from public law; they are subject to the administrative tutelage and supervision of central administrative authorities; and like other administrative agencies, their acts and actions are subject to judicial review not by general courts but by administrative courts. For all these reasons, their "public" character predominates, and constitutionally they are considered public corporate bodies. This does not mean, however, that they are mere appendices of the government. On the contrary, they often play a significant oppositional role, as most of them do today. Among these public professional organizations are the chambers of commerce and industry, chambers of agriculture, associations of small traders and artisans, bar associations, medical associations, and associations of dentists, veterinarians, pharmacologists, engineers and architects, notary publics, and their unions at the national level.[91]

Bianchi, writing about interest group politics in Turkey up to the 1980s, observed that "the existing institutional structure of Turkish associational life provides a much firmer base for the further expansion of corporatism than for the gradual development of pluralist democracy. . . . [I]n terms of organizational strength, financial soundness, control over rewards to and sanctions against members, and effective access to authoritative decision makers, the corporatist network enjoys a clear superiority over the still sprawling and fragmented pluralist network."[92] Developments in the post-1980 period, however, did not support this prediction. While public professional organizations are still important, the political weight of the pluralist voluntary associations grew much more rapidly. In particular, the two major associations of businessmen, TÜSİAD and MÜSİAD, play an increasingly active and important role as public-opinion makers not only in matters of purely economic policies, but in a wide range of social and political issues, even though their contribution to public policy-making is still somewhat limited.[93] To these economic interest associations, must be added a large number of think tanks, media and publishing companies, and similar organizations that provide the public with a much greater variety of opinions than used to be the case.

Conclusion

Our discussion so far indicates the difficulty of reconciling a pluralist society with a monolithic state structure. As so many democratic theorists from Dahl to Lijphart have argued, democracy in a plural society can be maintained only through highly consensual arrangements, recognition of cultural differences, a high level of toleration, and mutual guarantees. It has been pointed out in this chapter that some of the principles of the founding philosophy of the Turkish Republic are hardly favorable to the development and consolidation of a truly pluralist and consensual democracy. Elections in recent decades, particularly those of July 22, 2007 (parliamentary), and March 2, 2009 (local), clearly demonstrate the presence of four distinct subcultures in Turkey—the secularist CHP in Thrace and on the Aegean–Mediterranean seacoast; the ultra-nationalist Nationalist Action Party (MHP) in central Anatolia; and the Kurdish nationalist Democratic Society Party

(DTP) in the southeast—a situation considered particularly dangerous by Dahl.[94] At present, the conservative AKP seems to be the only truly national party with significant support in every geographical region of the country.

Against this historical and sociological background, Turkey's constitutional problem poses a major challenge to democratic consolidation. An important function of constitutions in a plural society is to provide mutual security guarantees to each segment of that society, without which a democratic regime cannot be expected to function properly. Turkey's constitutional challenge and the recent constitutional crisis will be analyzed in my other chapter in this volume.

Notes

1. Robert A. Dahl, *Dilemmas of Pluralist Democracy: Autonomy vs. Control* (New Haven, Conn.: Yale University Press, 1982), 5, 29.
2. Ibid., 36–37.
3. Juan J. Linz and Alfred Stepan, *Problems of Democratic Transition and Consolidation: Southern Europe, South America, and Post-Communist Europe* (Baltimore: Johns Hopkins University Press, 1996), 7.
4. Dahl, *Dilemmas of Pluralist Democracy*, 55–80; Samuel H. Beer, "Group Representation in Britain and the United States," in Roy C. Macridis and Bernard E. Brown, eds., *Comparative Politics: Notes and Readings* (Homewood, Ill.: Dorsey Press, 1962), 144–155, and *British Politics in the Collectivist Age* (New York: Knopf, 1965).
5. Philippe C. Schmitter, "Still the Century of Corporatism?" in Philippe C. Schmitter and Gerhard Lehmbruch, eds., *Trends Toward Corporatist Intermediation* (Beverly Hills: Sage, 1979), 13, 15.
6. Stein Rokkan, "Norway: Numerical Democracy and Corporate Pluralism," in Robert A. Dahl, ed., *Political Oppositions in Western Democracies* (New Haven, Conn.: Yale University Press, 1966), 107.
7. Dahl, *Dilemmas of Pluralist Democracy*, 68–71, 79–80.
8. Arend Lijphart, *The Politics of Accommodation: Pluralism and Democracy in the Netherlands* (Berkeley: University of California Press, 1975); *Democracy in Plural Societies: A Comparative Exploration* (New Haven, Conn.: Yale University Press, 1977); and *Democracies: Patterns of Majoritarian and Consensus Government in Twenty-one Countries* (New Haven, Conn.: Yale University Press, 1984).
9. Lijphart, *Democracy in Plural Societies*, 3–4.
10. Ibid., 25ff.

11. Ibid., 48.

12. Robert A. Dahl, "Governments and Political Oppositions," in Fred I. Green-stein and Nelson W. Polsby, eds., *Handbook of Political Science*, vol. 3, *Macropolitical Theory* (Reading, Mass.: Addison-Wesley, 1975), 152.

13. Benjamin Braude and Bernard Lewis, "Introduction," in Benjamin Braude and Bernard Lewis, eds., *Christians and Jews in the Ottoman Empire: The Functioning of a Plural Society*, vol. 1, *The Central Lands* (New York: Holmes and Meier, 1982), 1.

14. On corporate federalism, see Lijphart, *Democracies*, 183–185.

15. Braude and Lewis, "Introduction," 12–13. Their collection *Christians and Jews in the Ottoman Empire* includes excellent analyses and case studies; for the *millet* system, see in particular, Kemal H. Karpat, "*Millets* and Nationality: The Roots of the Incongruity of Nation and State in the Post-Ottoman Era," 141–169; and Benjamin Braude, "Foundation Myths of the *Millet* System," 69–88.

16. Kemal H. Karpat, *Ottoman Population, 1830–1914: Demographic and Social Characteristics* (Madison: University of Wisconsin Press, 1985), 72.

17. Ibid., 188.

18. Carter V. Findley, "The Acid Test of Ottomanism: The Acceptance of Non-Muslims in the Late Ottoman Bureaucracy," in Braude and Lewis, eds., *Christians and Jews in the Ottoman Empire*, 339–368.

19. Robert Devereux, *The First Ottoman Constitutional Period: A Study of the Midhat Constitution and Parliament* (Baltimore: Johns Hopkins University Press, 1963), 143–145. Enver Ziya Karal gives slightly different figures, such as sixty-seven Muslims and forty-eight non-Muslims, in "Non-Muslim Representatives in the First Constitutional Assembly, 1876–1877," in Braude and Lewis, eds., *Christians and Jews in the Ottoman Empire*, 394.

20. On the Young Ottomans in general, see Şerif Mardin, *The Genesis of Young Ottoman Thought: A Study in the Modernization of Turkish Political Ideas* (Princeton, N.J.: Princeton University Press, 1962).

21. Karal, "Non-Muslim Representatives in the First Constitutional Assembly," 396–398.

22. Feroz Ahmad, "Unionist Relations with the Greek, Armenian, and Jewish Communities of the Ottoman Empire, 1908–1914," in Braude and Lewis, eds., *Christians and Jews in the Ottoman Empire*, 404. Ahmad notes that the Greeks had twenty-six and the Armenians fourteen deputies in the 1908 Assembly (430n.26).

23. Karal, "Non-Muslim Representatives in the First Constitutional Assembly," 396.

24. Arus Yumul, "Azınlık mı Vatandaş mı?" in Ayhan Kaya and Turgut Tarhanlı, eds., *Türkiye'de Çoğunluk ve Azınlık Politikaları: AB Sürecinde Yurttaşlık Tartışmaları* (Istanbul: TESEV, 2005), 93. For the steady decline in non-

Muslim population, see also Dilek Güven, "Bugün Malınıza, Yarın Canınıza: Etnik ve Ekonomik Homojenleştirme, 6–7 Eylül 1955 Olayları," in *Türkiye'de Azınlık Hakları Sorunu: Vatandaşlık ve Demokrasi Eksenli Bir Yaklaşım* (Istanbul: TESEV, 2006), 38.

25. Ahmad, "Unionist Relations," 425–428.

26. Baskın Oran, *Türkiye'de Azınlıklar: Kavramlar, Lozan, İç Mevzuat, İçtihat, Uygulama* (Istanbul: TESEV, 2004), 38–41.

27. Ayhan Aktar, *Varlık Vergisi ve Türkleştirme Politikaları* (Istanbul: İletişim, 2000), 71–99.

28. Ibid., 172 and passim. See also Rıdvan Akar, "Tek Parti Dönemi: Varlık Vergisinin Ekonomik, Toplumsal ve Siyasi Boyutları," in *Türkiye'de Azınlık Hakları Sorunu*, 31–35.

29. Aktar, *Varlık Vergisi ve Türkleştirme Politikaları*, 207–208.

30. Güven, "Bugün Malınıza, Yarın Canınıza," 37.

31. Yumul, "Azınlık mı Vatandaş mı?" 92.

32. The subject of minorities has long been considered a taboo in Turkey even in academic writing. In recent years, however, there has been a growing and critical interest in parts of academia, the media, and literary circles. For a sample of such readings, see especially Oran, *Türkiye'de azınlıklar* (this paragraph is largely based on Oran's detailed account); Kaya and Tarhanlı, eds., *Türkiye'de Çoğunluk ve Azınlık Politikaları*; *Türkiye'de Azınlık Hakları Sorunu*; Aktar, *Varlık Vergisi ve Türkleştirme Politikaları*; Umut Özkırımlı, *Milliyetçilik ve Türkiye-AB İlişkileri* (Istanbul: TESEV, 2008); and Sevan Nişanyan, *Yanlış Cumhuriyet: Atatürk ve Kemalizm Üzerine 51 Soru* (Istanbul: Kırmızı, 2008).

33. Oran, *Türkiye'de Azınlıklar*, 41–45; Tahire Erman and Aykan Erdemir, "Aleviler ve Topluma Eklemlenme Sorunsalı," in Kaya and Tarhanlı, eds., *Türkiye'de Çoğunluk ve Azınlık Politikaları*, 127–144.

34. Mehmet Demiray, "Understanding the Alevi Revival: A Transnational Perspective" (master's thesis, Bilkent University, 2004), 57.

35. Oran, *Türkiye'de Azınlıklar*, 42–45.

36. For a discussion of the Alevi demands, see Erman and Erdemir, "Aleviler," 135–143; for Kurdish claims, see Bahar Şahin, "Türkiye'de Avrupa Birliği Uyum Süreci Bağlamında Kürt Sorunu: Açılımlar ve Sınırlar," in Kaya and Tarhanlı, eds., *Türkiye'de Çoğunluk ve Azınlık Politikaları*, 101–126.

37. For interesting observations, see Suavi Aydın, "Azınlık Kavramına İçeriden Bakmak," in Kaya and Tarhanlı, eds., *Türkiye'de Çoğunluk ve Azınlık Politikaları*, 145–170.

38. Taha Parla, *Türkiye'de Siyasal Kültürün Resmi Kaynakları*, vol. 1, *Atatürk'ün Nutuk'u* (Istanbul: İletişim, 1991), 13–16. See also Mustafa Erdoğan, *Demokrasi, Laiklik, Resmi İdeoloji* (Ankara: Liberte Yayınları, 2000).

39. For the difference between ideologies and mentalities, see Juan J. Linz, "Totalitarian and Authoritarian Regimes," in Greenstein and Polsby, eds., *Handbook of Political Science*, 3:266–269. According to Linz, ideologies are "systems of thought more or less intellectually elaborated and organized, often in written form, by intellectuals, pseudo-intellectuals, or with their assistance," whereas mentalities are "ways of thinking and feeling, more emotional than rational, that provide non-codified ways of reaction to situations." For an analysis of Kemalism along these lines, see Ergun Özbudun, "The Nature of the Kemalist Political Regime," in Ali Kazancıgil and Ergun Özbudun, eds., *Atatürk: Founder of a Modern State* (London: Hurst, 1981), 87–92.

40. Taha Parla, *Türkiye'de Siyasal Kültürün Resmi Kaynakları*, vol. 3, *Kemalist Tek-Parti İdeolojisi ve CHP'nin Altı Ok'u* (Istanbul: İletişim, 1992), 12, 21–22.

41. Parla, *Türkiye'de Siyasal Kültürün Resmi Kaynakları*, 1:13.

42. *Atatürk'ün Söylev ve Demeçleri*, vol. 1, *T.B.M. Meclisinde ve C.H.P. Kurultaylarında, 1919–1938* (Ankara: Türk İnkılâp Tarihi Enstitüsü, 1961), 196.

43. Taha Akyol, *Ama Hangi Atatürk* (Istanbul: Doğan Kitap, 2008).

44. Mete Tunçay, *Türkiye Cumhuriyeti'nde Tek-Parti Yönetiminin Kurulması, 1923–1931* (Ankara: Yurt Yayınları, 1981), 448–449. For the official translation of almost identical definition in the 1935 Program, see Suna Kili, *Kemalism* (Istanbul: Robert College, 1969), 78.

45. Parla, *Türkiye'de Siyasal Kültürün Resmi Kaynakları*, 3:42, 44. For similar assessments, see Tunçay, *Türkiye Cumhuriyeti'nde Tek-Parti Yönetiminin Kurulması*, 209; and Levent Köker, *Modernleşme, Kemalizm ve Demokrasi* (Istanbul: İletişim, 1990), 209.

46. *Atatürk'ün Söylev ve Demeçleri*, vol. 2, *1906–1938*, ed. Nimet Unan (Ankara: Türk İnkılâp Tarihi Enstitüsü Yayımları, 1952), 97–98, 82. The same themes were stressed in his election manifesto to the nation on April 20, 1931: Taha Parla, *Türkiye'de Siyasal Kültürün Resmi Kaynakları*, vol. 2, *Atatürk'ün Söylev ve Demeçleri* (Istanbul: İletişim, 1991), 213–215.

47. Parla, *Türkiye'de Siyasal Kültürün Resmi Kaynakları*, 2:217–219. For further elaboration, see also Ziya Gökalp, *Kemalizm ve Türkiye'de Korporatizm* (Istanbul: İletişim, 1989).

48. Parla, *Türkiye'de Siyasal Kültürün Resmi Kaynakları*, 2:262, 264.

49. Ibid., 3:126–136.

50. Ibid., 139–144. For a comparison between Kemalist corporatism and the Italian fascist corporatist state, see Feroz Ahmad, "The Search for Ideology in Kemalist Turkey," in *From Empire to Republic: Essays on the Late Ottoman Empire and Modern Turkey* (Istanbul: Istanbul Bilgi University Press, 2008), 184–192. On Kemalist corporatism, see also Taha Parla and Andrew Davison, *Corporatist*

Ideology in Kemalist Turkey: Progress or Order? (Syracuse, N.Y.: Syracuse University Press, 2004).

51. Parla, *Türkiye'de Siyasal Kültürün Resmi Kaynakları*, 3:71, 74, 78–85.

52. Ibid., 144; in the same direction, see Köker, *Modernleşme, Kemalizm ve Demokrasi*, 209, 226.

53. Parla, *Türkiye'de Siyasal Kültürün Resmi Kaynakları*, 3:112.

54. Ibid., 2:60.

55. Ibid., 224.

56. Ibid., 1:100.

57. The term belongs to Carl J. Friedrich and Zbigniew Brzezinski, *Totalitarian Dictatorship and Autocracy* (New York: Praeger, 1963), 57, 63, 82, 103, 132ff.

58. Şerif Mardin, "Opposition and Control in Turkey," *Government and Opposition* 1 (1966): 375–387.

59. Walter F. Weiker, *Political Tutelage and Democracy in Turkey: The Free Party and Its Aftermath* (Leiden: Brill, 1973), 68–69.

60. Ibid., 70; *Atatürk'ün Söylev ve Demeçleri*, 2:256; Çetin Yetkin, *Serbest Cumhuriyet Fırkası Olayı* (Istanbul: Karacan Yayınları, 1982). See also Metin Heper, *The State Tradition in Turkey* (Walkington: Eothen Press, 1985), 51–52 and passim.

61. Weiker, *Political Tutelage and Democracy in Turkey*, passim; Ahmad, "Search for Ideology in Kemalist Turkey," 184–186.

62. Parla, *Türkiye'de Siyasal Kültürün Resmi Kaynakları*, 3:128–129.

63. See, for example, Ergun Özbudun, *Contemporary Turkish Politics: Challenges to Democratic Consolidation* (Boulder, Colo.: Rienner, 2000), 21–24; Ahmad, "Search for Ideology in Kemalist Turkey," 175–176, 180, 187.

64. Parla, *Türkiye'de Siyasal Kültürün Resmi Kaynakları*, 3:19–20.

65. Ibid., 158.

66. Ibid., 162.

67. Samuel Huntington, "Social and Institutional Dynamics of One-Party Systems," in Samuel Huntington and Clement H. Moore, eds., *Authoritarian Politics in Modern Society: The Dynamics of Established One-Party Systems* (New York: Basic Books, 1970), 15–16. For an analysis of the CHP's single-party regime along similar lines, see Ergun Özbudun, "Established Revolution Versus Unfinished Revolution: Contrasting Patterns of Democratization in Mexico and Turkey," in ibid., 380–405.

68. Frederick W. Frey, *The Turkish Political Elite* (Cambridge, Mass.: MIT Press, 1965), 40.

69. Özbudun, "Nature of the Kemalist Political Regime," 93–94.

70. *Atatürk'ün Söylev ve Demeçleri*, 2:98, 224.

71. Parla, *Türkiye'de Siyasal Kültürün Resmi Kaynakları*, 3:28, 35.

72. Ibid., 110.

73. Ibid., 119–120.

74. Ergun Özbudun, "Milli Mücadele ve Cumhuriyet'in Resmi Belgelerinde Yurttaşlık ve Kimlik Sorunu," in Nuri Bilgin, ed., *Cumhuriyet, Demokrasi ve Kimlik* (Istanbul: Bağlam, 1997), 63–65. This volume contains many important contributions on the subject of Turkish identity. For a similar collection of articles on the same topic, see Artun Ünsal, ed., *75 Yılda Tebaa'dan Yurttaş'a Doğru* (Istanbul: Tarih Vakfı, 1998).

75. *Atatürk'ün Söylev ve Demeçleri*, 1:73–74. In fact, Atatürk's elaboration of his concept of the nation in his civic education textbook first printed in 1931 is not fundamentally different from his early speeches: A. Afet İnan, *Medeni Bilgiler ve M. Kemal Atatürk'ün El Yazıları* (Ankara: Türk Tarih Kurumu Yayınları, 1969), 18–25, 351–383.

76. For examples of the Turkification policies and the discriminatory practices against non-Muslim and Kurdish minorities, see Parla, *Türkiye'de Siyasal Kültürün Resmi Kaynakları*, 3:203–211; Baskın Oran, *Atatürk Milliyetçiliği: Resmi İdeoloji Dışı Bir İnceleme* (Ankara: Dost Kitabevi, 1988), 157–159, 231, 237; Aktar, *Varlık Vergisi ve Türkleştirme Politikaları*, passim; and Tanıl Bora, "Cumhuriyetin İlk Döneminde Milli Kimlik," in Bilgin, ed., *Cumhuriyet, Demokrasi ve Kimlik*, 53–62.

77. Parla, *Türkiye'de Siyasal Kültürün Resmi Kaynakları*, 3:36, 39.

78. Ahmet T. Kuru, "Passive and Assertive Secularism: Historical Conditions, Ideological Struggles, and State Policies Toward Religion," *World Politics* 59 (2007): 568–594. See also Charles Taylor, "Modes of Secularism" in Rajeev Bhargava, ed., *Secularism and Its Critics* (Delhi: Oxford University Press, 1998), 31–53; and Tunçay, *Türkiye Cumhuriyeti'nde Tek-Parti Yönetimi'nin Kurulması*, 218–225.

79. Ergun Özbudun, "Continuing Ottoman Legacy and the State Tradition in the Middle East," in L. Carl Brown, ed., *Imperial Legacy: The Ottoman Imprint on the Balkans and the Middle East* (New York: Columbia University Press, 1996), 135–139.

80. Ergun Özbudun, "State Elites and Democratic Political Culture in Turkey," in Larry Diamond, ed., *Political Culture and Democracy in Developing Countries* (Boulder, Colo.: Rienner, 1993), 247–268.

81. Robert Bianchi, *Interest Groups and Political Development in Turkey* (Princeton, N.J.: Princeton University Press, 1984), 105. Bianchi provides a perceptive analysis of the Ottoman-Turkish political culture with regard to interest groups (73–107).

82. Harun Çetintemel, "Kamu Kurumu Niteliğindeki Meslek Kuruluşları" (manuscript, available at the Council of State [Danıştay] Library, Ankara, 1976), 3, 12.

83. Bianchi, *Interest Groups and Political Development*, 139–140.

84. Çetin Yetkin, *Türkiye'de Tek-Parti Yönetimi, 1930–1945* (Istanbul: Altın Kitaplar, 1963), 30.

85. Ibid., 52–66, 78–86.

86. Bianchi, *Interest Groups and Political Development*, 155.

87. Ibid.

88. Ibid., 155–156. From the mid-1950s through 1968, the single largest category of voluntary associations was that of mosque-building associations, according to Ahmet Yücekök's figures in *Türkiye'de Dernek Gelişmeleri, 1946–1968* (Ankara: AÜSBF Yayınları, 1972).

89. *Türkiye Cumhuriyeti Devlet Başkanı Orgeneral Kenan Evren'in Yeni Anayasayı Devlet Adına Resmen Tanıtma Programı Gereğince Yaptıkları Konuşmalar (24 Ekim–5 Kasım 1982)* (Ankara: TBMM Basımevi, 1982), 37–38, 41, 48, 56–58, 70–77, 128.

90. Ergun Özbudun and Serap Yazıcı, *Democratization Reforms in Turkey, 1993–2004* (Istanbul: TESEV, 2004), 20–21.

91. Ergun Özbudun, "The Post-1980 Legal Framework for Interest Group Associations," in Metin Heper, ed., *Strong State and Economic Interest Groups: The Post-1980 Turkish Experience* (Berlin: de Gruyter, 1991), 46–49.

92. Bianchi, *Interest Groups and Political Development*, 350.

93. On the complicated love–hate relationship between the state and commercial groups, see Ersin Kalaycıoğlu, "Commercial Groups: Love–Hate Relationship with the State," 79–87, and Yeşim Arat, "Politics and Big Business: Janus-Faced Link to the State," 135–147, both in Heper, ed., *Strong State and Economic Interest Groups*; and Ayşe Buğra, "Class, Culture, and State: An Analysis of Interest Representation by Two Turkish Business Associations," *International Journal of Middle East Studies* 30 (1998): 521–539, and *Islam in Economic Organizations* (Istanbul: TESEV, 1999).

94. For an analysis of the March 29, 2009, local elections, see Ergun Özbudun, "Değişiklikler ve Süreklilikler," *Zaman* (daily), April 10, 2009; and "Merkez Partisinin İkilemleri," *Zaman*, April 11, 2009.

4

Laïcité as an "Ideal Type" and a Continuum

Comparing Turkey, France, and Senegal

AHMET T. KURU AND ALFRED STEPAN

On March 13 and 14, 2008, Turkish president Abdullah Gül attended the meeting of the Organization of the Islamic Conference (IOC) in Senegal. Turkey's membership to the IOC had been a domestically controversial issue because of its secular state structure. It took Turkey fifteen years (1969–1984) to be represented by its president in the IOC. Senegal is also a secular state but did not have a similar concern. Turkey is the only long-standing democracy with a Muslim-majority population in the Middle East, while Senegal is one of the world's few "electoral overachievers," in terms of combining low GDP per capita with competitive elections.[1] Both Senegal and Turkey were influenced by France in terms of modeling their secular states.[2]

A common characteristic of secular states (*états laïques*) is their lack of an established religion. In this regard, Turkey, Senegal, and France are similar to other secular states such as the United States, India, and Indonesia, while differing from states with an established church, such as the United Kingdom, Denmark, and Greece. The variations of secularism (*laïcité*) have been examined by several scholars. Alfred Stepan develops two models: the *separationist* model (e.g., the United States, France, and Turkey) and the *respect all, support all* model (e.g., India, Indonesia, and Senegal).[3] Ahmet Kuru defines secularism in two types—*assertive* and *passive*

TABLE 1

Variations of Secularism

	PASSIVE SECULARIST	ASSERTIVE SECULARIST
SEPARATIONIST	United States	France
		Turkey
RESPECT ALL, SUPPORT ALL	India	[By definition impossible]
	Indonesia	
	Senegal	

secularism. Assertive secularism requires the state to play an assertive role to exclude religion from the public sphere. This is the dominant ideology in France and Turkey. Passive secularism, conversely, demands the state to play a passive role by allowing public visibility of religion. It is dominant in the United States.[4] Table 1 combines these two typologies.

Documenting Variations of Laïcité

In Turkey and Senegal, French laïcité (laiklik in Turkish) literally and intellectually is the historical origin of the idea of the secular state. The opening articles of the constitution in all three countries identically refer to laïcité. Nevertheless, Senegal differs from Turkey and France with its *respect all, support all* model, which tolerates public religions and the state's close interaction with them. Although Turkey and France seem to be similarly separationist and assertive secularists, they have different policies toward religion, too. In France, religions have relatively more freedom in the public domain than they do in Turkey. In Jonathan Fox's dataset, the scores (of restricting majority and minority religions) of Turkey 15 (6 + 9), France 5 (0 + 5), and Senegal 1 (1 + 0) support our comparison.[5]

We will demonstrate the differences between these three cases by analyzing state restrictions over four issues: (1) the organization of the majority religion, (2) the organization of the minority religions, (3) (private and public) religious education, and (4) religious dress. First, in Turkey, all imams in around eighty thousand mosques have been employees of the governmental Directorate of Religious Affairs (Diyanet). The president of the Diyanet is jointly appointed by the president, the prime minister, and a minister. The Diyanet oversees the writing of the sermons given in mosques. Any other Islamic associations, either Sunni or Alevi, are illegal. In other words, associations independent of the Diyanet cannot run mosques or other Islamic sites, unless they define these as cultural, educational, and the like. The Diyanet, as the major instrument of the state to regulate religion, constitutes the major practical contradiction to Turkey's theoretical "separationism" between religion and the state. Due to the dominance of assertive secularist ideology in Turkey, the state pursues a policy to exclude Islam from the public sphere by confining it to the Diyanet-run mosques.

In France, the central government and local administrations have owned and funded the great majority of the 45,000 Catholic churches built before 1906.[6] They allow Catholics to use these buildings. Other than that and some other exceptions, such as the status of the Alsace-Moselle region, where the clergy are appointed and paid by the state, the state and the Catholic Church have been separated in France since the 1905 law.

In Senegal, the state does not have a direct supervisory role over Islamic institutions. Islamic groups, such as Sufis, are largely independent of the state and enjoy freedom of association. Around "90 percent of the population is . . . affiliated with two major—and several smaller—Sufi orders."[7] In short, the Senegalese state does not put restrictions over the majority religion—Islam.

Second, non-Muslim communities have faced difficulties in Turkey. Until recently, they experienced restrictions while trying to construct places of worship. A legal reform in 2003, as part of Turkey's adaptations for the European Union (EU), facilitated the construction of such places. Another reform in 2008, partially helped solving some other problems of these communities, such as their associations' ability to own property, in particular, and to act as a corporate entity, in general.

In France, there is general freedom to construct houses of worship and found religious associations, except for two restrictions. One is the bureaucratic and practical barriers Muslims have experienced while constructing mosques. The other is the recently founded governmental body that observes what the French have called 173 "dangerous cults," such as Jehovah's Witnesses and Scientology.

In Senegal, religious minorities, especially the Catholic minority, have enjoyed freedom of association and freedom to construct places of worship. There is no state restriction over minority religions' organization in Senegal comparable to that in Turkey and France.

In terms of our third criterion, that of religious education, in Turkey, private Islamic education has been banned since the founding era. Islamic instruction is provided only by the Diyanet's Qur'ān courses, by public Islamic (Imam-Hatip) high schools, and in religious instruction in all public schools. Even in governmentally controlled courses, it is not permitted to teach the Qur'ān to students under fifteen years of age (under twelve in summers). The nationwide university admission examination system discriminated against the graduates of Imam-Hatip schools by giving them a lower coefficient while calculating their scores. The religious instruction in schools has been mainly designed to teach a state-crafted version of Islam—a concern of individual conscience. Christians in Turkey also have some problems in terms of their religious education. For example, the state has not allowed the reopening of the Greek Orthodox Church's Theology Seminar in Istanbul.

In France, there is no religious instruction in public schools. Yet since the late 1880s, a weekday (now Wednesday) has been made free (or partially free) in public schools so that students who want to go to churches (or other religious institutions) may do so in order to receive religious education. About 20 percent of all students attend private schools, 95 percent of which are Catholic schools. These schools are free to teach religion and to organize prayers. Most of them sign contracts with the state to receive public funding in exchange for following the national curriculum and being open to all students regardless of their religions. Public funding covers teaching salaries and thus compensates about 80 percent of these schools' budgets.[8] Around 60 percent of the French public schools have Catholic chaplains for responding to student requests for religious counseling.[9] Following the recent headscarf ban in French public schools, many Muslim students began to attend Catholic private schools or newly opened Islamic schools. There are now four Islamic private schools in France.[10] These schools are still in the process of applying for state funding.

In Senegal, mandatory religious instruction was introduced in public schools in 2002. Its implementation "remains unclear, but it was generally well received by all religious groups, including the small Christian minority, since it will give students the choice of Christian or Muslim instruction."[11] In addition to public schools, there is a vast and expanding network of private schools, ranging from simply Qur'ānic schools to formal "Franco-Arabic" schools, which particularly provide Islamic education. The state

TABLE 2

Turkey, France, and Senegal: State Restrictions over Religion

STATE RESTRICTIONS OVER:	MAJORITY RELIGION'S ORGANIZATION	MINORITY RELIGIONS' ORGANIZATION	PRIVATE RELIGIOUS EDUCATION	RELIGIOUS DRESS
Turkey	Yes	Some	Yes	Yes
France	No	Some	No	Yes
Senegal	No	No	No	No

funds the "schools operated by religious institutions that meet national education standards. Christian schools, which have a long and successful experience in education, receive the largest share of this government funding. The majority of students attending Christian schools are Muslims."[12] In sum, there is no state restriction over majority Islamic or minority Catholic education in Senegal.

Finally, in terms of our fourth criteria, religious dress: in Turkey, wearing the Muslim headscarf has been banned for students, teachers, professors, civil servants, and elected politicians. The French state has recently banned all religious symbols in public schools, without imposing such restriction on private schools or universities. The ban on wearing headscarves in France is also extended to civil servants. In Senegal, there has been an encompassing freedom to wear religious dress and to display religious symbols publicly, including at public institutions.

Table 2 summarizes the comparison of these three cases regarding state restrictions in the four areas. This comparison illustrates that Senegal, where passive secularism is the dominant ideology, differs from Turkey and France, where assertive secularism is dominant. Yet France is more tolerant toward public religions than is Turkey. The difference between Turkey and France, despite their ideological similarity, reveals that secularism is a matter of degree. States exist on a continuum between the Weberian ideal types of passive and assertive secularism, because no case is perfectly passive secularist (completely tolerating religions in the public sphere) or assertive secularist (prohibiting any public visibility of religion). Although brief analyses can present assertive and passive secularist ideal types in a dichotomy, a detailed analysis should acknowledge the difference within these types and therefore put the cases on a continuum.

TABLE 3
Turkey, France, and Senegal: Official Holidays, 2009

	TURKEY	FRANCE	SENEGAL
Secular holidays	New Year (January 1)	New Year (January 1)	New Year (January 1)
	National Sovereignty Children's Day (April 23)	Labor Day (May 1)	Independence Day (April 4)
	Commemoration of Atatürk, Youth, and Sports Day (May 19)	V-E Day (May 8)	Labor Day (May 1)
	Victory Day (August 30)	Bastille Day (July 14)	
	Republic Day (October 29)	Armistice Day (November 11)	
Majority religious holidays	Eid al-Adha (September 20)	Easter Monday (April 13)	Eid al-Adha (September 21)
	Eid al-Ramadan (November 27)	Ascension Day (May 21)	Eid al-Ramadan (November 27)
		Whit Monday (June 1)	Ashura (January 8)
		Assumption Day (August 15)	The Prophet's Birthday (March 10)
		All Saints' Day (November 1)	
		Christmas Day (December 25)	

	TURKEY	FRANCE	SENEGAL
Minority religious holidays	None	None	Easter Monday (April 13)
			Ascension Day (May 21)
			Pentecost Monday (June 1)
			Assumption Day (August 15)
			All Saints' Day (November 1)
			Christmas Day (December 25)

Source: "Q++ Worldwide Public Holidays," http://www.qppstudio.net/publicholidays.htm (accessed January 19, 2009).

Separationism also indicates a Weberian ideal type, while real cases are located along a continuum. In neither France nor Turkey are the state and religion totally separated. In Senegal, they are not fully entangled either. Senegal, with its *respect all, support all* model, experiences close state interactions with religions, especially majority Islam and main minority Catholicism. The Senegalese government "assists Muslim participation in the annual Hajj. It also provides similar assistance for an annual Catholic pilgrimage to the Vatican." It even provides "free plane tickets to Muslim and Christian citizens to undertake the pilgrimage to Mecca or to Rome and the Holy Land."[13]

Another illustration of religion–state relations is the number of holidays a state grants to its majority and the minority religions. Table 3 shows that Senegal differs from separationist Turkey and France in terms of recognizing minority religions. It lists the secular, majority religion, and minority religion holidays in Turkey (5, 2, and 0), France (5, 6, and 0), and Senegal (3, 4, and 6). Neither France nor Turkey recognizes a holiday for a minority religion, whereas Senegal has six (two more than it has for the majority religion).

Explaining Variations of *Laïcité*

Why did Senegal produce an inclusive understanding and practice of *laïcité*, whereas Turkey developed a version that has been more exclusionary than even *laïcité* in France? We argue that certain historical conditions, especially the existence or absence of an ancien régime at the time of secular state-building, have resulted in this variation. The ancien régime is based on the alliance between monarchy and hegemonic religion against the republicans.[14] In France, the founding period of the secular state was the early Third Republic—from the Constitutional Laws of 1875 to the 1905 law separating church and state. At that time, the secular republicans struggled with the conservative Catholics who sought to reestablish the monarchy and to preserve the Catholic establishment. During the founding of the Republic of Turkey, from its establishment in 1923 to the constitutional amendment enshrining secularism in 1937, the Westernist secularists fought with Islamists who wanted to maintain the official status of Islam. The Republic of Senegal, however, did not have such an ancien régime. It was founded in 1960 following the end of French colonialism, which had lasted for more than a century, rather than replacing a local monarchy. In Senegal, Islamic groups were not an ally of an old regime against the new republic. Moreover, the Sufis in Senegal established friendly relations with the secular French colonial regime in the late nineteenth century based on mutual accommodation and the "rituals of respect." In other words, the Senegalese state was created by the French colonial power, which had already established a version of *laïcité* that accommodated Sufi elites. This positive relationship between the secular state and the Sufis was inherited by the new state after decolonization. This historical legacy is important for understanding the religious-friendly version of *laïcité* in the independent Senegal.

In France and Turkey, the severe conflict between the secular republicans and the religious groups resulted in the dominance of assertive secularism, whereas in Senegal, the accommodating relations between these two groups led to the dominance of passive secularism. Moreover, since the Catholic minority played an important positive role in the founding of Senegal, the secular state recognized Catholicism, as well as Islam, which led it to the *respect all, support all* model, instead of unfriendly state–religion separationism.

This argument, which claims an ideological path dependence,[15] does not imply a historical determinism.[16] On the one hand, the secular state-building, assertive/passive secularist ideologies, and separationist/*respect all, support all* models have largely preserved their dominance in the three countries through public education and institutional socialization. On the other hand, these ideologies and models have been challenged by sociopolitical forces and experienced conceptual and practical transformations. In short, both ideological path dependence and ideological struggles are crucial dimensions of the public-policy formation process. We will examine the historical emergence of two types of secularism and contemporary ideological struggles between the defenders of various interpretations and implementations of these secular ideologies in the three cases.

Before analyzing each case separately, we want to examine the differences between France and Turkey despite their historical and ideological similarities. French and Turkish ancien régimes had different characteristics. In France, the Catholic Church represented a hierarchical organization relatively isolated from society. Certain of its features, such as the pope's supranational authority and the clergy's celibacy, contributed to that isolation. There was a tension between several segments of French society and the church regarding issues such as the church's large properties since the time of feudalism. In Turkey, however, religion had played a relatively different role in the ancien régime. Islamic institutions, from the *ulema* in Istanbul to Sufi lodges in local areas, were very diverse. These institutions were comparatively more deeply embedded in society because there was not an extraterritorial pope or isolated clergy who were celibate. The pious foundations, for example, were seen as a shared value of society, not the property of the *ulema*. In this regard, there was no monolithic polarization between the "mosque" and certain segments of the "people." The tension occurred between the Westernist elite and Islamic leaders in the late Ottoman and early republican periods. The Islamists in Turkey, unlike the Catholic Church in France, did not try to reestablish the monarchy. Yet the Turkish republican elite still saw the Islamists as the representatives of the ancien régime, in terms of the hegemony of the Islamic way of life.

For these reasons, assertive secularism was largely imposed as a top–down elite project in Turkey, while it was established through a relatively more bottom–up process in France. Assertive secularism in Turkey was the pillar of the Westernization project, which alienated the traditional culture of the masses by importing a new—European—way of life. In France, assertive secularism was more indigenous. That is why the assertive secularists have become successful under multiparty democracy in France, whereas they have needed authoritarian means in Turkey. This historical difference has an impact on contemporary differences between democracy in France and semi-authoritarianism in Turkey. From the secular state-building in the late nineteenth century to the present, assertive secularism in France has coexisted with multiparty democracy and has gained substantial popular support. Secularist parties, for example, increased their votes in the elections a year after they passed the 1905 law that disestablished Catholicism.[17] Assertive secularism in France was challenged by Catholic movements that supported the reestablishment of monarchy and authoritarian rule, such as the Vichy regime (1940–1944). Thanks to democracy, the opponents of assertive secularism have had the political means to criticize certain policies, and the assertive secularists have made compromises from their utopian ideological views. In Turkey, by contrast, assertive secularism was established by an authoritarian single-party rule in the early twentieth century and has been defended since 1960 by several military and judiciary coups d'état against democratically elected governments. In the Turkish elections, assertive secularist politicians have always received far fewer votes than the conservatives and liberals, who have largely embraced passive secularism. That reflects the tension between assertive secularism and democracy in Turkey. Under the shadow of the authoritarian military and judiciary, it has been much more difficult to oppose assertive secularist policies. The assertive secularists, therefore, have rarely accepted policy compromises. Nevertheless, very recently, democratization has also caused relative moderation of assertive secularist policies in Turkey.

France

In the late eighteenth century, French republicans were largely anti-clerical, mainly in reaction to the marriage between the monarchy and the Catholic establishment. Following the 1789 revolution, tens of thousands of the clergy who refused to submit loyalty oaths to the state fled France or were imprisoned.[18] During this period, the state expropriated the lands of the church and guillotined about three thousand priests.[19] Yet that meant neither the elimination of the church's power nor the end of the dichotomy between secularists and clergy. Instead, several regime changes, back and forth between French monarchies and republics, intensified the antagonism between these two sides. Since republicanism was not the dominant regime until the late nineteenth century—except the short-lived Second Republic (1848–1852)—Catholicism preserved its privileged position in French sociopolitical life.

The republicans challenged the Catholic establishment following the foundation of the Third Republic in 1870. Léon Gambetta formulized their enmity with his famous slogan: "Le cléricalisme, voilà l'ennemi!" (Clericalism, that is the enemy!).[20] The conservative Catholics, on the contrary, perceived the Third Republic as fragile and sought a new monarchy to consolidate their established status.[21] The conflict between these two groups turned into the "war of two Frances." One France was the inheritor of the 1789 revolution's values—republican, anti-clerical, and secularist. It included leftist parties, some civic associations (e.g., Freemasons, Freethinkers, and League of Education), and religious minorities (Protestants and Jews). The other France was tied to the ancien régime, based on the marriage between the Catholic Church and the monarchy. It included the clergy, conservative press, and conservative politicians.[22]

The main fault line between the secularists and the conservative Catholics was education, since both aimed to shape the worldviews of the young generation. Jules Ferry, the republican minister of education, played a vital role in the establishment of "free, obligatory, and secular" education. Secularist republicans excluded thousands of clerical teachers from the education system, as well as closing about fifteen thousand Catholic schools.[23] The Catholics tried to oppose these policies. Nevertheless, they were not effective in party politics and parliament. In 1905, the republicans proposed the bill that would separate the church and the state. Despite the opposition of conservative Catholics, the bill was approved in the Assembly (341–233) and the Senate (179–103).[24] Pope Pius X, the French clergy, and the Catholic press condemned the law. Throughout the Third Republic, the Catholic hierarchy preserved its opposition to secularism. The French Assembly of Cardinals and Bishops, for example, declared in March 1925 that "secularism in all spheres is fatal to the private and public good. Therefore the secularization laws are not laws."[25] Assertive secularism in France emerged as a result of this severe conflict.

The conflict between the republican secularist and monarchist Catholics continued until the end of World War II. Following the collapse of the Vichy regime, the church and conservative politicians recognized that restoration of the monarchy or reestablishment of Catholicism was no longer possible. In November 1945, the French Episcopate declared that it accepted secularism as church–state separation and religious freedom, while still opposing secularism as an anti-religious ideology.[26] When secularism became a fundamental principle of the 1946 Constitution, the church and the conservative politicians did not directly oppose it. In the following period, assertive secularist policies were moderated through state concessions to the Catholics, such as public funding of Catholic schools.

The rising Muslim population in France in the late 1980s reshaped the debates on state–religion relations.[27] Until that time, the leftists, who embraced assertive secularism, were opposed by the conservative rightists. Regarding the Muslim question, the majority of the leftists reiterated their commitment to assertive secularism and allied with the anti-immigrant and Islamophobic rightists.[28] On the other side, multiculturalist leftists and rightists came together to support passive secularism, which would tolerate public visibility of religion and respect increasing cultural diversity in France. The headscarf debate polarized these two coalitions. Passive secularists, such as the influential League of Education, opposed a general ban on headscarves in public schools.[29] Assertive secularists, such as the Freemasons, pressed for such a ban.

In 1989, the Council of State decided that students' religious symbols are not inherently incompatible with secularism.[30] Until 2004, many students wearing headscarves were tolerated by the school administrators or returned to their schools by local court rulings. Of the forty-nine cases that reached it from 1992 to 1999, the council overturned forty-two by taking the side of students.[31] In the early 2000s, the right–left coalition against headscarves became visible in the polls. The supporters of the headscarf ban reached 72 percent of the population—71 percent of leftists and 79 percent of the rightists.[32] The 2002 presidential elections indicated the rise of the far right, a major supporter of the headscarf ban. In the first round of the elections, Jean-Marie Le Pen, the leader of the extreme nationalist, anti-immigrant, and Islamophobic National Front received 17 percent of votes, while central-rightist incumbent Jacques Chirac won only 20 percent and leftist prime minister Lionel Jospin won only 16 percent.

After his reelection, President Chirac took a clearly negative position against headscarves. He appointed a commission headed by a former minister, Bernard Stasi, to evaluate the issue. All but one member of the commission were assertive secularists. The commission submitted its final report, proposing a law that would ban students' religious symbols. The Stasi Commission had several other propositions, such as making one Jewish and one Islamic holiday official.[33] The French president and legislators neglected the other proposals while embracing that on prohibiting religious symbols. Both the National Assembly (494–36, with 31 abstentions) and the Senate (276–20) voted by a large majority for the legislative bill against religious symbols in public schools. On March 15, 2004, Chirac signed it into law. The number of students wearing headscarves was 1,465 in the 2003/2004 academic year. The new law was applied a year later and led to the expulsion of forty-seven Muslim female students from their schools, in addition to three Sikh male students who wore turbans.[34] Other Muslim students removed their headscarves, transferred to private Catholic schools, studied at home, went to another country for education, or left school entirely.[35]

Following the headscarf ban, the coalition between the assertive secularist left and the Islamophobic right seemed to end. In December 2007, the newly elected rightist president, Nicolas Sarkozy, criticized assertive secularism in his first visit to the Vatican.[36] He spoke about the importance of France's Catholic roots, using a conservative rightist discourse.[37] A month later, Sarkozy visited Saudi Arabia, where he stressed the importance of religion for civilization and human life.[38] Nonetheless, the recent law banning the wearing of a face veil on the street and further debates on Islam have indicated the persistence of the left–right coalition against Muslim symbols in France.

To conclude, the French ancien régime created a path dependence that led to the conflict between republican secularists and Catholic monarchists, and finally resulted in the dominance of assertive secularism. Democracy in France, however, has moderated the state's assertive secularist policies toward Catholicism. The French state's policies toward Islam, in contrast, have become much more exclusionary, given the support of both the assertive secularist left and the Islamophobic right.

Turkey

The doctors of Islamic sciences, the *ulema*, were a strong pillar of the Ottoman monarchial order. In the late nineteenth and early twentieth centuries, the Ottoman elite received a Western, including positivistic, education, which led them to regard Islam as a defender of traditionalism and a barrier against their reform projects. They began to blame Islam for the decline of the empire and the "backwardness" of the society. As a result, there occurred a conflict between the Westernist and Islamist elites.[39]

M. Kemal Atatürk and his cadre (the Kemalists), who founded the republic in 1923, were intellectual inheritors of Ottoman Westernists. They eliminated the Islamists, tried to exclude Islam from the public sphere, and made assertive secularism the dominant ideology of the new republic. The Kemalists abolished the caliphate, founded the Diyanet, and banned all Islamic communities. They created a secular legal structure by importing European codes. To oppress the Islamist and Kurdish opposition, they founded special tribunals and passed the Law on the Maintenance of Order, under which "nearly 7,500 people were arrested and 660 executed."[40] In 1928, the Kemalists removed the reference to Islam as the official religion from the constitution. In 1937, they added the principle of secularism to the constitution (art. 2). Şükrü Kaya, the minister of the interior, explained the government's support to this amendment in parliament with the following words: "We are determinists in our view on history and pragmatist materialists in our affairs. . . . We note that religions should stay in individuals' consciences and temples without intervening in material life and worldly affairs. We are not letting them intervene and we will not let them intervene."[41]

Although the Kemalist reforms included a broad range of issues—such as enforcing the wearing of the top hat, banning the Arabic *ezan* (call to prayer), and adopting the Latin script and the Western calendar—they focused mainly on education.[42] In the 1920s, the Kemalists closed all the 479 *medreses* (religious schools), eliminated religious instruction from the school curricula, and removed Arabic and Persian classes.[43] They shut down all Imam-Hatip schools in 1930 and the only department of theology of the country in 1933. From that time until 1949, there was no legal teaching of Islam in Turkey except for a few rural Qur'ān courses.

The Republican People's Party (CHP) ruled the country from 1923 to 1946 as the single party, with two abortive second-party experiences.[44] The

Democrat Party won the first fair elections in 1950 and stayed in power for a decade. It provided more religious freedom by policies such as lifting the ban of the Arabic *ezan*. The military coup in 1960, which was followed by coups in 1971, 1980, and 1997, stopped this process. Since 1960, the military has been the guardian of assertive secularism and is supported in this mission by its allies in the judiciary, politics, media, business, and civil society. The Constitutional Court elaborates these groups' views while defining secularism as "not separation of religion and the state," but as "separation of religion and worldly affairs [including] social life, education, family, economics, law, manners, dress codes, etc."[45]

The overwhelming majority of Turkish society has opposed assertive secularist policies. Unlike France, where only 28 percent of people oppose the headscarf ban in public schools,[46] 78 percent of people in Turkey are against the headscarf ban at universities.[47] Another unpopular assertive secularist policy is the restrictions over the Imam-Hatip school graduates' admittance to universities, except departments of theology, which is also opposed by 85 percent of Turkish society.[48] That is mainly why assertive secularist parties have never won the majority in parliament through a democratic election. Although passive secularist parties have received around 70 percent of votes in elections for the past three decades, their impact on the moderation of assertive secularist policies has remained limited because of the assertive secularist dominance in the military and the judiciary.

In 2008, the ruling Justice and Development Party (AKP) joined with the Nationalist Action Party to lift the headscarf ban. Despite the assertive secularist opposition, parliament overwhelmingly (411–103) voted the following two amendments, and President Gül signed them into law (to art. 10, where the additional part is emphasized): "State organs and administrative authorities shall act in compliance with the principle of equality before the law in all their proceedings *and in benefiting from all public services*" and (to art. 42) "No one can be deprived of his or her right to higher education for reasons not openly mentioned by laws. The limits of the use of this right will be determined by law." The amendments focus on (1) equality for students while receiving education as a public service, to keep the ban on headscarves for the faculty and staff, and (2) the freedom of higher (college and graduate) education, to continue the ban on schools. The CHP and another assertive secularist party, the Democratic Left Party, applied to the Constitutional Court. The court struck down the amendments as anti-secular and claimed that if some students wore headscarves at universities that would be a pressure to those who did not wear them. It also noted that the courts should be active in banning headscarves because parliament was unable to "limit religious freedoms" given the fact that it was "a political institution" elected by the people and "majority of the people in [Turkey] was affiliated with a particular religion [Islam]." Haşim Kılıç, president of the court and a passive secularist, stressed in his dissenting opinion that the court violated the balance of power by disregarding article 148 of the constitution, which prevented it from evaluating the contents of constitutional amendments. He also emphasized that there is no other modern country that banned religious symbols at universities.[49]

Motivated by the headscarf debate, the prosecutor of the High Court of Appeals opened a closure case against the AKP with the Constitutional Court and asked for a five-year ban from politics for President Gül, Prime Minister Recep Tayyip Erdoğan, and sixty-nine AKP politicians. The case contributed a new term to Turkish political lexicon: "judicial coup d'état." Because of several external and internal factors, this attempt remained abortive. Although six of the eleven Constitutional Court judges upheld the prosecutor's accusations, the case was rejected because seven votes were needed. Yet the court, by a vote of 10 to 1, decreed the AKP to be a basis of anti-secular activities and cut half of its annual public funding for one year (in an amount equaling U.S. $20 million).[50]

In short, the Kemalists have perceived Islam as a major component of the Ottoman ancien régime and an impediment to their Westernization reforms. This pejorative perception has affected their assertive secularist ideology and policies to exclude Islam from the public sphere. Conservative Muslims and liberals have tried to resist these policies and support passive secularism as an alternative. Despite popular opposition and the democratization process, assertive secularist policies have persisted in Turkey, mainly because of the authoritarian interventions of the military and the judiciary.

From 2007 to 2010, Turkey experienced a series of elections and referendums that weakened the assertive secularist domination in politics and judicial bureaucracy. Lowers courts' recent activism against hundreds of military officers, who allegedly planned coups, also restricted the military's political influence. The decline of Kemalist judicial and military tutelage over Turkish democracy has had some policy implications. In 2010, the Council of Higher Education (YÖK) alleviated the university admission conditions for Imam-Hatip schools' graduates. It could do so only in a very limited manner because of the assertive secularist courts' adamant resistance. Again in 2010, the YÖK asked the professors to only report the students wearing headscarves, instead of expelling them from the classrooms. This de facto ended the headscarf ban in many universities. These changes indicate that democratization will eventually result in the liberalization of the state practice of *laïcité* in Turkey. Historical path dependence matters, but it does not impose a deterministic and unchangeable understanding of *laïcité*.

Senegal

The French colonial power in Senegal, unlike that in Algeria and Tunisia, was relatively accommodating regarding the local people's political participation and religious laws, due to different circumstances in these colonial contexts. Even French republicans altered their anti-clerical domestic policies and tried to be seen as a religiously friendly "Muslim power" in Senegal.[51] As Donal Cruise O'Brien comments: "France was short of legitimacy in Senegal, short also of staff and money, and it made good sense to support the local Muslim leaderships." Therefore, the Sufi orders "may have in the nineteenth century been identified by the French policy makers as instruments of holy war, but in the twentieth-century colonial setting it was quite possible to come to an understanding on the solid ground of shared material interests."[52] The Senegalese people succeeded in gaining the rights of legal citizenship and political representation (even in the French parliament),[53] as well as in retaining some aspects of Muslim personal law.[54] This French policy in the late nineteenth century facilitated the turn of Sufi leaders away from the ideas of jihad against the French colonialist and also the necessity of a complete fusion of religion and the state. This constituted the historical legacy for the accommodation between the secular state and the Sufis in the independent Senegal.

Moreover, Senegal, unlike France and Turkey, did not have an ancien régime. The Republic of Senegal was founded in 1960 following the end of French colonialism, instead of replacing a local monarchy. Therefore, the secular elite did not see Islamic actors, such as Sufis, as an ally of the old regime and an enemy of the new republic. Additionally, although Islam was the majority religion at the time of state-building, the Catholic minority, which constituted about 5 percent of the population, was politically influential as a result of the long-term French colonization. Léopold Senghor, the first president of Senegal, also a poet and member of the Academy of France, was Catholic.[55] Given these factors, Sufi–secular mutual respect started in the late nineteenth-century colonial period and continued during the republican era.

That respect led to Senegal's construction of *"laïcité bien comprise"* (*laïcité* well understood [and properly practiced]). The second president of Senegal, Abdou Diouf, elaborates this particular interpretation:

> *Laïcité* in itself is a manifestation of respect of others. It acts in this way if it is *laïcité* well understood and properly practiced. Such *laïcité* cannot be anti-religious, but neither if it is a true *laïcité* can it become a state religion. I would say further that such a *laïc* state cannot ignore religious institutions. . . . Respect of religion does not only mean tolerance, it does not mean only to allow or to ignore, but to respect the beliefs and practices of the other. *Laïcité* is the consequence of this respect for the other, and the condition of our harmony.[56]

The existence of a particular Senegalese version of *laïcité* does not mean the absence of debates on it. On the contrary, following his election in 2000, the third president, Abdoulaye Wade, was criticized by the secular media and intellectuals for omitting the article on *laïcité* in the new draft constitution, which was later added again. The secular elite also disliked the introduction of obligatory religious (Islamic or Christian) instruction in public schools.[57] Yet *laïcité* is well established in Senegal, and "outside a very small urban minority there is virtually no opposition to the much-touted principle of *l'état laïc.*"[58]

Senegalese understanding of *laïcité* matches our concepts of passive secularism and the *respect all, support all* model. Senegalese state actors frequently participate in meetings of religious communities to emphasize their close relations and mutual respect.[59] Similar to their inclusive support to Muslim and Catholic pilgrimages, the state rulers attend the meetings of both Muslims and Catholics. There is also a deep level of tolerance between Muslim and Catholic societal actors in Senegal. It is not rare that they help each other build mosques or churches.[60] Due to the religious-friendly environment in Senegal, as well as their minority status, Catholics in Senegal, unlike conservative Catholics in French history, are the greatest defenders of *laïcité*.[61]

In his essay on the "twin tolerations," Stepan argues that mutual toleration between the state and religions and the recognition of each other's sphere, rather than a hostile state–religion separation, are necessary conditions for a healthy democracy. He also notes that all religions are "multivocal," in a sense that they have both anti-democratic and democratic interpretations. He concludes that this necessarily implies, contra John Rawls, that it would be a mistake to "take religion off the agenda."[62] Proponents of some human rights–violating policies often use religious arguments to justify their positions. An effective counterresponse can come from a local respectful figure, who, from within the core values of the religion and culture of the country, makes a powerful, religiously based argument against the specific human right violation. Senegal is an important example of such a counterresponse.

The constant mutual display of respect between religions and the Senegalese state has facilitated policy cooperation on issues such as anti-AIDS and anti–female genital mutilation policies. It has created an atmosphere where religious leaders have felt free to make arguments from within Islam against practices and policies that violate human rights. N'Diaye, the secretary general of Senegal's National Association of Imams (ANIOS), publicly argued that there was nothing in the Qur'ān commanding female genital mutilation (FGM), and that there was no evidence that the Prophet had his own daughters circumcised.[63] A law banning female circumcision was passed in 1999. To avoid the law being a dead letter, ANIOS helped governmental health authorities train imams on how to speak authoritatively about the health problems FGM presented and to help with anti-FGM talks by imams on radio and television. Since patterns of FGM were closely related to perceptions of marriage eligibility, the government, ANIOS, and national and international women's rights organizations worked together to develop policies of "coordinated abandonment" of FGM, so as to preclude jeopardizing marriage prospects within participating villages. Moreover, Professor Abdoul Aziz Kebe, who had close ties with the largest Sufi order in Senegal, the Tijans, wrote a powerful forty-five-page report to attack FGM. The report systematically argues that FGM is a violation of women's rights, bodies, and health, with absolutely no justification in the Qur'ān or in approved *ḥadīth*s. Kebe argues that not only is there no Islamic justification for FGM, but that given current medical knowledge, and current Islamic scholarship, there is a moral obligation for communities and individuals to bring a halt to FGM. The report was distributed by Tijan networks, secular ministries, and the World Health Organization.[64] FGM is still a problem in Senegal, with an estimated 28 percent of women from the ages of fifteen to forty-nine having undergone it, according to UNICEF. However, the same source lists Egypt at 96 percent. Senegal's three contiguous Muslim majority countries have much higher rates: Mali (92 percent), Guinea (95 percent), and Mauritania (71 percent). Although ethnic and tribal differences may also be important factors behind this variation, religious activism against FGM in Senegal is still crucial for the lower percentage in that case.[65]

Another area of policy cooperation between religious groups and secular state authorities concerns AIDS. A United Nations Development Programme (UNDP) report on anti-AIDS policies in Muslim-majority countries notes:

> In Senegal, when political leaders realized that a change in sexual behavior was necessary to contain HIV/AIDS, they undertook multiple strategies, an important one of which was to enlist the support of religious leaders. Religious leaders were given training to equip them with knowledge for advocacy work. HIV/AIDS then became a regular issue of Friday prayer sermons in mosques throughout the country and religious leaders talked about HIV/AIDS on television and radio. Brochures and information were distributed through religious teaching programs. Since the early 1980s, Senegal has managed to keep their HIV prevalence rates low, less than 1%.[66]

Some observers may think that the Muslim pattern of male circumcision alone accounts for this low AIDS rate. However, they should bear in mind that AIDS rates in some other Muslim-majority African states, where male circumcision is also the norm, such as Chad, Guinea, Eritrea, Mali, and Djibouti, are two to five times higher. This is, of course, not to speak of the extremely high AIDS rates in some non-Muslim states such as South Africa (21 percent) and Botswana (37 percent).[67] Again, although it is difficult to pinpoint the exact reasons for various AIDS rates in the region, religious activism in Senegal seems to be playing a positive role.

In sum, the "overlapping consensus" between secular state rulers and Sufi leaders in Senegal has resulted in a particular version of *laïcité* that tolerates public visibility of religion. This consensual relationship has empowered both the state and Sufi groups.[68] Some may regard close relations between the state and the Sufis as a violation of *laïcité*. Such close relations do not seem to be a violation of Senegalese interpretation of *laïcité* or democracy.

Conclusion

Comparative analysis of multiple secularisms is a new but growing research agenda. This chapter contributes to the emerging literature by showing that not only secularism in general, but also *laïcité*, a particular conception of secularism with a historical and normative background, has multiple interpretations. Typologies and continua, such as "passive versus assertive secularism" and "*respect all, support all* model versus separationism" help analyze different understandings and implementations of *laïcité* in Senegal, France, and Turkey. The existence of an ancien régime is a major reason for the historical dominance of an assertive and separationist interpretation of *laïcité* in France and Turkey. The distinctions between their ancien régimes, as well as their diverse levels of democratization, are also important for understanding policy variation between these two countries. Senegal substantially differs from these two in its own version of *laïcité*, which can be defined as both passive secularism and *respect all, support all* model. The analysis of Senegal reveals that cooperation between the state and public religions can be productive, as seen in the examples of anti–female genital mutilations and anti-AIDS policies, as long as there are "twin tolerations" between the state and religions.

With its cross-religion analysis of Turkey (99 percent Muslim), France (83 percent Catholic, 8 percent Muslim, and 2 percent Protestant), and Senegal (94 percent Muslim and 5 percent Catholic),[69] the essay problematizes essentialist generalizations about Islam. The Turkish Constitutional Court echoed the perception of some Turkish and Westernist essentialists when it argued that an assertive secularism was required in a Muslim-majority society because "Islam, unlike Christianity, had peculiar characteristics."[70] Yet the Senegalese case indicates that a Muslim society can coexist with secularism, even if the latter is not assertive. Furthermore, passive secularism in Senegal has produced much less state–society tension than has assertive secularism in Turkey. Assertive secularism historically created and still creates restrictions for public religions (Islam, Catholicism, or any other public religion). That is why certain groups have opposed it in France and Turkey. In Senegal, passive secularism did not result in such restrictions and did not face similar opposition. But religions, including Islam, are all "multivocal." An "assertive" interpretation of Islam that insists on state–religion amalgamation would not be compatible with any version of secularism.

Further research is needed to examine the relationship between multiple versions of secularism and multiple interpretations of religion. More specifically, scholars can examine former French colonies in sub-Saharan Africa (e.g., Mali and Niger) and in North Africa (e.g., Algeria and Tunisia) to reveal the entire continuum of the variations of *laïcité*.[71]

Notes

The authors thank Leonardo Villalón and Mirjam Künkler for their helpful comments. Portions of this essay were adapted from Ahmet T. Kuru, *Secularism and State Policies Toward Religion: The United States, France, and Turkey* (New York: Cambridge University Press, 2009); and Alfred Stepan, "Rituals of Respect: Sufis and Secularists in Senegal" (manuscript). These portions are reprinted with permission.

1. Alfred Stepan with Graeme B. Robertson, "An 'Arab' More Than 'Muslim' Electoral Gap," *Journal of Democracy* 14 (2003): 34. Freedom House codes countries as "free," "partly free," and "not free" based on their scores of political rights (PL) and civil liberties (CL), with 1 as the highest score and 7 as the lowest score of democratization. In 2007, it coded only Senegal and Indonesia as "free" among Muslim-majority countries, with PL (2) and CL (3), while coding Turkey and Albania as "partly free" with scores of PR (3) and CL (3). See http://www.freedomhouse.org/template.cfm?page=363&year=2007. Polity IV Country Reports 2007 gives the score of +10 to the most democratic countries and –10 to the least democratic ones. Albania has the highest score among Muslim-majority countries (+9), while Senegal and Indonesia have +8, and Turkey has +7. See http://www.systemicpeace.org/polity/polity06.htm (both accessed February 15, 2009).

2. For Turkey, see Jean-Paul Burdy and Jean Marcou, "*Laïcité/Laiklik*: Introduction," *Cahiers d'études sur la Méditerranée orientale et le monde turco-iranien*,

January–June 1995, 5–34. For Senegal, see Djibril Samb, *Comprendre la laïcité* (Dakar: Les nouvelles éditions Africaines du Senegal, 2005).

3. Alfred Stepan, "The Multiple Secularisms of Modern Democracies and Autocracies," in Craig Calhoun, Mark Juergensmeyer, and Jonathan VanAntwerpen, eds., *Rethinking Secularism* (New York: Oxford University Press, 2011). Stepan's ideas on the *respect all, support all* model in India are based on his field research and inspired by three essays by Rajev Bhargava: "The Distinctiveness of Indian Secularism," in T. N. Srinivasan, ed., *The Future of Secularism* (Oxford: Oxford University Press, 2006), 20–53; "Political Secularism," in John S. Dryzek, Bonnie Honig, and Anne Phillips, eds., *The Oxford Handbook of Political Theory* (New York: Oxford University Press, 2006), 636–655; and "What Is Secularism For?" in *Secularism and Its Critics* (Delhi: Oxford University Press, 1998), 486–542.

4. Kuru, *Secularism and State Policies Toward Religion*, esp. 11–14.

5. Jonathan Fox, *A World Survey of Religion and the State* (New York: Cambridge University Press, 2008), 109–110, 219–220, 253–255.

6. Conseil d'Etat, "Rapport public: Réflexions sur la laïcité," 2004, http://lesrapports.ladocumentationfrancaise.fr/BRP/044000121/0001.pdf (accessed March 20, 2008), 318. Half of the Protestant churches and one-tenth of synagogues also have the same status. See Jean René Bertrand, "State and Church in France: Regulation and Negotiation," *GeoJournal* 67 (2006): 296, 299.

7. Leonardo A. Villalón, "ASR Focus: Islamism in West Africa. Senegal," *African Studies Review* 47 (2004): 63.

8. Jean Baubérot, "Brève histoire de la laïcité en France," in Jean Baubérot, ed., *La laïcité à l'épreuve: Religions et libertés dans le monde* (n.p.: Encyclopaedia Universalis, 2004), 150; Guy Coq, "Les batailles de l'école," *L'Histoire*, July 2004, 101.

9. Bérengère Massignon, "Laïcité et gestion de la diversité religieuse à l'école publique en France," *Social Compass* 47 (2000): 363n.2. There are also Catholic, Protestant, Muslim, Jewish, and Orthodox chaplains in the French military. Conseil d'Etat, "Rapport public: Réflexions sur la laïcité," 315n.262. In Turkey, however, there is no Muslim or non-Muslim chaplain in schools or the military.

10. Katrin Bennhold, "French Muslims Find Haven in Catholic Schools," *New York Times*, September 30, 2008.

11. Villalón, "ASR Focus: Islamism," 67.

12. U.S. Department of State, "Senegal: International Religious Freedom Report 2008," http://www.state.gov/g/drl/rls/irf/2008/108388.htm (accessed January 20, 2009).

13. Ibid. See also Samb, *Comprendre la laïcité*, 140–144.

14. For the role of the ancien régime in the formation of passive or assertive types of secularism in several other countries, see Kuru, *Secularism and State Policies Toward Religion*, 22–30; and Ahmet T. Kuru, "Passive and Assertive Secularism: Historical Conditions, Ideological Struggles, and State Policies Towards Religion," *World Politics* 59 (2007): 568–594.

15. Paul Pierson, "Increasing Returns, Path Dependence, and the Study of Politics," *American Political Science Review* 94 (2000): 251–267.

16. Kathleen Thelen, "How Institutions Evolve: Insights from Comparative Historical Analysis," in James Mahoney and Dietrich Rueschemeyer, eds., *Comparative Historical Analysis in the Social Sciences* (New York: Cambridge University Press, 2003), 208–240.

17. Othon Guerlac, "The Separation of Church and State in France," *Political Science Quarterly* 23 (1908): 280.

18. T. Jeremy Gunn, "Religious Freedom and Laïcité: A Comparison of the United States and France," *Brigham Young University Law Review* 24 (2004): 435–436.

19. Jean Baubérot, *Histoire de la laïcité en France* (Paris: Presses Universitaires de France, 2004), 14.

20. Quoted in Mona Ozouf, *L'Ecole, l'Eglise et la République: 1871–1914* (Paris: Cana, 1982), 50.

21. Stathis N. Kalyvas, *The Rise of Christian Democracy in Europe* (Ithaca, N.Y.: Cornell University Press, 1996), 114–166.

22. Maurice Larkin, *Church and State After the Dreyfus Affair: The Separation Issue in France* (New York: Barnes and Noble, 1973).

23. Ozouf, *L'Ecole, l'Eglise et la République*, 233–234.

24. Guerlac, "Separation of Church and State in France."

25. Quoted in Guy Bedouelle and Jean-Paul Costa, *Les laïcités à la française* (Paris: Presses Universitaires de France, 1998), 15.

26. Ibid., 12–13.

27. The Muslim population reached 4 to 5 million, 7 to 8 percent of the French population, half of whom are French citizens, according to Haut conseil à l'intégration, *L'Islam dans la République* (Paris: La documentation française, 2001), 37–38. There are 1,685 mosques in France, according to "L'islam nationalisé?" *Libération*, December 8, 2004, 4–5.

28. Ahmet T. Kuru, "Secularism, State Policies, and Muslims in Europe: Analyzing French Exceptionalism," *Comparative Politics* 41 (2008): 1–19.

29. Alain Seksig, Patrick Kessel, and Jean-Marc Roirant, "Ni plurielle ni de combat: La laïcité," *Hommes & Migrations*, March–April 1999, 64–75.

30. French Council of State, November 27, 1989; no. 346,893.

31. Haut conseil à l'intégration, *L'Islam dans la République*, 66.

32. Jean-Louis Debré, *La laïcité à l'école: Un principe républicain à réaffirmer. Rapport de la mission d'information de l'Assemblée nationale* (Paris: Odile Jacob, 2004), 179.

33. Stasi Commission, "Rapport au président de la République," December 11, 2003, http://lesrapports.ladocumentationfrancaise.fr/BRP/034000725/0000.pdf.

34. Ministère de l'éducation nationale de l'enseignement supérieur et de la recherche, "Application de la loi du 15 mars 2004 sur le port des signes religieux ostensibles dans les établissements d'enseignement publics," http://lesrapports.ladocumentationfrancaise.fr/BRP/064000177/0000.pdf (accessed July 2, 2005).

35. Xavier Ternisien, "Des organisations musulmans évoquent 806 'victimes,'" *Le Monde*, March 14, 2005.

36. "La République a besoin de croyants, dit Sarkozy," *Le Monde*, December 21, 2007.

37. "L'intérêt de la République, c'est qu'il y ait beaucoup d'hommes qui espèrent," *Le Monde*, December 21, 2007.

38. "Sarkozy ramène l'Eglise dans l'Etat," *Libération*, January 16, 2008.

39. Niyazi Berkes, *The Development of Secularism in Turkey* (1963; rpt., New York: Routledge, 1998).

40. Erik Jan Zürcher, *Turkey: A Modern History* (New York: Tauris, 2004), 173.

41. T.B.M.M., *TBMM Kavanin Mecmuası*, vol. 17, *Devre V, İçtima 2* (Ankara: TBMM Matbaası, 1937), 60–61.

42. Nur Yalman finds a similarity between the Kemalists reforms in Turkey and the Cultural Revolution in Mao's China, in "Some Observations on Secularism in Islam: The Cultural Revolution in Turkey," *Daedalus* 102 (1973): 139–168.

43. Elisabeth Özdalga, "Education in the Name of 'Order and Progress': Reflections on the Recent Eight-Year Obligatory School Reform in Turkey," *Muslim World* 89 (1999): 418.

44. Sibel Bozdoğan and Reşat Kasaba, eds., *Rethinking Modernity and National Identity in Turkey* (Seattle: University of Washington Press, 1997).

45. Turkish Constitutional Court, January 16, 1998; no. 1998/1.

46. Debré, *La laïcité à l'école*, 179.

47. About 63 percent of women wear some sort of headscarf in Turkey, according to Ali Çarkoğlu and Binnaz Toprak, *Değişen Türkiye'de Din, Toplum ve Siyaset* (Istanbul: TESEV, 2006), 58, 71.

48. Ibid., 55. In the 1996/1997 academic year, the Imam-Hatip schools were at their peak with 511,502 students, which constituted about 10 percent of all students. As a result of the closure of their secondary branches and restrictions over their graduates imposed following the 1997 military coup, the number of

students in these schools had decreased to 64,534 by the 2002/2003 academic year. See İrfan Bozan, *Devlet ile Toplum Arasında* (Istanbul: TESEV, 2007), 20, 22. Prime Minister Erdoğan is also a graduate of Imam-Hatip schools.

49. Turkish Constitutional Court, June 5, 2008; no. 2008/116.
50. Turkish Constitutional Court, July 30, 2008; no. 2008/2.
51. The French rulers in Senegal provided support for pilgrimages to Mecca, construction of mosques, and Arabic-language training. See David Robinson, *Paths of Accommodation: Muslim Societies and French Colonial Authorities in Senegal and Mauritania, 1880–1920* (Athens: Ohio University Press, 2000), 75–96; and Donal Cruise O'Brien, "Towards an 'Islamic Policy' in French West Africa," *Journal of African History* 8 (1967): 303–316.
52. Donal Cruise O'Brien, *Symbolic Confrontations: Muslims Imagining the State in Africa* (London: Hurst, 2004), 194. See also Robinson, *Paths of Accommodation*, 218.
53. According to Mamadou Diouf, "In 1848, Senegal was granted a seat in the Chamber of Deputies in Paris" ("The French Colonial Policy of Assimilation and the Civility of the Originaires of the Four Communes [Senegal]: A Nineteenth-Century Globalization Project," *Development and Change* 29 [1998]: 674).
54. Michael Crowder, *Senegal: A Study of French Assimilation Policy* (London: Methuen, 1960). This combination of rights was refused by the French colonial power to Algerians, who never attained the Senegalese-type voting status.
55. Janet G. Vaillant, *Black, French, and African: A Life of Léopold Sédar Senghor* (Cambridge, Mass.: Harvard University Press, 1990). Senghor was also a member of a linguistic and ethnic minority—Serer. The largest ethno-linguistic group of Senegal has been Wolof.
56. Doudou Ndoye, ed., *Constitution of Senegal* (Dakar: EDJA, 2001), 48–49.
57. Villalón, "ASR Focus: Islamism," 67.
58. Leonardo A. Villalón, *Islamic Society and State Power in Senegal: Disciples and Citizens in Fatick* (New York: Cambridge University Press, 1995), 2. See also Leonardo A. Villalón, "From Argument to Negotiation: Constructing Democracy in African Muslim Contexts," *Comparative Politics* 42 (2010): 375–393; and Carrie S. Konold, "Shari'ah and the Secular State: Popular Support for and Opposition to Islamic Family Law in Senegal" (Ph.D. diss., University of Michigan, 2010).
59. Leonardo A. Villalón. "Sufi Rituals as Rallies: Religious Ceremonies in the Politics of Senegalese State–Society Relations," *Comparative Politics* 26 (1994): 415–437.
60. "Une famille, deux religions," *Le Soleil* (Senegal), October 23, 2001.
61. During his interviews in Senegal's capital, Dakar, in December 2006, Alfred Stepan realized that almost none of his Muslim interviewees felt com-

fortable with the concept of "apostate," but they did feel comfortable with the fact that the famous Catholic cardinal Thiandoum of Dakar came from a Muslim family.

62. Alfred Stepan, "The World's Religious Systems and Democracy: Crafting the 'Twin Tolerations,'" in *Arguing Comparative Politics* (New York: Oxford University Press, 2001), 227–229.

63. Habibou Bangré, "Croisade musulmane contre l'excision: Les imams rétablissent la vérité sur cette tradition," *Walfadiri* (Senegal), June 8, 2004.

64. Abdoul Aziz Kebe, *Argumentaire religieux musulman pour l'abandon des MGF's* (Dakar: Organisation Mondiale de la Sante, 2003).

65. It should be acknowledged that in addition to social policy, ethnic traditions are also important. The Wolofs, an important ethnic group in Senegal, traditionally have not practiced FGM. However, it is worth noting that among ethnic groups that have a high rate of FGM, the rates inside Senegal are lower. For example, the Pular in neighboring Mali have more than a 90 percent rate and the Pular in Senegal have a 62 percent rate. All FMG rates are from UNICEF, "Multiple Indicator Cluster Surveys, MICS 1995/2005," http://www.childinfo.org/mics.html (accessed November 30, 2006).

66. UNDP, "The Role of Religious Leaders in the Fight Against HIV/AIDS," www.undp.org.my/uploads/Role_of_Religious_Leaders_in_Fight_Against_HIV.pdf (accessed November 30, 2006), 19.

67. UNICEF, http://www.unicef.org/french/sowc05/Table4 F.xls, table 4 (accessed November 30, 2006).

68. Andrew F. Clark, "Imperialism, Independence, and Islam in Senegal and Mali," *Africa Today* 46 (1999): esp. 165; O'Brien, *Symbolic Confrontations*, 49. According to O'Brien, "[T]he secular state has accommodated [religious] differences in Senegal very well, much better than any 'Islamic republic' is likely to do so. Perhaps the secular state is the Sufi's secret love" (63).

69. CIA–The World Factbook, https://www.cia.gov/library/publications/the-world-factbook/ (accessed January 6, 2010). The percentage of Catholics in France mostly reflects cultural identification. Surveys that question the numbers of French people believing in the pillars of Catholic faith give results as low as 45 percent. See Dominique Vidal, "La France des 'sans-religion,'" *Le Monde diplomatique*, September 2001, 22–23.

70. Turkish Constitutional Court, March 7, 1989; no. 1989/12.

71. Tunisian understanding and implementation of *laïcité*, for example, has generally been defined as more exclusionary toward public religions than that of Turkey. See Edward Webb, "Civilizing Religion: Jacobin Projects of Secularization in Turkey, France, Tunisia, and Syria" (Ph.D. diss., University of Pennsylvania, 2007).

5

A New Politics of Engagement

The Turkish Military, Society, and the AKP

ÜMIT CIZRE

The central task of this chapter is to explain the shifting dynamics and emerging features of the relationship between the Turkish military and society, in the context of a bitterly fought contest between secular forces and Islamic political activism. This confrontation has gained in intensity since 1997, when the military-dominated National Security Council (NSC) forced the resignation of a coalition government headed by the predecessor party to the now-ruling Justice and Development Party (AKP), thereby making the military institution the most prominent player on the secular side. Today, the military institution is still a leader in this conflict, having forged partnerships with segments of the judiciary dealing with regime and national security issues (including public prosecutors and the Constitutional Court); with high echelons of the civilian bureaucracy (especially the Foreign Ministry, which has historically formulated and conducted foreign policy in close coordination with the General Staff); and, as this essay will show, with significant sectors of Turkish secular civil society.

With the AKP's rise to power in 2002 and party victories in five subsequent elections, this security-conscious secular establishment has stepped up its ideologically and emotionally charged efforts to portray the ruling party's postures and policies as an "internal threat" to the "security" of the republic, understood as the regime's "secular" character. The hypothesis of this chapter is that, in this energetic struggle against the ruling party's "true" (i.e., Islamic) intentions—and in seeking to establish the hegemony of its own understandings of secularism, security, and democracy—the establishment has shifted its strategy from state-centered to society-centered discourse. Although continuing to act politically as top–down promoter of secularism as the hallmark of security, the Turkish Armed Forces (TAF) has changed its social strategy from a traditional dependence on education and military service (in order to produce passive reverence, fear, and indifference) to initiating more direct contact with the masses (in order to produce active popular consent). This new strategy involves creating, sponsoring, supporting, and mobilizing secular urban associations and think tanks, at times encouraging them to organize mass meetings and demonstrations, all in order to make the "Islamic question" an enduring component of everyday language and social relations. This strategy of communitizing by the state[1] is matched by the AKP's own communitizing efforts, although in the military's case the methods used are marked by a discourse of threat, blame, and "imminent catastrophe." This discourse, aiming to create and sustain a community of believers, pervades Turkish public life, reinforcing deep divisions and undermining the prospect of an inclusive, democratic, and positive-thinking society.

From one perspective, the situation examined by this chapter has global implications. Much has been written on contemporary versions of political Islam and its relations with democracy, society, and politics; but in the complex and challenging context of the past decade or so, academic studies have not yet sufficiently acknowledged substantial changes in the military traditions and policies of some democracies, including Turkey's—where a politically autonomous and secular military is pitted against a popularly elected government sympathetic to Islam within the context of a relatively robust democracy. Observers see little threat of a return to direct military rule in an international environment discouraging overt military intervention in politics, but they also fail to account for the ways in which military power is in fact exercised in most democracies. There is a need for better empirical understanding of what is happening in a context such as Turkey, where military power has taken on substantially different forms since the rise of Islamic political activism.

To make a crude distinction for the purposes of this chapter, the question of the military's relation to society can be considered on two basic levels—bearing in mind that the TAF's de jure powers have coincided with its de facto roles in neither case. The first is the level of an official role in public political decision making; this gets to the problematic nature of Turkish "democracy" itself and raises an enormous question—How does a civilian government control its military?—a question beyond the strict limits of this study. The second level incorporates ways in which a military creates, shapes, or mobilizes societal platforms, groups, and movements in general. Success in this capacity requires significant leverage and control over political culture and the moral imaginary of the public, exercised through policies both legal and extra-legal, discursive and nondiscursive. This second level is the axis of reference for this chapter.

Historical Trends and Problems of the Military–Society Relation

At the heart of the ongoing conflict between the ruling AKP and Turkey's secular military establishment is an official narrative of the state, the modernizing and secularizing mandate known as Kemalism—after Mustafa Kemal Atatürk (1881–1938), the founder of the regime. Conventional wisdom holds that current tensions are normal, even inevitable, given the military's traditional role as a last line of defense guarding Turkey's secular tradition and politically entrenched opposition to pro-Islamic conservatism. In such a view, the traditional state approach to political manifestations of Islam seems hardly to have changed during the past two decades.

This chapter contends that it has in fact changed considerably and that society has become the battleground for this defense; it accepts the apparent schism between the secular establishment and the ruling party, but it does not take such a schism for granted as natural or inevitable. The typical portrayal of the contemporary Turkish political landscape, with secular republican ideology pitted against the AKP, dangerously disguises the true dialectical relationship between the two sides, both in fact incorporated "within a Turkish discourse of state-centered nationalism."[2] More to the point, the secular state—far from holding to a stylized and invariable strategy of clashes with Islamic political activism—has historically negotiated, sought compromises, and even shifted its position to incorporate Islamic vocabulary into the official discourse.[3]

The Military's Early Role

The early years of the Turkish republic in the 1920s were marked by the rule of a single party, the Republican People's Party (CHP), led by the leader of the Turkish revolution, Atatürk, and a small political cadre of former officers. Atatürk deliberately kept the military from direct involvement in politics as soon as its support was no longer essential to the post-independence power configuration, so as to avoid a rival challenge.[4]

The critical point here is the limited role given to the TAF in the drive to "modernize the countryside"—considered more backward and tradition-bound than urban areas, and so more in need of social and cultural reform. However, in his sourcebook on the role of Middle East armies in social change (based on Frederick W. Frey's pioneering study of rural attitudes in the 1950s), J. C. Hurewitz argues that the contribution of the TAF in rural areas was less than previously thought.[5] Whether or not this indicates a conscious effort on the part of the state to keep in check the military's role in society, it is clear that the army was unable to act as the sort of populist national force more typical in post-revolutionary countries. This inability can, in turn, be regarded as indicating a lack of "active popular impetus" for the Turkish revolution, with a distance between the republican elite and the masses inherited from the Ottoman tradition of statecraft but also accentuated by the new regime.[6] Still, the overriding focus of education efforts in the early republic was on mobilizing the populace and redefining power relations, institutions, and leaders for a new political culture. That said, one unspoken consideration in the minds of the Kemalist leaders must have been whether the armed forces might turn their weapons against their own people in the event of a religious reaction to secular reforms, and whether such a situation might escalate beyond the capacity of civilian forces to manage it.

It is safe to say that the "civilizing mission" of the army—that of co-opting the masses to the purposes and values of the republic—has in some form continued ever since. Male draftees, for instance, are trained not only in the martial arts but in the social and cultural codes of modern life. However, with capitalism and democracy gaining some momentum in the multiparty years after 1950, the civilizing function of the army was superseded by the proliferation of other modernizing forces, institutions, and agents in the public sphere.[7] The already rather limited social role of the military can be said to have dwindled in substance even further over time.

The Grand Paradox

Before the military intervention of 1997, the army had taken control of politics on three occasions: in 1960, 1971, and 1980. When the radicalization of left and right and the ensuing anarchy and violence led to the 1971 and 1980 interventions, the high command took aim at the left–right polarization in qualitatively different ways than it had in 1960. Then, the subsequent 1961 Constitution had brought checks and balances to parliamentary majorities by introducing the mechanism of a multiparty system and robust institutions to uphold the rule of law. The 1971 and 1980 interventions, by contrast, sought a more centralized and restrictive configuration, more intent on injecting illiberal and conservative values into the bloodstream of politics and society. The readiness of the military to step into politics in the multiparty era had as much to do with its receding political power and social status as it did with its defense of Kemalism.

On none of these occasions did the high command face serious problems in establishing legitimacy in the eyes of the populace; in each case, the military stepped into a void it claimed was created by dysfunctional civilian politics and politicians. According to some research, public acceptance of the 1980 coup was also due to its leader's (General Kenan Evren) conformity to the "average Turk's image of a leader, seeming to combine both traditional and modern characteristics"[8]—an image drawing on both the Ottoman tradition of a supreme and wise authority and the republican one of an absolutist but enlightened figure with whom society could identify. Granted that "supreme and wise" is too extravagant a phrase for the post-1980 military leadership, such a view explains how even a rather pedestrian leader can exploit such legacies, invoking qualities that have very little to do with reality in order to forge a bond with the public in exceptional and unaccountable conditions.

Interesting and useful though this characterization may be, it leaves unexplained the enduring paradox in Turkish military–society relations: having repeatedly imposed its own political will, to the extent of eliminating or appointing particular ruling parties, military leaders have invariably found themselves in situations where the electorate's preferences turned out to be different from the army's in post-intervention elections. To deepen the paradox, the Turkish electorate gave overwhelming support to the high command's projects for reshaping state and society on these occasions—as evidenced by wide support for constitutional referenda after the 1960 and

1980 interventions. However, support for the legal frameworks of reorganization and for the expediencies of political engineering did not entail support for the military's own choices of parties, leaders, and processes of Turkish governance. On the contrary, it became a predictable pattern in post-intervention elections for the masses to opt for the very parties and leaders reincarnated after dissolution by the TAF.

One hallmark of contemporary Turkish politics, then, has been a persistent disjunction between the popular political will and the military establishment's attempts to impose its own "concept of Turkey." As a result, the military bureaucracy has been unable to prevent the rise of the new Islam-friendly capitalist elite, which emerged as a product of Cold War urbanization and industrialization. The limits of Turkish military power are revealed in the fact that Turkey entered the new millennium with a ruling party born of a previously banned Islamist party; a ruling party that won five consecutive elections over five years—two general (2002 and 2007), two local (2004 and 2009), and one presidential (2007)—and that received in the most recent general election (July 22, 2007) nearly 50 percent of the popular vote, more than twice as much as the next-largest rival party, from a turnout of well over 80 percent.

Still, less than a year after this enormous win, on March 14, 2008, the prosecutor general launched proceedings in the Constitutional Court to close down the party. The players of the secular bloc had failed to learn the lesson of the "grand paradox": that political dynamics do not necessarily obey the establishment's logic or will; that party closures invariably lead to the rise of renewed and more robust successors, equally unpalatable to the establishment, thus defeating its attempt to divert electoral support to more favorable platforms. This inability to read past events and reconfigure future actions further underscores the gulf between the intentions and the outcomes of military interventions.

The ambivalence of large sectors of society toward the military's own image of Turkey can be understood as a version of "preference falsification,"[9] whereby individuals who have lost confidence in the political process, driven by insecurity and fear about their future, opt for a disciplined, ordered, incomplete, and military-controlled democracy. While harboring negative sentiments regarding the military's policies and views—and particularly toward continuing casualties of the war in the southeast—the Turkish public retains a positive symbolic notion of the armed forces. The result is a further paradox in the nature of Turkish nationalism, an unintended consequence of the "constructed" nature of national identity: citizens are taught and socialized to uphold nationalist discourse to the utmost extent, with death for one's country understood to be the extreme manifestation; but on the level of everyday personal behavior, the focus of these same citizens shifts from patriotic altruism to criticism of the laws, norms, and codes established by the state.

The Problems of Conservative-Religious Education and Conscription

One enduring fact of Turkish military–society relations, then, is that when the TAF returned to its barracks after each intervention, it invariably found itself with fewer allies and without the support of any party or interest group in society.[10] During the 1980 post-intervention process of political reconfiguration, in an attempt to reunify the nation against Communism, the military high command strengthened its institutional bonds with society through direct intervention in the education system, including the revision of school textbooks in favor of religious and military discourse.[11] In a detailed analysis of the school curricula and pedagogical policies of the period, Sam Kaplan comes to the interesting conclusion that increased numbers of religious-track schools and "greater religious instruction in the secular-track school system" in the period sought to homogenize the concept of Islam for Turkish schoolchildren—but, no less important, sought also to militarize it.[12] With textbooks portraying the Turkish soldier as a "pious defender of the nation" and military service as a holy duty,[13] the next generation was encouraged to "imagine and identify with a primordial military ethos common to all Turks."[14] The military's collaboration with the sponsors of the "Turkish-Islamic" synthesis as a marked feature of the period can be understood as a further pragmatic strategy to appeal to the conservative-religious subculture in order to bolster the legitimacy of a new economic model requiring greater discipline and obedience from the population.[15] Such strategies indicate an attempt to instrumentalize religion in order to consolidate and perpetuate respect for military values, rather than an attempt to seek accommodation and compromise with the Turkish-Islamic school of thought. Indeed, with the cards once more reshuffled in the period following the 1997 intervention, these strategies were reversed in favor of an exclusionary approach.

In addition, as was explained earlier, the army's "civilizing mission" has continued in the form of compulsory military service, requiring all male citizens at the age of twenty to be drafted and trained not only in military methods but also in the social and cultural codes of modern life. The system of military conscription in Turkey stems from specific historical conditions, including a deliberate political choice to maintain a large military force (second only to that of the Unites States within NATO),[16] especially during the Cold War, when the nation served as a buffer state between the former Soviet Union and the Western alliance (of which Turkey was a member). In the 1990s, with the escalation of the civil war between Kurdish groups and the regular army, conscription became a much-needed source of manpower for the high command. Still, conscription could not succeed in resolving the civil–military tensions. On the contrary, increased military casualties in the early years of this century have caused many to question the military's motivations and strategies in its fight against the Kurdish separatists.

If the "preference falsification" explanation outlined earlier is correct, conscription provides one of those outlets for the population, which symbolically reaffirms its respect and loyalty to the army (by celebrating, for instance, when new recruits board the bus to go to their training place), while simultaneously questioning the fairness of only socioeconomically disadvantaged youth being drafted and killed in the war in the southeast.

The Problems of a Military "Above" Politics and a "Papa State"

It is clear that one source of unresolved tensions between the military elite and large segments of the populace has been the failure on the part of the former to grasp the fundamental reality that no degree of political and constitutional engineering can generate sufficient sociopolitical support for targeted institutional intervention in opposition to the autonomous and irrepressible forces of ongoing social change. Disinclined to understand that societal and political dynamics are the true drivers of conflict and change, the military bureaucracy has historically underestimated the purpose, value, and utility of social forces, movements, and institutions in undertaking its political agenda.

In an attempt to make its own proactive role viable and legitimate, it portrays itself as an entity "above" particular interests, representing the whole of the society and of "the nation." Thus military–society relations in Turkey are subsumed under the state–society relationship, and the institutional and political bias of the army is skewed in favor of what the military institution considers to be in the "state interest." The military's perception and portrayal of itself as being "above" society—as a "neutral" player within the realm of the state, acting as guarantor for the Kemalist order—provides the armed forces with the rationale to potentially and (in its view) legitimately alter the life of society both normatively and institutionally.

But the military faces serious obstacles to such a proactive guardian role. Informing the army's mission is an ideological predisposition toward "anti-political" reasoning, which opposes any "political" mediation among societal, economic, and military powers.[17] This anti-political ideology reflects an understanding of the army's obligation in a democracy as being a matter of political responsibility and rationality rather than responsiveness to society.[18] In such an understanding, progress is perceived as contingent on order, conflict is perceived as zero-sum, and criticism and opposition are perceived as threats to the canons of the regime. According to one insightful observer:

> [The TAF's] power position, as the defenders and carriers of a pre-politically defined above-politics common good, is constructed on an anti-political foundation, which in turn results in a tendency to be disinterested in understanding societal developments as a determinant of politics. This is because, drawing from Gadamer's claim that good knowledge has an identity cost, understanding the societal developments has the potential to transform one's political identity and thus one's approach to power, as well as have an impact on the actor's power position. Hence, the secular establishment understands neither the AKP, nor the societal dynamics that produced and brought it to power. . . . Rather, it displays a suspicion about the capacities of the ordinary people to make rational decisions and thus, for example, dismiss election results as irrational.[19]

Corresponding with this proclaimed position "above politics," the military bureaucracy has typically identified itself in its rhetoric and behavior as a "papa-state" (*Devlet Baba*). In keeping with this role, the TAF has historically maintained an attitude toward society marked by a reluctance to fraternize and a tendency to formalize all contact, thus maintaining an elitist distance from the inherent conditions and qualities of the populace. The "papa" concept, though, has in fact been responsible for the TAF's failure to develop genuine links with society: the high command has justified its interventionist role not by having risen from the common people, sharing their values and belief patterns, but by sitting above in a patriarchal enclave, with no accountability and with the capacity to control, manipulate, and mobilize the populace.

The Problems of Populism and Secularism

Any discussion of Turkish civil–military relations must consider "populism" as an important component of the founding ideology of the republic and of Turkish democracy. Although the term has had different meanings at different times,[20] the Republican People's Party's Program in 1931 essentially "reflect[ed] an elitist—'for the people, with or without the people'—kind of populism."[21] In other words, the Turkish military's autonomy from both the general populace and the political class is not simply an effect of its lacking structural links with those elements of society; it results from a form of populism that disdains society as unenlightened and irrational, prone to manipulation by self-interested, incompetent, shortsighted, and greedy politicians. This prevailing notion is reinforced by the military education system, which inculcates a less-than-democratic ideology among the officer corps, thereby seriously obstructing democratic civilian oversight. Elitist disdain of society became even less morally and politically sustainable when globalization led to the emergence in Turkey of less state-centered and more fragmented understandings of personal and national identity. Among the officers, however, a vision of nation and society as absolutely integrated has continued to prevail. In this view, society is collapsible into a homogeneous, monolithic, state-endorsed collective unity devoid of diverse social, economic, and cultural coordinates, experiences, identities, or imaginations.

Most armies with a political role seem to share what military sociologist Alfred Stepan, in one of his pioneering works on Latin America, calls an "organic and corporatist view of society and politics,"[22] which denigrates ordinary citizens, civilian politicians, and democratic politics. In Turkey, this mind-set also reduces political life to a dichotomy between the "traditionally oriented" masses and a "modernizing, secular elite," spearheaded by the military bureaucracy. Collapsing society and nation into one camp "masks the profound contradictions and cleavages within the political-

social landscape," causing officers to see the world around them in simplistic modern/traditional, secular/anti-secular dichotomies.[23]

Equally important as a term to consider in studying the military's approach and policy toward Islamic activism is "secularism," the framing
narrative of the hegemonic public discourse.[24] The trajectory of Turkish
secularism is an example of the "different meanings" and "unexpected intensity" that Western modernity takes as it travels into different contexts.[25]
"It is possible to speak of an excess of secularism, when secularism becomes a fetish of modernity. Modern social imaginaries cross boundaries
and circulate, but take a different twist and a slightly modified accent in
non-Western contexts—they take on a sense of extra. We can read *extra*
both as external to the West and as additional and unordinary."[26] This "extra" or "excessive" nature of Turkish secularism has had bearings on the
statist elite's view of society and Islam—a view that positions the two as
inseparably linked, with religion permeating the whole of social and political life. This view imagines neither secularism within Islam nor the de-
mise of Islam when secularism sets in.[27] In framing Islam as a perennial
"problem" in public life, the republican elite justifies the establishment
of "unspoken, implicit borders and the stigmatizing, exclusionary power
structure of the secular public sphere."[28]

These, then, are the typical beliefs of an officer of the Turkish army: a
rigid understanding of secularism as a life-and-death matter, as an ersatz
religion in its own right to be handled by a whole branch of bureaucracy;[29]
and a view of classic modernization processes as the only way to free individuals from the shackles of tradition and Islam. The secularist narrative
further extends to include a fetishist belief in an overcentralized system of
education (*egitim*) and school curricula as the sole means of enabling Turkey to catch up with Western civilization and enabling its citizens to aspire
to lead good lives in conformity with republican values. However, as Perry
Anderson brilliantly puts it, "religion was never detached from the nation,
becoming instead an unspoken definition of it."[30]

Reinvention of Security as a Means of Social Control: The February 28 Process

February 28, 1997, signaled the start of a new military plan to refashion
Turkey's political landscape along what it considered the rightful Kemal-

ist lines, when on that date the National Security Council sought to bring an end to the "Islamization" of Turkey with pressure on the coalition government led by the Islamist Welfare Party (RP). In the aftermath of the 1997 intervention, the phrase "February 28 process" came to refer to "not only the far-reaching implications of the NSC decisions, but also the suspension of normal politics until the secular correction was completed. This process has profoundly altered the formulation of public policy and the relationship between state and society. No major element of Turkish politics at present can be understood without reference to the February 28 process."[31]

In the new context that emerged, the TAF's first priority with regard to society was to ensure predictability in pursuit of its own ideas of "secularism." To do so, the military emphasized the task of restructuring societal thinking and behavior through an ideological awakening to Kemalist ideals and precepts, leading to a moral consensus opposing the rising power of the pro-Islamic RP. The new strategy involved two components. The first was a project to monitor, securitize, and militarize the society: the General Staff announced a radical change to the country's National Military Defense Concept on April 29, 1997, declaring Kurdish separatism and forms of Islamic activism to be internal threats to the character of the Turkish state, and putting greater emphasis on securitizing the regime.[32] One of the most controversial new structures set up in this direction was the Western Study Group (Batı Çalışma Grubu [BÇG]), which assigned officers from all forces the task of collecting information regarding the political orientations of politicians, intellectuals, academics, and bureaucrats. Some of the BÇG's intelligence mandates were highly irregular: officers' families, for example, would be required to report about "Islamists" within their communities.[33]

The second component of the general strategy followed the methodology of the post-1980 "pedagogical state":

All primary and secondary school curricula were altered again so as to emphasize both the secularist history and character of the republic and the new security threats posed by political Islam and separatist movements. Teachings on Atatürkism were expanded to cover all courses taught at all levels and types of schools. The secondary school system for prayer-leaders and preachers (*imam hatip*) was scrapped and an eight-year mandatory schooling system was introduced. Appointments of university chancellors since then were pointedly made from among staunch Kemalists. Orientation programs in Kemalist principles, the struggle against reactionism, and national security issues were also extended to bureaucrats and prayer leaders. Finally, military institutions and personnel were actively involved in administering the programs. If we add to these measures the closing down of the Islamic parties and the banning of their key policy makers from active politics, it is clear that the architects of the process aimed to ensure that the key political players toe the line—namely, comply with the need to both stabilize the rule of the original Kemalist project and revive the myth of a homogenous nation and society.[34]

By contrast, the "neo-republican" policies of the military rule between 1980 and 1983 had incorporated Islamic values into school curricula and public discourse to provide a moral basis against the Communist threat and to reintroduce social solidarity and obedience in the face of global capitalism. This policy allowed for negotiation between Turkey's pro-Islamic forces and the establishment. In the new pattern of military–society interaction after 1997, however, the military displaced its own post-1980 attempts to broaden the scope of modernity by giving some place to an Islam-transpired discourse and identity; it returned instead to a more narrowly secular version of the nationalist project.

This new set of goals entailed the military's entry into society at the level of day-to-day practices, values, attitudes, and opinions through education, intelligence gathering, and dissemination of media messages. The greatest challenge to the military's new approach was that the necessary departure from its traditional "above politics" position led some to question the military's political position and prerogatives:

Particularly in the Islamist mass media, the military came to be associated with Marxism, imperialism as well as with the militantly secularist, heterodox Alevi sect. Scenarios of "Syrianization" and Marxist dictatorship within the army have been suggested. A differentiation between the military as an institution and its commanders has been made. While the legitimacy of the former has never been questioned, the legitimacy of the latter's actions were [sic] severely attacked. Some others advanced the view that such an active involvement of the military in politics might also be detrimental to its professional cohesion.[35]

The military elite's new set of strategies was a result of the failure of its strategy of hegemony in the previous era and a response to the fatal puncturing of the republican power configuration by the Islamist Welfare Party, a party that outflanked the secular conservative political forces and drew its support from those on the margins of society, while acting as a surrogate social democratic movement in Turkey. The military institution saw itself not only as the key player on the macro level, making or breaking the government on a large scale; but also as a cultural broker on the micro level, focusing on the national community, remoralizing it in line with the principles of Atatürk, and defending it against the threat of an Islamist takeover of society.

From Pedagogical State to Dependence on "Quamingos": The TAF Since 2002

The explosion of internal security threats in the 1990s promoted the hegemonic role of the military by sustaining a state-sponsored nationalism and by validating a more proactive vigilance on its part. Heightened focus on security precluded any genuine connections with the ideas, values, sensibilities, and symbols of broad segments of society beyond those urban, educated, and Westernized groups identifying themselves with "state interests." In stark contrast, the AKP's recent election victories mark its substantial rise in power among the Turkish middle classes: as Turkey's conservative-religious commercial classes become a middle-class nouveau riche, the party becomes the emblem of this new social force. With the AKP now reflecting the interests of those working in the booming private sector, along with blue-collar families, rural populations, and lower-class migrant suburbs around Istanbul and other cities, the traditional military-led secular elite have found themselves in a disadvantageous position for top–down orchestration of society and politics.

The sense of "rivalry" with the AKP plays a central role in the military strategy to mobilize popular support more actively than before: "The community-based brotherhoods and other faith-based networks promoting their own versions of pro-modern Islam, a major constituency for the AKP, compete with the state-sponsored religion while also cooperating with it where necessary for survival and self-advancement."[36] While the nation's "secularists understand that radical Islamism has little potential to rule in

Turkey"[37]—due to republican modernization's success in promoting a persistent (if not consistent) worldliness and Western lifestyle—they object to the AKP's brand of Islam precisely because it is "moderate," rivaling that of the state's own "moderate Islam." Their objection sheds light on the unprecedented scale of the establishment's mobilization against conservative-religious supporters of the AKP, who have become "more secular and thus more visible, while remaining assertively religious."[38] With pro-AKP businessmen having acquired large media companies, and with the party securing the power troika of legislature, government, and presidency in the elections of 2007,[39] the establishment's sense of urgency and alarm has been reinforced by a new fear that the balance of power between the two camps has shifted unalterably.

The AKP's complex networks of societal support have attracted a large body of literature, much of which criticizes the importance that AKP leaders attach to everyday social practices:

> AKP leaders are not theoreticians of Islam. They are not interested in ideology. What they are interested in is promoting "everyday Islam": taxes on alcohol, or looking the other way when someone in a school distributes literature that celebrates the Prophet's birthday. It is not a question of the state imposing an Islamic agenda, but of spontaneous actions by lower-level officials who believe that it is part of their mission. It is a dynamic phenomenon with possibilities that cannot be predicted.[40]

What is overlooked in this literature, though, is the secular establishment's own contribution to producing such everyday practices as a societal realities—not by "excluding," "repressing," "censoring," "masking," and "concealing" "the other" (i.e., the AKP-faithful),[41] but by incessantly and vocally projecting secular fears and concerns. Fears about the eventuality of restrictions on public life—regarding, for instance, gender relations, headscarves, adultery, alcohol licenses, and fasting during Ramadan—carry "effects of truth,"[42] because such fears become issues central to the government and to "lower-level officials" enthusiastic about enforcing such strictures; thus secular fears and hostilities are "self-fulfilling prophecies,"[43] and "what was feared [is] realized."[44]

Such fears have also motivated the TAF's attempts to communitize. Menderes Çinar, one of those rare scholars who captures the essence of twenty-first-century politics of Turkey as mired in "communitization" by both secular state institutions and the ruling party, explains that problematizing the AKP on the basis of the Islamist pedigrees and conservative lifestyles of its members rather than its policy proposals has reinforced the definition of the secular state as a community: "Since the state-as-community has become the main characteristic of Turkish politics,"[45] the tendency for the AKP's own communitization, and thus polarization, has increased as well.[46]

The shift in the orientation of the Islamic movement from macropolitics on the state level to communities and daily micropractices represents a challenge not only to the institutional boundaries and meanings of traditional secular political activity but also to social legitimacy in politics and the prospect of socioeconomic compromise in Turkish politics:

> According to its [AKP's] posture, what is important is not to hijack state power but to democratize it predicated on the notion that a democratically structured state apparatus will guarantee a safe living space for Muslims in socio-cultural and economic terms. The AKP is a concrete manifestation of the capacity of Turkey's Islamic movement . . . to change politically not just in structure but also in content. The AKP's acceptance of civil society as the basic realm of visibility for religion and its abandonment of the state-centric salvationist approaches is a radical breakaway.[47]

There is an increasing sense on the part of the secular community that the command-and-control model of the state is being overtaken by Islam-influenced forms of existence, community, private, and sub-state. These various levels do not necessarily represent autonomous centers of power seeking complete independence from state authority. On the contrary, as explained earlier, there is significant interaction between state agencies and such subgroups aimed at negotiation and compromise, with a shared undemocratic discourse in opposition to common opponents such as liberals, intellectuals, minority groups, and the West. While the TAF and the secular elite have at times marginalized and even more often disciplined what they call "the irresponsible use of Islam for partisan purposes," they have in fact demonstrated a dynamic approach in encountering politically active Islamic forces, their supposed adversary—while the latter have also kept their identity and strategy vis-à-vis the secular camp fluctuating and inconclusive.

The TAF's Quest for Populism

The secular elite's sense of threat is now so strong as to make its traditional strategies—blocking legislation or government appointments, taking advantage of biases already built into the political system—seem less sufficient and effective than ever. As the perception grows among the high command that popular respect for the armed forces must be made to keep up with growing popular support for the AKP, the TAF as an institution comes increasingly to resemble a political party, in direct and immediate relation with organized and unorganized sectors of society. With a sense of lost political influence culminating in the 2007 election of President Abdullah Gül and the subsequent electoral success of the AKP, the TAF has come to view society as the central front in a battle to maintain support for its guardian mission.

In March 2007, the current affairs weekly *Nokta* published excerpts of a diary alleged to have been written by Admiral Özden Örnek, the former navy commander. The diary entries contain detailed plans for a military coup, prepared jointly by commanders of the army (Aytaç Yalman), navy (Örnek himself), air force (İbrahim Fırtına), and gendarmerie (Şener Eruygur) in 2004. One significant aspect of the alleged coup plans recorded in the diary was the author's pointed and repeated emphasis on the need to build up public support among key figures of the media, business world, and trade unions, as well as rectors of universities, in order to undermine support for the government. By acting from "above" and calling for organized sectors of society to stand either "for" or "against" the AKP—which is another way of saying either "for" or "against" the secular state—the military elite continues to contribute to the degrees of intolerance on both sides and to the reproduction of the vicious and insecure cycle of the secular–Islamist dichotomy. In working to spread secular republican ideology and enhance its own influence in society, the military institution and its civilian allies have been making effective inroads to public and private spheres such as associations and universities, where they have had no apparent presence in the past.

A number of important new features characterize such current strategies on the part of the military in navigating the new electoral realities and asserting the power of its role in society. First, the military has targeted a more diversified and informal cluster of addressees—including citizens, civil-societal groups, academia, university students, think tanks, and media. Second, the military high command has been visibly proactive in working for the creation of new networks and alliances within civil society as conduits for the secular bloc's influence. Third, recent events represent a break with the conventional wisdom that the TAF is always careful to base political interventions on some legalistic foundation:[48] revelations of military entanglement in alleged coup attempts and in illegal gangs opposing the AKP government show that such concern for "legality" is past.[49] Perhaps the most striking feature of the military's new strategy toward society is the attempt to play on the fears of urbanites who are particularly sensitive to the threat that a "backward" Islamic lifestyle may pose to secular consumer identity. Crowds in the streets protesting "anti-secular" government practices are also restless consumers of a lifestyle privileging individualistic modernity, which they believe to be dependent on the survival of Kemalism. The name of one prominent NGO, the Association for the Protection of Modern Life (Çağdaş Yaşamı Koruma Derneği), suggests exactly the type of fearful reaction on which the secular elite has come to depend.[50]

But the TAF's active attempts to capitalize on these fears raises a question: Does the record of the AKP government confirm them? At first glance, visible examples of "the AKP's pious free-market conservatism" abound in municipalities around Istanbul, like Sultanbeyli and Ümraniye, where "urban citizen-consumers," shopping malls, gated communities, chic restaurants, and tennis clubs are found alongside "semi-rural life-styles and impoverished Islamist-stronghold neighborhoods."[51] Cihan Tuğal points to the useful synthesis the AKP has achieved in "combining the construction of high-rise office buildings and shopping malls with a proliferation of domes, minarets, Islamic clothes shops, reconstructed Ottoman neighborhoods, Ramadan festivities and Quran schools, retaining the votes of the poor while remaking Istanbul to cater to the whims of global finance."[52] However—and this is the key to the kind of alarm invoked by the secular establishment—the integration of the AKP's conservative voters into the marketplace exacerbates rather than lessens the fears of the secular middle classes in Turkey. Urbanite secularists now voice their discomfort and anger at having to share their lifestyle with "foes" whom they regard as invading a modern space that is rightfully theirs. The central paradox of Turkey's state elite and their urban-secular supporters is that, as the vanguard in "modernizing" the republic, they stand simultaneously as a blockade against modernization's more encompassing spread.

How "Civil" Are Quamingos?

From its traditional repertoire of civil and military bureaucracies and schools, the TAF has come to rely increasingly on what could rightly be termed "quasi-military non-governmental organizations" (Quamingos), two prominent examples being the earlier-mentioned Association for the Protection of Modern Life and the Association for Atatürkist Thought (Atatürkçü Düşünce Derneği). Organized by the secular power elite to shift the ground from under the AKP and to frustrate its European Union–ordained reforms, these NGOs often are chaired by former military personnel or recruit retired military officers as board members. They have acquired a quasi-military character, being intimately aligned with the TAF in unequivocally defending the principles and assumptions of the modern secular tradition of the Turkish state. Quamingos have legal status, but their political stance is mostly incompatible with democratic ideals; they expect a uniform subscription to official ideology, view political diversity as undermining the unitary state and secular regime, and portray those who call for the military's compliance with principles of transparency and accountability as traitors conspiring with foreign forces.

But that is not all: it is a well-known fact that most secular NGOs, considered in theory to be autonomous vis-à-vis the state, have in reality been defined, structured, and mobilized as secularist frontline partisans in the ongoing war against the regime's "anti-secular enemies." Former President Ahmet Necdet Sezer (2000–2007) gave a last-minute declamation before his term ended in May 2007, warning that the secular republic faced its biggest threat since its foundation and asserting that the "ideology of the modern Turkish Republic contained in Atatürk's principles is a state ideology that all citizens should take as their own."[53] Sezer's words sum up the intersection between state and civil society and illuminate the enveloping, totalizing, ordering, structuring, regulating ideology of the state with which the Quamingos have identified.

At first glance, the existence of a strong body of embattled secularist NGOs opposing, criticizing, or positively influencing the "unsecular" practices of the AKP government seems a credible method, one used in many democracies around the world. However, as a document leaked to *Nokta* revealed, in extracting favors and resources from the secular elite, these NGOs do not operate on a level field: the Turkish military is actively engaged in classifying associations, dailies, professors, journalists, and intellectuals in pro- and anti-TAF terms,[54] and then opening its arms to the "friendly" ones while ostracizing the others. Working to delineate civil society in this divisive manner, the TAF undermines the self-direction, purpose, and credibility of those rallying behind it.

The real danger of the Quamingos for Turkish democracy is the "negativism" that undermines their legitimate oppositional role as civil-societal actors: because they lack all tolerance for the AKP and consider Islamic political activism a high internal security risk, they are unable in their discourse to articulate any positive nuance. Although as secular societal actors they have begun to construct their own political space and establish their own practices in Turkey, with the explicit goal of broadening their support and increasing their influence, their reach into society is quite restricted. More often than not, Quamingos take as their organizing principles references to the members and values of a secular community rather than those of a broader one. Nor do they seem concerned with democracy and an equitable "contemporary life-style."[55] Rather, they translate the universal principles of Kemalism into almost "religiously upheld community" values; they act as members of a community obeying a higher authority, "just as a believer is supposed to serve God within the terms of rules" not of his or her own making, safeguarded by reference to tradition and threats of punishment.[56] It would be quite apt to characterize members of Quamingos as a "community of believers." Lacking independence from the state, lacking self-reliance and creativity in problem solving, lacking even any projects of their own, the Quamingos lead to statism by default.

The military's proactive drive for societal support in undermining the popularly elected government recently took yet another turn. As part of its radical departure from past strategies of social connectivity, the General Staff prepared an action plan to be instituted in September 2008, published the preceding June by *Taraf*, an Istanbul daily.[57] This plan proposed to "bring the public opinion to the same level of agreement with the General Staff on issues about which the General Staff is sensitive and to prevent incorrect impressions being formed about the TAF" by the recruitment of "civil associations that are fully controllable, can be influenced and activated; or suitable media organs; or those sharing the same approaches with the TAF."[58] To the extent that such actions contradict any known example in the modern democratic world, they offended the sensitivities of Turkey's thinking elite, regardless of their own criticisms of the government.

The TAF's strategic methods for ensuring that recruited civil associations are "fully controllable" have included creating new and sympathetic ones and encouraging retired generals and officers to take over existing ones. In the action plan, the actors with whom "contact should be maintained so that they should be 'made' to act parallel to the TAF" are listed as "those which have the power to create public opinion, that is, universities, the high echelons of high courts, media, and artistic communities."[59] The plan can be characterized not as an initiative for further integration with society or for the restructuring of society in line with Kemalist principles, but as a project of "operational jointness" (in civilian terms: "reaching consensus") with society. Another way of assessing the plan would be to see it as a vehicle for communication with those secular urbanites with whom the General Staff has been cultivating a collaborative relationship since the February 28, 1997, intervention.

In the post-2002 context, Atatürk's principles are the real measures against which the political elite's capacity to rule are held. However, given that there are multiple interpretations of Kemalism (just as there are multiple interpretations of Islam), it would be unreasonable to expect complete uniformity in the Quamingos' subscriptions to Kemalist principles. Still, these groups retain the most essential characteristics, allowing them to be defined as nationalist-Kemalist. The Turkish example, then, reveals serious shortcomings in the assumption that civil-societal groups universally supersede all forms of nationalism and instead place a higher value on citizens' identification with the ideals of civil society, along with the assumption that such groups exemplify resistance to the irregular practices of the state. Such assumptions are problematic, especially in those parts of the world where security traditions are radically different from those in the West and where security actors are instruments of control over civil society.[60]

Conclusion

While the era of military interventions may be past, clearly the old questions about the military institution's role and prerogatives in politics and society are still valid—especially in a context like Turkey, where the specter of a democratically elected Islam-sensitive government presents an unprecedented challenge to a strongly secular military. As the military institution wages a battle to defend its political role in the system, society is the battleground. Historical legacies of the military–society nexus in any region obviously do not tell us much about whether those legacies are sustainable. However, attention to such legacies is critical for understanding the parameters of founding moments and their sustaining dynamics. More important, as political context provides the substance of the military–society relationship, those legacies may offer warnings of what to expect if the politics do not change.

An analysis of the political landmarks shaping the Turkish military's basic assumptions and actions in society inevitably involves an analysis of the military's general perception of its own position, role, and rationale within civilian politics and the broader society. The military's fundamental view of the masses as unreliable and unruly results from its always having held a seat of power in the state system. The TAF holds sway by virtue of its role in pioneering modernization and guarding secularism. Furthermore, anti-political reasoning forms an instrumental link between the TAF and society. Its positions, views, and practices are presented to society not so much as "good," but as "necessary"; not as "desirable," but as "rational" and "in the national interest." Society is thus left with no acceptable means of expressing dissatisfaction.

However, the advent of the February 28 process has brought a major transformation in the orientation of the General Staff toward at least some sizable segment of urbanites, motivated by the emergence of new Islamic actors who have adopted a more worldly stance in order to engage with intellectual, economic, and political domains and capture the hearts and minds of millions of Turks. This new context has convinced the establishment that the moment has come to access, activate, mobilize. and develop a more cohesive "groupthink" among the already existing community of Kemalist believers. The result for the TAF has been a new strategy toward society, headed with the word "populism." The Turkish case presents an example of a military's adaptive political influence in secular public life being shaped by an electorally powerful conservative-religious government, with democratization pushing traditional military intervention out of the foreground.

In an era of increasing Islamic activism in Muslim countries ranging from Algeria, Egypt, and Morocco to Malaysia and Indonesia, the TAF's attempts to restructure the thoughts and behavior of Turkish citizens so as to consolidate support for its opposition of Islamic activity provides a significant case for the comparative study of civil–military relations, and of the links between Islam-sympathizing conservative parties and militaries in strongly secular settings. In other words, the old questions about the military institution's role and prerogatives in politics and society are still relevant—though the answers to these questions may well have changed.

Notes

1. Menderes Çınar, "The Justice and Development Party and the Kemalist Establishment," in Ümit Cizre, ed., *Secular and Islamic Politics in Turkey: The Making of the Justice and Development Party* (New York: Routledge, 2008), 113–120.

2. Yael Navarro-Yashin, *Faces of the State: Secularism and Public Life in Turkey* (Princeton, N.J.: Princeton University Press, 2002), 58.

3. Ümit Cizre, "Parameters and Strategies of Islam–State Interaction in Republican Turkey," *International Journal of Middle Eastern Studies* 28 (1996): 231–251.

4. Daniel Lerner and Richard O. Robinson, "Swords and Ploughshares—the Turkish Army as a Modernizing Force, 1960–61," *World Politics* 13 (1960): 21.

5. J. C. Hurewitz, *Middle East Politics: The Military Dimension* (London: Praeger, 1969), 431.

6. Perry Anderson, "Kemalism," *London Review of Books*, September 11, 2008.

7. For an overall account of the modernizing role of the army, see Serdar Şen, *Geçmişten Geleceğe Ordu* (Istanbul: Alan Yayıncılık, 2000).

8. Kemal Karpat, "Military Interventions: Army Civilian Relations in Turkey Before and After 1980," in Ahmet Evin and Metin Heper, eds., *State Democracy and the Military in the 1980s* (Berlin: de Gruyter, 1988), 156.

9. The core idea here is the distinction between "private" preferences and their "public" expressions. "Preference falsification" as a term is borrowed from Timur Kuran, *Private Truths and Public Lies: The Social Consequences of Preference Falsification* (Cambridge, Mass.: Harvard University Press, 1995).

10. Karpat, "Military Interventions," 148–149.

11. Sam Kaplan, *The Pedagogical State: Education and the Politics of National Culture in Post-1980 Turkey* (Stanford, Calif.: Stanford University Press, 2006), 187.

12. Ibid., 191.

13. Ibid., 187.

14. Ibid., 182.

15. Ümit Cizre and Erinç Yeldan, "Politics, Society, and Financial Liberalization: Turkey in the 1990s," *Development and Change* 31 (2000): 481–508.

16. Lale Sariibrahimoğlu, "Turkish Armed Forces," in Ümit Cizre, ed., *Democratic Oversight and Reform of the Security Sector in Turkey* (Zurich: Geneva Center for the Democratic Control of Armed Forces, 2007), 78.

17. Ümit Cizre, "Ideology, Context, and Interest: The Turkish Military," in Reşat Kasaba, ed., *The Cambridge History of Turkey*, vol. 4, *Turkey in the Modern World* (Cambridge: Cambridge University Press, 2008), 306.

18. Metin Heper, "The Strong State as a Problem for the Consolidation of Democracy: Turkey and Germany Compared," *Comparative Political Studies* 25 (1992): 170.

19. Menderes Çınar, "The Justice and Development Party as a Catalyzer of the Secular Regime in Turkey" (paper presented at the Kokkalis Program of the Kennedy School of Government, Harvard University, Cambridge, Mass., February 5, 2009), 13.

20. See, for example, Ali Kazancıgil, "The Ottoman-Turkish State and Kemalism," in Ali Kazancıgil and Ergun Özbudun, eds., *Atatürk: Founder of a Modern State* (London: Hurst, 1997), 51; and Paul Dumont, "The Origins of Kemalist Ideology," in Jacob Landau, ed., *Atatürk and the Modernization of Turkey* (Boulder, Colo.: Westview, 1984), 30.

21. Kazancıgil, "Ottoman-Turkish State and Kemalism," 51.

22. Alfred Stepan, *The State and Society: Peru in Comparative Perspective* (Princeton, N.J.: Princeton University Press, 1978), 26–45.

23. Cizre, "Ideology, Context, and Interest," 301–332.

24. For the deflation of a number of myths related to the Turkish understanding of "secularism," see Ahmet T. Kuru, "Secularism in Turkey: Myths and Realities," *Insight Turkey* 10 (2008): 101–110. Also relevant in the Turkish case is José Casanova's paradigm of secularization as the "differentiation of the secular spheres from religious institutions and norms" (*Public Religions in the Modern World* [Chicago: University of Chicago Press, 1994], 211).

25. Nilüfer Göle, "Islam in Public: New Visibilities and New Imaginaries," *Public Culture* 14 (2002): 184.

26. Ibid.

27. Niyazi Berkes, "Historical Background of Turkish Secularism," in Richard N. Frye, ed., *Islam and the West* (The Hague: Mouton, 1957), 45.

28. Göle, "Islam in Public," 178.

29. Anderson, "Kemalism."

30. Ibid.

31. Ümit Cizre and Menderes Çınar, "Turkey 2002: Kemalism, Islamism, and Politics in the Light of the February 28 Process," in Sibel Irzık and Güven Güzeldere, eds., "Relocating the Fault Lines: Turkey Beyond the East–West Divide," special issue, *South Atlantic Quarterly* 102 (2003): 370.

32. Ümit Cizre, "Demythologizing the National Security Concept: The Case of Turkey," *Middle East Journal* 57 (2003): 213–229.

33. Fikret Bila, "Batı Çalışma Grubu" [Western Study Group], *Milliyet*, July 12, 1997, and "İşte Tartışılan Belgeler" [These are the documents under discussion], *Milliyet*, July 11, 1997. For a time, the BÇG's operations included warning the public not to patronize commercial enterprises owned by "Islamists." It also prepared a report on religious reactionism in universities, presented to the NSC at its April 29, 1998, meeting. Additional units set up for similar purposes followed: one was the Prime Ministerial Crisis Management Center, seemingly responsible to the prime minister but in reality answering to the NSC. Another, the Prime Ministerial Monitoring Council (Başbakanlık Takip Kurulu, or BTG), was instituted to replace the BÇG. In its March 2001 meeting, the NSC agreed, on the basis of a report prepared and submitted to it by the BTG, that the struggle against Islamic reactionism should not end, but on the contrary should accelerate. See Murat Gürgen, "BTG: İrtica Bitmedi" [Religious reactionism is not over], *Radikal*, March 31, 2001. It is clear that the BÇG had been established in consideration of the fact that, since the National Intelligence Agency (Milli İstihbarat Teşkilatı, or MİT) answers to the prime minister and the police intelligence answers to the minister of the interior (himself answering to the prime minister), intelligence reporting on extreme Islamic activities would inevitably be tempered by the more permissive attitudes of these civilians. Therefore, the General Staff felt it safer to set up the BÇG as its own intelligence department vis-à-vis Islamic activity.

34. Cizre and Çınar, "Turkey 2002," 312–313.

35. Menderes Çınar, "Rebuilding the Center: Mission Impossible," *Private View* 1–2 (1997): 75.

36. Murat Somer, "Moderate Islam and Secularist Opposition in Turkey: Implications for the World, Muslims, and Secular Democracy," *Third World Quarterly* 28 (2007): 1277.

37. Ibid.

38. Ibid., 1278.

39. Niels Kadritzke, "Headscarves, Generals, and Turkish Democracy," *Le Monde diplomatique*, February 1, 2008.

40. Şerif Mardin, interview, in Angel Rabasa and F. Stephen Larrabee, *The Rise of Political Islam in Turkey* (Santa Monica, Calif.: RAND, 2008), 56.

41. Navarro-Yashin, *Faces of the State*, 31.

42. Ibid., 32.

43. Ibid., 31.

44. Ibid., 33.

45. Menderes Çınar, "The Justice and Development Party and the Kemalist Establishment," in Cizre, ed., *Secular and Islamic Politics in Turkey*, 115.

46. Ibid.

47. Ahmet Yıldız, "Problematizing the Intellectual and Political Vestiges: From 'Welfare' to 'Justice and Development,'" in Cizre, ed., *Secular and Islamic Politics in Turkey*, 56–57.

48. The military high command has justified its incursions into politics in the past not only by invoking the popular readiness against the breakdown of law and order but also by referring to its own internal rules and to the TAF's duties as broadly inscribed in the constitution.

49. When grenades were found in the Istanbul home of a retired military officer in June 2007, the investigation into a coup plotted by an anti-government network named Ergenekon resulted in the arrest of some 130 people, including retired four-star generals, prominent politicians, journalists, and academics. The plans were motivated by commanders' indignation regarding the positive turn of Turkish accession to the EU since 2004, and the fears they shared with other nationalists that this might require Turkey to grant concessions on Cyprus, to give greater freedoms to minorities, and to develop a more democratic political system.

   According to the indictment, the plotters were hoping to bring down the AKP by causing enough chaos through terror attacks and high-level assassinations that the military would be forced to intervene in 2009. The conspirators were linked with various politically motivated murders, including the assassination of the Armenian intellectual Hrant Dink. Among those arrested were retired generals Veli Küçük, Hurşit Tolon, and Şener Eruygur; the last two were sent to prison in Istanbul on July 5, 2008, pending investigation. The Ergenekon incident lends credence to the accounts of retired admiral Örnek's diaries about the two coup attempts by the force commanders.

50. The largest demonstrations in Turkish history were held on Saturday, April 14, 2007, in Ankara, against the potential presidential candidacy of Recep Tayyip Erdoğan; and on Sunday, April 29, 2007, in Istanbul, against the anti-secular tendencies of the AKP. Over three hundred NGOs from across the country were involved in organizing these so-called republican meetings; one of the most prominent such groups was the Association for Atatürkist Thought, established to promote Atatürk's ideals and chaired by Şener Eruygur, a retired former commander of the Turkish gendarmerie currently under investigation for allegedly plotting a coup against the AKP government in 2004. Another sizable constituency was made up of associations representing secular-modern women, identified by Nilüfer Göle as principal actors in the process of secularization in a Muslim context.

51. Cihan Tuğal, "The Greening of Istanbul," *New Left Review* 51 (2008): 78.

52. Ibid., 79.

53. Nicholas Birch, "Ankara Protest Opens Window on Turkey's Brewing Culture War," *Eurasianet*, April 16, 2007, http://www.eurasianet.org/departments/insight/articles/eav041607final.shtml.

54. *Nokta*, April 5–11, 2007; *Radikal*, February 17, 2007; *Radikal*, March 8, 2007.

55. In direct contrast with Turkey's Kemalist civil-societal actors, which fail to represent autonomous grassroots dynamism vis-à-vis the state, NGOs in some other parts of the world have in the past decade begun to take issue with the power dynamics of capitalism and hierarchy and to organize more vocally around the goal of social change. Marina Sitrin provides one of the most original ethnographic accounts of the autonomous upsurge of civil-societal organizations among the middle classes declassed following the Argentinian economy's collapse in 2001, in "Introduction," in Marina Sitrin, ed., *Horizontalism: Voices of Popular Power in Argentina* (Oakland, Calif.: AK Press, 2006), 1–20. Because the movement aims to break from the vertical hierarchy of the clientelist system and to try to form links with unemployed and underemployed workers, the term *horizontalidad* is used to characterize its organizational principles.

56. Haldun Gülalp, "Enlightenment by Fiat: Secularization and Democracy in Turkey," *Middle Eastern Studies* 41 (2005): 363.

57. "Genelkurmay'ın Türkiye'yi Biçimlendirme Planı," *Taraf*, June 20, 2008.

58. Ibid.

59. Ibid.

60. Jane Chanaa, *Security Sector Reform: Issues, Challenges, and Prospects*, Adelphi Paper 344 (Oxford: Oxford University Press, for International Institute for Strategic Studies, 2002), 53.

6

The Turkish Constitutional Court and Political Crisis

ERGUN ÖZBUDUN

That Turkey has a constitutional problem is admitted by most observers, Turkish and foreign alike. It is paradoxical that Turkey, after more than six decades of multiparty competitive politics, has not been able to fully consolidate its democratic regime, and thus lags behind some of the newer, "third-wave" democracies, such as the three southern European and many eastern European democracies.

The immediate blame for this failure may be put on the 1982 Constitution, the product of the military regime of 1980 to 1983 (National Security Council [NSC] regime). The military rulers of this period blamed the excessive (in their opinion) liberalism of the 1961 Constitution for the breakdown of law and order in the late 1970s. Consequently, they set out to make a constitution in order to strengthen the authority of the state at the expense of individual liberties and to create a set of tutelary institutions that would exercise a strict control over elected civilian authorities. This meant a considerable narrowing down of the legitimate area of democratic politics. It has often been observed that the primary goal of the 1982 Constitution was to protect the state against the actions of its citizens, rather than to protect the citizens against the encroachments of the state—that is, what a democratic constitution should do. The constitution also provided strong exit guarantees for the outgoing NSC regime by granting the military vaguely defined tutelary powers and reserved domains. Finally, the 1982 Constitution reflected the strong distrust of the military for civilian politics and political parties by putting the activities of political parties in a virtual straight jacket surrounded by numerous and formidable bans. The same distrust was also shown for all other civil society institutions by banning them from all political activities and from collaborating with political parties, as alluded to in my other chapter in this volume.

It is no wonder that the 1982 Constitution, prepared through entirely undemocratic and unrepresentative procedures that left the final say to a five-member military council, led to a constant wave of criticism and demands for change as soon as civilian authority was restored in the fall of 1983. Consequently, the constitution has undergone fifteen amendments— some major, some minor—since 1987. The general direction of constitutional change has, no doubt, been towards liberalization and democratization, so much so that the European Commission observed that Turkey "has sufficiently satisfied the Copenhagen political criteria," thus opening the way to the start of accession negotiations at the beginning of 2005. It is commonly admitted, however, that such reforms were not sufficient to completely eradicate the authoritarian, statist, and tutelary legacy of the NSC rule.[1]

It would be a simplification to blame Turkey's constitutional problems entirely on the NSC's legacy, however. As I have tried to explain, deeper problems can be found in the incompatibility between the requirements of a truly liberal democracy and some of the principles of the founding philosophy of the Turkish Republic. Indeed, the 1982 Constitution bears strong traces of the "founding philosophy of the republic," or the Kemalist legacy, particularly of its three pillars: Turkish nationalism, secularism, and a unitary, highly centralized state. The single-party ideology's "passion for unanimity" is strongly reflected in this constitution. Thus the territorial and national unity of the state, or "the indivisible unity of the State with its territory and nation," in the words of the constitution, is mentioned sixteen times in the constitution (twice in the preamble, thrice in article 28, and once in articles 3, 5, 14, 26, 30, 68, 118, 122, 130, 143), and there are eight references to Atatürk (twice in the preamble, and in articles 2, 42, 58, 81, 103, and 134). While the meaning of "territorial integrity" is reasonably clear, the term "national integrity" may mean different things to different people. Thus it can be and has been used as a constitutional pretext against the claims for cultural recognition by linguistic, ethnic, and religious minorities.[2]

This is most clearly seen in the provisions of the Law on Political Parties, also passed during the NSC regime. Thus article 80 of this law bans political parties that aim to change the unitary nature of the state, although of course the protection of the territorial integrity of the state does not necessarily entail a unitary state. Article 81 contains an even more draconian provision, according to which political parties

- Cannot maintain that there are minorities in the territory of the Republic of Turkey, based on differences of national or religious culture, or race, or language.
- Cannot pursue the aim of harming, or engage in activities harmful to, national unity by way of creating minorities in the territory of the Republic of Turkey through protecting, developing, or spreading languages and cultures other than the Turkish language or culture.
- Cannot use or distribute posters, placards, audio and video tapes, brochures, and declarations written in languages other than Turkish in the writing and publishing of their statutes and programs, congresses, open or closed hall gatherings, public meetings, and propaganda activities; nor can they remain indifferent to these actions perpetrated by others. However, their status and programs may be translated into a foreign language not prohibited by law.

Clearly, article 81 of the law goes far beyond the legitimate aim of protecting the territorial unity of the state, and therefore is unconstitutional. The prohibition regarding the protection, development, and spreading of languages and cultures other than the Turkish language and culture reminds one of a "cultural genocide," in the words of a leading Turkish constitutional scholar.[3]

Another constitutional reflection of this exclusionary ethnic Turkish nationalism is found in the bizarre phrase "languages prohibited by law" in articles 26 and 28 of the constitution. Thus a law passed by the NSC (law no. 2932) prohibited the "expression, dissemination, and publication of opinions in any language other than those of the first official language of the states recognized by the Turkish State." This was indeed a very ingenious way of banning all public use of Kurdish without having to pronounce the word "Kurdish," since Kurdish is not the first official language of any state, but the second official language of Iraq. This law was repealed in 1991, and the scandalous phrase "languages prohibited by law" was deleted from the constitution in 2001. However, the prohibitions in the Law on Political Parties still remain in force.

The 1982 Constitution repeated the commitment of its predecessor, the 1961 Constitution, to secularism, another pillar of the Kemalist ideology. It enumerated "secular state" as one of the unamendable characteristics of the republic (articles 2 and 4) and repeated verbatim the ban in article 19 of its predecessor: "No one shall use and abuse in whatsoever manner religion, or religious sentiments, or things deemed sacred by religion with the aim of even partially basing the fundamental social, economic, political or legal orders of the State on religious rules, or of obtaining political or personal benefits or influence" (art. 24). Activities against the principle of secular state are also a cause for the prohibition of political parties (art. 68). These bans are elaborated and expanded in articles 84 to 89 of the Law on Political Parties. Ironically, however, the 1982 Constitution made the teaching of "religious culture and morals" compulsory at primary and secondary schools (art. 24). This may have been due to the NSC regime's desire to use a Turkified version of official Islam (the so-called Turkish-Islamic synthesis) as a bulwark against what they perceived as a leftist-Communist threat.

At a more symbolic, but no less meaningful, level is the sublimation of the state (always with a capital S) in the 1982 Constitution. The first paragraph of the preamble (repealed in 1995) used the adjective "sacred" for the "Turkish State." Paragraph 2, which is still in force, uses the term "Sublime [*Yüce*] Turkish State." It is interesting that in the preamble and in some of the articles (e.g., art. 14 before the 2001 amendment) the term "Turkish State," instead of the official name of the state, "the Republic of Turkey," is used. Such sublimation of the state is strongly reminiscent of Recep Peker's statements in the 1930s as quoted in my earlier chapter in this volume. Also reminiscent of the solidarist-corporatist discourse of the 1930s are the terms "societal peace" and "national solidarity" referred to in the unamendable article 2. The constitution and other legislation contain many more phrases expressing commitment to Kemalism. Under article 42 of the constitution, "education and instruction shall be carried out . . . in the direction of Atatürk's principles and reforms." Article 58 stipulates that the state shall take measures "to bring up and develop the youth . . . in the direction of Atatürk's principles and reforms." The Law on Political Parties requires political parties to carry out their activities "in the direction of Atatürk's principles and reforms" (art. 4). The Law on Higher Education (law no. 2547) entrusts the Council of Higher Education (YÖK) with the task of seeing to it that "students are imbued with a consciousness in loyalty to Atatürk nationalism in the direction of Atatürk's reforms and principles" (art. 5). Finally, the 1982 Constitution substituted the phrase "committed to Atatürk's nationalism" for the more neutral term "national state" used by its predecessor, in its unamendable article 2.

More important, the 1982 Constitution's statist-solidarist-tutelary philosophy is not limited to such abstract and philosophical notions, but is supplemented by a carefully designed elaborate tutelary mechanism. The chief tutelary mechanism was conceived as the "Office of the Presidency of the Republic." This office was designed as an impartial, above-party one, controlled by the state elites, with extensive supervisory powers over civilian politics. Through his broad appointive powers, the president was expected to influence the composition of other tutelary agencies, such as the Constitutional Court, other parts of the higher judiciary, and YÖK.

It is pertinent to remember here that General Kenan Evren, the leader of the 1980 coup, got himself elected as president of the republic for a period of seven years (1982–1989) through a procedure whose democratic legitimacy was extremely questionable. The election of the president was combined with the constitutional referendum: a yes vote for the constitution also meant a yes vote for Evren, the sole candidate. Evren frequently declared himself as the guardian of the new constitution. Apparently, it was hoped that after Evren's term of office, the new president would also be someone acceptable to the military through the Nationalist Democracy Party, which was created by the NSC and expected to win the transition election of 1983. The unexpected electoral victory of Turgut Özal and his Motherland Party (ANAP) changed this picture somewhat, and the two presidents who succeeded Evren, Turgut Özal (1989–1993) and Süleyman Demirel (1993–2000), were civilian politicians and the leaders of their parties. However, the tutelary role of the president remained embedded in the constitution, and Ahmet Necdet Sezer (2000–2007), the former president of the Constitutional Court and a compromise candidate among political parties, used his tutelary powers even more often and more eagerly than General Evren, thus leading to frequent frictions with both the coalition government of Bülent Ecevit and the Justice and Development Party (AKP) governments of Recep Tayyip Erdoğan. The latter was also in constant conflict with the Constitutional Court and YÖK, both strongly influenced by Sezer's appointments.

Another important tutelary agency is the National Security Council, first created by the 1961 Constitution but substantially strengthened by its successor. Before the constitutional amendment of 2001, the military and civilian members were represented in equal numbers in the council, assuming that the president of the republic, who presides over the council, is a person of civilian background. Furthermore, under article 118 of the constitution, the Council of Ministers had to give "priority consideration" to the recommendations of the NSC. The 2001 constitutional amendment gave the civilian members a majority and underlined the advisory character of the NSC's recommendations. The amendment was followed by the changes in other laws, particularly in the one on the NSC secretariat adopted in 2003. The net effect of these reforms was a significant degree of civilianization of the political system. Yet it is no secret that the military still enjoys much greater power and influence compared with that in any consolidated democracy, much beyond what the letter of the constitution and the relevant laws suggest.[4]

The experience of other democratizing countries suggests that the removal of such vestiges of former military regimes, or "exit guarantees," is not impossible in the long or even medium run. Two important, interrelated factors that affect the long-term viability of exit guarantees are the probability of a new military coup and the degree of unity or disunity among civilian political forces with regard to the military's role in politics. In this sense, a credible threat of a coup fundamentally alters the expectations and calculations of civilian political actors, leading them to act in ways that detract from democratic consolidation—such as seeking alliances with the military or inviting the military to intervene. The second factor is also very important because disunity among civilian political forces over the proper role of the military gives the latter a powerful incentive to intervene in politics and to attempt to maintain or increase its political influence. Commenting on the Latin American experience, Felipe Agüero observes that "by failing to display a united front, civilians have shown no common understanding of the obstacles which the military present for the prospects of democratic consolidation. A critical deterrent against the military, which would increase the costs of military domestic assertiveness, is thus given away, opening up civilian fissures for utilization by the military."[5]

This analysis seems to fit the present Turkish case. The complete civilianization of the regime and the elimination of other tutelary features are obstructed by a numerically not so large but politically strong coalition of civilian forces, such as the main opposition party, the Republican People's Party (CHP), the Constitutional Court, the higher judiciary, an important part of the mainstream media, and academia. The uniting factor is their deep attachment to the Kemalist legacy and their fear that the present governing party, the conservative AKP, may lead the country to an Islamic regime. Indeed, a 2006 survey has shown that, although only 8.9 percent of the respondents preferred an Islamic government based on the *sharia*, 22.1 percent thought that secularism was in danger, 36.7 percent believed that the AKP aimed at reversing the republican acquisitions in the field of women's rights, 43.8 percent were of the opinion that the AKP was trying to Islamize public services with its own supporters, and 50.2 percent felt that the AKP aimed at establishing an Islamic way of life in Turkey (not necessarily the same thing as establishing a *sharia*-based government). Other interesting findings are that 26.8 percent believed that Turkey's problems could be solved not by elected governments but only by a military regime, and 24.8 percent thought that the people cannot protect secularism without the support of the military.[6] It can be inferred from such findings that a nonnegligible portion of Turkish society sees the military as the ultimate, last-resort guarantee against a possible attempt to establish an Islamic regime in Turkey.

Such fears and anxieties also led the opposition bloc to feel lukewarm or outright suspicious about Turkey's European Union (EU) project. Ziya Öniş has pointed out that the predominant cleavage is no longer between left and right, center and periphery, or secularists and Islamists, but between what he termed "conservative globalists" (i.e., the pro-EU forces) and "defensive nationalists" (i.e., the anti-EU forces), although it may be argued that this new cleavage may still carry some elements of the older ones. While many groups within the defensive nationalist camp are broadly supportive of the EU membership in principle, they "tend to be uncomfortable with key elements of EU conditionality," which they see as leading to the erosion of national sovereignty and endangering the territorial integrity and/or unitary character of the Turkish state. This group consists of much of the state elite and the two major opposition parties, the CHP and the Nationalist Action Party (MHP), also joined by radical Islamists, while the globalist camp includes the moderate Islamists (or conservative democrats, as they prefer to call themselves), secular liberals, and Kurdish reformers. An interesting paradox of Turkish politics is that a party with Islamist roots (AKP) has become the leading supporter of the accession to the EU and the reform process associated with it.

An equally striking paradox is the increasing alienation of the CHP, the chief protagonist of Westernization and a Western style of life in Turkey, from the objective of EU membership.[7]

In the case of such deep societal division, it is difficult to expect the normal functioning of democratic institutions. Thus the AKP government had to face not only the parliamentary opposition, but the opposition of many state institutions: the former president Ahmet Necdet Sezer (until the end of his term in August 2007), the military, the Constitutional Court and the higher judiciary in general, and the YÖK (until quite recently). Of these state institutions, the Constitutional Court deserves special attention since in recent years it has become an active participant in the ongoing political conflict. The Turkish Constitutional Court was established by the 1961 Constitution as one of the earliest and strongest constitutional courts in Europe. The court was designed by the makers of the 1961 Constitution (essentially, the state elites and their representatives, the CHP) as a mechanism of self-protection against the unchecked power of elected parliamentary majorities (at that time represented by the Democrat Party). As such, it was viewed as the guardian of the fundamental values and interests of the state elites, and their Kemalist ideology.[8] The 1982 Constitution, also the product of the state elites, did not significantly change the powers of the Constitutional Court.

It can be argued that the Turkish Constitutional Court, in its practice of close to a half-century, has behaved essentially according to the expectations of the state elites who created and empowered it. In other words, it has acted as the guardian of the two basic pillars of the Kemalist ideology, the national and unitary state and the principle of secularism. As opposed to the practice in most Western states, fundamental rights and freedoms of individuals were put on the backstage when they seemed to be in conflict with these values in the eyes of the Constitutional Court judges. A Turkish constitutionalist describes this attitude of the Constitutional Court as representing an "ideology-based" paradigm in contrast to a "rights-based" paradigm.[9]

The state-oriented attitude of the Constitutional Court can most clearly be observed in the party prohibition cases. The court has consistently closed down Islamic and Kurdish ethnic political parties through an extremely rigid interpretation of the constitution and the Law on Political Parties. Thus the court ruled in the Democracy Party (DEP) case that the concept of territorial integrity of the state also encompassed the protection of the unitary nature of the state:

The principle of the indivisible integrity encompasses the protection of the independence and the territorial and national integrity of the state. This historical characteristic of the Turkish Republic, which has been a unitary state since its establishment, has been reflected in the Constitutions and strict sanctions have been provided for its protection. . . . This structure is the raison d'étre of the nation, and it cannot be compared with the conditions of other multinational countries. No concessions can be made with regard to this fundamental principle. . . . The Constitution, which is based on the principle of *unitary* state, does not permit *federal* state. Therefore, political parties cannot include federal system in their programs, and cannot advocate such a structure. . . . As the principle of nation-state does not permit the notion of multinational state, there is no room for a federal structure in such a system. In a federal system, (multiple) sovereignties are exercised by the federated states. Whereas, in a unitary state, there is only one sovereignty.[10]

In the same ruling, the court precludes even regional states by stating that "the Constitution is closed to such discriminatory procedures as autonomy or self-rule for regions," even though regional state is a variant of a unitary state. Furthermore, the court commits another juridical error by arguing that in a federal state, federated states also exercise their sovereignties. Sovereignty, by its very nature, cannot be exercised by more than one unit. What the federated states exercise in a federal state is not sovereignty but a limited state power defined by the federal constitution. Another problem involves the court's confusing multinationalism with federalism. Obviously, not all federal states are multinational states. The Turkish court reiterated the same reasoning in an earlier ruling concerning the Socialist Party.[11]

The court has been equally rigid in its interpretation of national integrity. Thus in its ruling on the Democracy Party case, it asserted:

The recognition of minority status based on differences of race and language is incompatible with the notion of territorial and national integrity. Just as citizens of other origins, the citizens of Kurdish origin are not prohibited from expressing their identity; it has been stipulated, however, that they are not a minority or a different nation, that they cannot be conceived outside the Turkish nation, and that they are placed in the integrity of the state. Citizens of Kurdish origin do not carry a characteristic conforming to the sociological and legal definitions of a minority; nor is there any legal rule that differentiates them from other citizens. It does not make any sense to transform unlimited rights into limited rights, and to transform being a nation itself into being a minority. It is clear that the aim is to accomplish secession. . . . One cannot violate the constitutional principle of national integrity by differentiating between Turkish and Kurdish nations. In the state of the Republic of Turkey, there is one state and one nation, not more than one nations. Even though there are individuals of different origins in the Turkish nation, they are all placed in the unity of the Turkish nation. . . . It is impossible to recognize validity to such dangerous aims derived from certain political causes and foreign factors . . . and intensified by claims of human rights and freedom.

The relevant passage of the Constitutional Court's decision ends with the rather rhetorical and emotional statement that "the State is SINGLE; the territory is a WHOLE; the nation is ONE.[12]

The court's attitude has been no more tolerant with regard to allegedly Islamist parties. So far, the court has closed down five parties on account of their alleged anti-secular activities: the National Order Party (May 20, 1971), Turkey Peace (Huzur) Party (October 25, 1983), Freedom and Democracy Party (November 23, 1993), Welfare Party (January 16, 1998), and Virtue Party (June 22, 2001). More recently, the Constitutional Court refused to dissolve the AKP, but ruled that it had become a focal point of anti-secular activities and so deprived it of half of its state subsidies. In these decisions, as well as others related to secularism, the Constitutional Court defined secularism not as the simple separation of the state and religion, but as a total philosophy, a way of life, reminiscent of Comteian positivism and scientism. Thus in its ruling banning the wearing of headscarves at universities, it asserted:

Secularism has separated religiosity and scientific thought . . . it speeded up the march toward civilization. In fact, secularism cannot be narrowed down to the separation of religion and state affairs. It is a milieu of civilization, freedom, and modernity whose dimensions are broader and whose scope is larger. It is Turkey's philosophy of modernization, its method of living humanly. It is the ideal of humanity. . . . The dominant and effective power in the state is reason and science, not religious rules and injunctions. It is the last stage of the intellectual and organizational evolution of societies. . . . In a secular order religion is saved from politicization, ceases to be an instrument of government, and left to the individuals' conscience, its real and respected place. Thus, science and law become the basis of political life.[13]

In recent years, the Constitutional Court got more intensely involved in the opposition against the AKP government. Three extremely controversial rulings by the court in 2007 and 2008 made it appear as one of the active parties in the ongoing political conflict. The first involved its decision on the parliamentary quorum to elect a president of the republic at the end of Ahmet Necdet Sezer's term of office. The court's interpretation of the decisional quorum (two-thirds of the full membership of the assembly on the first two rounds and an absolute majority on the third and fourth rounds) as also valid for the opening of the session effectively prevented Abdullah Gül, the AKP's candidate, from getting elected.[14]

This was clearly at variance with the literal and teleological interpretation of the constitution. Article 96 of the constitution stipulates that "unless there is a provision in the constitution to the contrary, the Turkish Grand National Assembly shall open its sessions with the presence of at least one-third of its total membership and decide with the absolute majority of those present; however, the decisional quorum shall in no case be less than one-fourth of its total membership." While the constitution contains a number of provisions on special decisional quorums, it has no special or exceptional provision with regard to the quorum for the opening of its session. Therefore, in accordance with the general rule in article 96, the presence of at least one-third of the assembly's total membership (184 members) should have been sufficient. Furthermore, the Constitutional Court's ruling is also against article 102 of the constitution, on the election of the president of the republic. While this article requires a two-thirds majority of the total membership on the first two rounds, it requires only an absolute majority of the total membership on the third and fourth (final) rounds. Thus the court's interpretation enables one-third of the deputies to effectively obstruct the process by not attending the first round. This amounts to an unacceptable veto power for the minority and makes the constitutional provision regarding the third and fourth rounds practically inapplicable.

The second case involved the annulment of the constitutional amendment designed to lift the ban on wearing headscarves at universities.[15] Even though article 148 of the constitution empowers the Constitutional Court to exercise only a procedural review over constitutional amendments, the court exercised a substantive review in this case and annulled the amendments on account of their alleged incompatibility with the unamendable articles of the constitution.

Indeed, article 148 of the constitution not only limits the court's review of constitutional amendments to a merely procedural review, but also defines the scope of such review to three specific issues: whether the amendment is proposed and adopted by the requisite majorities, and whether it is debated twice. No provision of the constitution empowers the court to review the compatibility of amendments with the three unamendable articles of the constitution. Furthermore, such a review is bound to be a substantive review clearly precluded by the constitution. As observed by a recent report of the Venice Commission (Commission of Democracy Through Law), "the scope of democratic politics is further eroded by the constitutional shielding of the first three articles of the Constitution, in such a way as to prevent the emergence of political programs that question the principles laid down at the origin of the Turkish Republic, even if done in a peaceful and democratic manner."[16] Indeed, the terms used in the first three articles are so broad and vague that this ruling amounts to an almost complete usurpation of the constituent power by the Constitutional Court.

The third case involved the suit brought about by the chief public prosecutor of the Court of Cassation for the closure of the AKP. The Constitutional Court did not close down the AKP, but concluded, as mentioned earlier, that it had become a focal point of anti-secular activities and deprived it of half of its state subsidies.[17] In fact, six judges out of eleven voted in favor of closure, and the AKP was saved only thanks to the constitutional amendment of 2001 that requires a three-fifths majority of the court for closure rulings. Interestingly, the court admitted that no proof had been obtained to show that the AKP "aimed to destroy democracy and the secular order or the essential principles of the constitutional order by the use of force and intolerance," nor "did it present a danger that will weaken the fundamental rules of social peace in a way incompatible with universal values." The court also approvingly cited the democratic constitutional and legal reforms accomplished by the AKP in the EU accession process. However, the court still concluded that the AKP had become a focal point of anti-secular activities.

One of the main reasons leading the court to such a conclusion was the constitutional amendment referred to earlier and certain statements by party leaders and deputies in favor of lifting the ban on headscarf-wearing at universities. Clearly, the court continued to stick to its sui generis positivist or assertive notion of secularism with probably no parallel in any Western democracy. These three decisions of the Constitutional Court are widely regarded as based on political, rather than juridical, considerations, and as amounting to an extreme example of juristocracy. It can also be concluded that the Turkish Constitutional Court has been acting in the direction of the expectations of the secularist state elites who created the court in the first place, thus lending support to Ran Hirschl's theory of "hegemonic preservation." What makes the problem even more difficult to resolve is that, after the court's ruling on the headscarf amendment, it seems difficult to liberalize and democratize the constitution by way of partial amendments, since almost any amendment runs the risk of being found incompatible by the court with the first three unamendable articles.[18]

The total picture, however, is not altogether bleak. Since 1999, when its candidate status was recognized by the EU, Turkey has accomplished an impressive number of democratizing and liberalizing reforms. An analysis of these reforms is beyond the scope of this study.[19] It is true, though, that the resistance of the pro–status quo state elites has considerably slowed down the reform process. The result can be summarized as a "two steps forward, one step back" approach. But as Baskın Oran sarcastically states, if one subtracts one from two, there still remains one step forward.[20] To use another metaphor, the jinni seems to be out of its bottle, but not yet strong enough to create miracles.

Addendum

In the spring of 2010, the Turkish Constitution underwent a radical amendment, changing or abolishing twenty-four articles and adding two provisional articles. The amendment law (law no. 5982) was adopted by the Grand National Assembly on May 7, 2010, with a majority between the three-fifths and the two-thirds of the full membership of the assembly; in accordance with article 175 of the constitution, it was submitted to a mandatory referendum. The law was adopted by referendum on September 12, 2010, with a 58 percent majority.

The most controversial provisions of the amendment package were those related to the composition of the Constitutional Court and the High Council of Judges and Public Prosecutors, as will be explained. Other changes involved the introduction of constitutional complaint; the establishment of an office of ombudsman; the restriction of the area of competence of military courts in favor of civilian courts; the addition of certain new fundamental rights, such as the protection of personal data and the protection of children; the introduction of affirmative action (positive discrimination) in favor of children, the elderly, the handicapped, and war veterans and their widows and children, in addition to strengthening affirmative action in favor of women, some improvements in union rights, and the abolition of judicial immunity in respect to the decisions of the Supreme Military Council and the High Council of Judges and Public Prosecutors.

The composition of the Constitutional Court and the High Council of Judges and Public Prosecutors was radically changed by the constitutional amendment package adopted in the referendum of September 12, 2010, without, however, reducing the role of the president. Under the new arrangement, the number of the Constitutional Court judges is raised from eleven to seventeen, three of whom shall be elected by parliament from among three candidates for each seat nominated by the Court of Accounts (two) and the presidents of the bar associations (one). Four members shall be directly selected by the president from among judges and public prosecutors, reporting judges of the Constitutional Court, practicing lawyers, and high-level public administrators. The president shall choose three members among three candidates for each seat nominated by the YÖK. YÖK's nominees have to be professors in the fields of law (two of the three must be in this field), economics, and political science. Finally, the president shall choose three members nominated by the Court of Cassation, two by the Council of State, one by the Military Court of Cassation, and one by the High Military Administrative Court, again from among three nominees for each vacant seat. Thus the president maintains his strong role in the selection of the Constitutional Court judges, directly or indirectly selecting fourteen out of seventeen members. These changes were intended to limit the tutelary role of the Constitutional Court in line with widely accepted European standards.

The 2010 constitutional amendment also changed the structure of the High Council of Judges and Public Prosecutors. Under the new arrangement, the number of members is raised from seven to twenty-two. Seven regular and four substitute members shall be elected by the judges and public prosecutors of all ordinary courts, three regular and two substitute members by the judges and public prosecutors of administrative courts, three regular and three substitute members by the Court of Cassation, two regular and two substitute members by the Council of State, and one regular and one substitute member by the Academy of Justice. The president's role in the selection of these members coming from the judiciary is eliminated. But the president is entitled to appoint four regular members from among law professors and practicing lawyers. The minister of justice and the undersecretary of the Ministry of Justice remain as ex officio members The minister is still the president of the council; however, his role is reduced to a mainly symbolic and ceremonial one. The change was intended to break the monopolistic domination of the two high courts over the council, and to make it more representative of the judiciary as a whole by allowing the judges and public prosecutors of the lower-level courts to be strongly represented in the council.

Notes

1. For details, see Ergun Özbudun and Ömer Faruk Gençkaya, *Democratization and the Politics of Constitution-Making in Turkey* (Budapest: Central European University Press, 2009); and Ergun Özbudun and Serap Yazıcı, *Democratization Reforms in Turkey, 1993–2004* (Istanbul: TESEV, 2004).
2. On the influence of the Kemalist legacy on the 1982 Constitution, see also Taha Parla, *Türkiye'de Anayasalar* (Istanbul: İletişim, 2007), 34–40, 45; and Taha Parla and Andrew Davison, *Corporatist Ideology in Kemalist Turkey: Progress or Order?* (Syracuse, N.Y.: Syracuse University Press, 2004), 39–40.
3. Bülent Tanör, *Türkiye'de Demokratikleşme Perspektifleri* (Istanbul: TÜSİAD, 1997), 44–45.
4. Serap Yazıcı, *Türkiye'de Askeri Müdahalelerin Anayasal Etkileri* (Ankara: Yetkin Yayınları, 1997); Özbudun and Yazıcı, *Democratization Reforms in Turkey*, 32–41.
5. Felipe Agüero, "The Military and the Limits to Democratization in South America," 177; and J. Samuel Valenzuela, "Democratic Consolidation in Post-Transitional Settings: Notion, Process, and Facilitating Conditions," 67–68, both in Scott Mainwaring, Guillermo O'Donnell, and J. Samuel Valenzuela, eds., *Issues in Democratic Consolidation: The New South American Democracies in Comparative Perspective* (Notre Dame, Ind.: University of Notre Dame Press, 1992).
6. Ali Çarkoğlu and Binnaz Toprak, *Değişen Türkiye'de Din, Toplum ve Siyaset* (Istanbul: TESEV, 2006), 75–77, 87.

7. Ziya Öniş, "Conservative Globalists Versus Defensive Nationalists: Political Parties and Paradoxes of Europeanization in Turkey," *Journal of Southern Europe and the Balkans* 9 (2007): 247–260. For a perceptive analysis of the alliance between religious conservatives and secular liberals, see Haluk Şahin, *Liberaller, Ulusalcılar, İslamcılar ve Ötekiler* (Istanbul: Saf Yayınları, 2008).

8. Ergun Özbudun, "Political Origins of the Turkish Constitutional Court and the Problem of Democratic Legitimacy," *European Public Law* 12 (2006): 213–223. Ran Hirschl, comparing the emergence of constitutional review in four countries (Canada, Israel, New Zealand, and South Africa), has reached a similar conclusion: that the main cause of such change was the desire of once-dominant and now-threatened political elites to protect their status by means of constitutional guarantees (*Towards Juristocracy: The Origins and Consequences of the New Constitutionalism* [Cambridge, Mass.: Harvard University Press, 2004], esp. 50–99). Those political elites who perceive their declining electoral support and do not wish to submit their fundamental values and interests to the uncertainties of the mechanisms of majoritarian democracy have preferred to leave the protection of such interests to an independent judiciary whom they hoped to influence more easily.

9. Zühtü Arslan, "Conflicting Paradigms: Political Rights in the Turkish Constitutional Court," *Critique: Critical Middle Eastern Studies* 11 (2002): 9–25.

10. Constitutional Court decision, E. 1993/3, K. 1994/2, June 16, 1994; *Anayasa Mahkemesi Kararlar Dergisi (AMKD)* (Constitutional Court Reports) 30.2:1201, 1199.

11. Constitutional Court decision, E. 1991/2, K. 1992/1, July 10, 1992; *AMKD* 28.2:696–831, esp. 804–805.

12. Constitutional Court decision, E. 1993/3, K. 1994/2, 1199. The same views were also expressed in the court's decision on the Freedom and Democracy Party (ÖZDEP), See Constitutional Court decision, E. 1993/1, K. 1993/2, November 23, 1993; *AMKD* 30.2:912–913.

13. Constitutional Court decision, E. 1989/1, K. 1989/12, March 7, 1989; *AMKD* 25:144–148. On the sui generis nature of Turkish secularism, see Ahmet T. Kuru, "Passive and Assertive Secularism: Historical Conditions, Ideological Struggles, and State Policies Toward Religion," *World Politics* 59 (2007): 568–594; and Ergun Özbudun, *Türk Anayasa Hukuku*, 9th ed. (Ankara: Yetkin Yayınları, 2008), 86–89.

14. Constitutional Court decision, E. 2007/45, K. 2007/54, May 1, 2007; *Resmi Gazete* (Official Gazette), June 27, 2007, no. 26565.

15. Constitutional Court decision, E. 2008/16, K. 2008/116, June 5, 2008; *Resmi Gazete*, October 22, 2008, no. 27032.

16. Venice Commission, "Opinion on the Constitutional and Legal Provisions Relevant to the Prohibition of Political Parties in Turkey," adopted at the Seventy-eighth Plenary Session, Venice, March 13–14, 2009, CDL-AD (2009)006, para. 108.

17. Constitutional Court decision, E. 2008/1, K. 2008/2, July 30, 2008; *Resmi Gazete*, October 24, 2008, no. 27034.

18. On the rule of the Constitutional Court in the political crisis, see Özbudun and Gençkaya, *Democratization*, chap. 6; Ergun Özbudun, "Anayasa'nın Değiştirilemez Hükümlerinin Bağlayıcılığı," *Zaman*, December 15–16, 2008; Zühtü Arslan, "Başörtüsü, AK Parti ve Laiklik: Anayasa Mahkemesi'nden İki Karar ve Bir Gerekçe," *Seta Analiz*, January 2009; and Sami Selçuk, "Ardışık Hukuk Yanılgılarının Tarihe Not Düşen Örneği: AYM'nin 367 Kararı," in *Prof. Dr. Ergun Özbudun'a Armağan–Essays in Honor of Ergun Özbudun*, vol. 2, *Constitutional Law* (Ankara: Yetkin Yayınları, 2008), 579–633.

19. See, however, Özbudun and Yazıcı, *Democratization Reforms in Turkey*, passim.

20. Baskın Oran, *Türkiye'de Azınlıklar: Kavramlar, Lozan, İç Mevzuat, İçtihat, Uygulama* (Istanbul: TESEV, 2004), 126.

7

Turkey's Accession to the European Union and the Role of the Justice and Development Party

JOOST LAGENDIJK

In December 1999, the European Union (EU) decided to give candidate status to Turkey. In 1987 Turkey had applied to become a member of the EU. It took more than ten years before the EU formally decided to allow the Turkey accession process to begin. Many in Turkey had lost hope that the union they wanted to join would ever give them the green light. In fact, the 1999 decision did not mean that negotiations between the EU and Turkey would start immediately. As had happened before with the countries of central and eastern Europe that wanted to join the EU, Turkey had to fulfill the so-called Copenhagen criteria on democracy and human rights before the real accession process could start.

In 2000 and 2001, the Turkish government worked to comply with EU standards but did not make substantial progress because the three parties making up the government were divided among themselves on the benefits of EU membership for Turkey. The liberals were strongly in favor, the nationalists had strong doubts, and the leading social democrats were somewhere in between. Despite that built-in brake on fast reforms, the government of Bülent Ecevit managed to introduce some remarkable changes, with the most visible reform being the abolishment of the death penalty. The coalition government fell in June 2002, and, to the surprise of many, the elections in November 2002 were won by a new party, the

Justice and Development Party (AKP), which had been founded one year before as a successor to an Islamist party with a strong anti-Western and anti-EU platform. That party had ruled briefly in 1996 and 1997 and had been banned by the Turkish Constitutional Court after the party had to step down following the nonviolent, postmodern coup d'état by the military.

For those reasons, many in Turkey and the EU were curious, not to say suspicious, about AKP's handling of the EU dossier. What I will try to do in this chapter is to describe how the AKP, as the party in power since 2002, has dealt with the most complicated and controversial dossier that any Turkish government could possibly be faced with: the accession process to the EU. I will work on the basis of two different types of information. First and foremost is my experience as the chairman of the European Union's Parliamentary Committee on Turkish Accession from January 2002 until July 2009. In that capacity, I traveled the whole country and met with all the major players. Second, I will draw from the growing pile of books and articles that have been written on the AKP and on Turkish EU accession over the last few years.

Golden Years

In December 2004, the EU decided that Turkey had sufficiently fulfilled the Copenhagen criteria on democracy and human rights and that negotiations could start in October 2005. It was a reward for the way the AKP had acted as a governing party. Many former skeptics, at home and abroad, had to agree that the AKP had done more to bring Turkey closer to the EU than previous governments had. An impressive range of reform proposals had been brought to the parliament and had been supported by large majorities of ruling party and opposition members.

The Ecevit coalition government had already introduced three so-called harmonization packages in 2002, and the AKP tabled another six packages in 2003 and 2004. All these packages involved changes in a number of laws, aimed at harmonizing Turkish legislation with EU rules and regulations and at implementing important constitutional amendments that were made in 2001 and 2004. The packages dealt with many of the problems that had been identified in the reports of the European Commission and the European Parliament. Freedom of expression and freedom of the press were improved, albeit partially. It became easier to try perpetrators of torture and mistreatment. Civil–military relations were restructured by diminishing the role of the National Security Council (NSC). There were almost revolutionary changes in Turkish law that permitted the use of local languages other than Turkish in radio and television broadcasting, although with certain important restrictions.

In hindsight, one could call the years 2003 and 2004 the "golden years" of EU reform in Turkey. It convinced the EU member states to start negotiations. Maybe more important, it created substantial majorities in public-opinion polls in Turkey and in most EU member states in favor of Turkey's accession to the EU. The fact that a substantial majority of Turks in 2004 was in favor of starting talks with the EU is taken for granted. There is a strong tendency to think that the start of negotiations with Turkey on full EU membership was a European elite project from the start that did not take into account the lack of appetite for further enlargement among EU citizens. That impression is not based on facts. Opinion polls in the autumn of 2004 in Germany and the Netherlands, two countries known for their decreasing public support after 2005, showed that around 60 percent in both countries supported the start of negotiations in the run-up to the EU summit in December 2004.[1] This welcoming attitude was based mainly on two years of positive news coming out of Turkey, showing to a skeptical European public opinion that things were really changing in the most populous and first Muslim-majority candidate country. For most elites and citizens of EU member countries, this was reason enough to give Turkey, and the AKP, the benefit of the doubt.

Slowdown

That positive perception started to change in the years 2005, 2006, and 2007. In Turkey, there was a clear slowdown in reforms, while inside the EU the mood changed. The French and Dutch "no"'s to the Constitutional Treaty in May and June 2005 delivered a big blow to Europe's self-confidence. All of a sudden, the EU did not know where to go and turned inward, trying to find an answer to the question of why so many EU citizens had lost faith in their leaders' capacity to govern Europe at a supra-national level.

As time passed, one of the explanations that gained popularity was so-called enlargement fatigue. According to many observers, the enlargement of the EU by means of ten new members in 2004 had not been properly digested. Many "old Europeans" did not feel at ease anymore in the new enlarged EU, and that was one of the main reasons why a majority of the French and the Dutch voted against the Constitutional Treaty. One must be careful here. It is true that the impact of the 2004 enlargement was underestimated by the political class in Brussels and in most EU capitals. But one should not overestimate these feelings either. During the referendum campaign in the Netherlands, the issue of previous or future EU enlargements was hardly ever mentioned as an argument to vote against—or in favor—of the Constitutional Treaty. Opinion polls held the day after the French and Dutch rejection clearly show that the main reason people in France and the Netherlands voted against the Constitutional Treaty was that they simply did not understand what it was about, they were afraid that their national identity was in danger of being overruled, and they were concerned that the "bureaucrats in Brussels" were getting too powerful.[2]

For a majority of no-voters, Turkish accession to the EU was not a reason to vote against the treaty. Still, as time went by, the "anti-Turkish accession vote" thesis became more and more popular. This was a self-fulfilling prophesy, creating a growing distance between the EU, where enthusiasm for Turkey's accession went down (or, at least, was perceived as going down), and Turkey, where support for accession began to decline when some government leaders and many citizens felt betrayed and confirmed in their suspicion that Europe did not want them to join anyway. French president Nicolas Sarkozy's vocal opposition to Turkey's accession after his election in 2007 only strengthened this perception that Turkey would be left out in the end.

As a result of this growing feeling of being the outsider in the European game, the tide increasingly turned in Turkey. Nationalist opposition to EU accession, which had always been there, came to the forefront much more prominently than in the years before. In the media and on the streets, resistance grew stronger. The adversaries used the classic argument of a loss of national identity that we have seen among many EU opponents throughout the union. On top of that was an almost-national consensus on the view that the EU had made a big mistake in 2004 by allowing Cyprus to join. This happened after the Turkish Cypriots, with the support of the Turkish government, had voted in favor of a United Nations–sponsored plan for reunification of the island. The Greek Cypriots rejected the plan but were still admitted into the EU. From then on, Cyprus used its veto power inside the union to make life difficult for Turkey and for the Turkish Cypriots. The fact that the EU allows the Cypriots to do so has created a strong anti-European sentiment that unifies many who strongly disagree on other issues.

With enthusiasm going down and resistance going up, the government, especially Prime Minister Recep Tayyip Erdoğan, opted for electoral opportunism and consolidation of his parliamentary majority, instead of sticking to a clear and visible pro-reform policy. In the long run-up to the elections in 2007, the AKP shied away from further reforms as they became afraid that movement on such sensitive issues as freedom of speech or the rights of religious and ethnic minorities would be used by the nationalist opposition to lure voters away from the AKP.

Strange Coalition

Many inside the EU were willing to accept this slowdown for some time. Most EU observers still understood that the times had changed and recognized the big achievements of the AKP government prior to the December 2004 EU summit. However, over the course of 2006 and 2007, disappointment in pro-Turkey circles in Europe grew stronger, and some started to have doubts whether the AKP was really committed to EU-inspired reforms. In Turkey, criticism from the main opposition party, the Republican People's Party (CHP), and mainstream media was growing. They tried to exploit the old fears about the AKP and its alleged "secret agenda" of Islamizing the country. The only convincing reaction of Erdoğan would have been to implement more EU-related reforms, but he choose not to do so. This slowdown of reform in Turkey created a situation that became harder and harder to explain inside the EU.

Almost from its start as a governing party, the AKP had received the most support in Europe from parties that belonged to a different "political family" from the AKP, which billed itself as a modern "conservative" party. But in the European Parliament and in most member states' parliaments, the parties that spoke out most clearly in favor of Turkish accession were the social democrats, the liberals, and the greens. But since the AKP declared itself to be a conservative party, it sought to become a member of the family of European Christian Democrats. Because the latter are strongly divided on the Turkish accession issue, they kept their distance from the

AKP. The result was an unnatural coalition in favor of Turkish EU accession between European progressives and Turkish conservatives.

All went well as long as the AKP was the driving force behind reforms that many in Turkey and in the EU, for good reasons, saw as making the country more democratic and more modern. The European progressive Turkey supporters knew that their Turkish partner was a conservative party with which they disagreed on many points. But there was agreement on the need to reform the country for the sake of democracy in Turkey and for Europeans. As long as the reforms continued, it was sometimes difficult but not impossible to explain this ad hoc coalition to skeptical European citizens. But once the reforms almost came to a halt, and the opposition against the AKP in Turkey became more vocal, the doubts set in among large parts of the population in Europe and thus among politicians. Maybe the AKP was not such a modern party after all. Maybe the AKP opponents in Turkey had a point when they claimed that the party leaders had not really changed position since the end of the 1990s, when they left the Islamist predecessor of the AKP. This started a debate on what kind of party AKP really was and how to assess its roots, its policies, and its plans for the future.[3]

Post-Islamist

From the very start of the party in 2001, there have been many in Turkey and in the EU who do not believe that the AKP is really different from its Islamist predecessors.[4] Deep down, some Europeans are still convinced that Recep Tayyip Erdoğan and Abdullah Gül, the two most important AKP leaders, have not really changed their goals and objectives but only their tactics. It is hard to argue against this "secret agenda" theory because one can never fully exclude the possibility that, even after many years of moderate conservatism, the AKP might decide to return to its Islamist roots. However, European analysts still agree that there is more to the visible move away from Islamism than deceit or a temporary and superficial change of mind. They underline the structural reasons behind the AKP's acceptance of a liberal economy and democracy by pointing at the needs and wishes of the party's key supporters. Successful businessmen in Anatolia want the Turkish economy to open up to the global economy. They want to get rid of the restrictions and impediments that are a result of the strong ties between the Istanbul-based monopolies that have dominated the Turkish economy for so long and the state bureaucracy that protects their interests. Large parts of the religious and conservative AKP electorate are convinced that the strong grip of the secular establishment on Turkish society can be weakened only if there is more democracy and less tutelage.[5]

In the end, the only way to check whether the AKP is a different kind of party from its Islamist predecessors is to look closely at the AKP's statements, policies, and record in government. On all three accounts, many analysts argue that the AKP is an example of a "post-Islamist" party. For the AKP, religion is important as a source of inspiration in the same way as it is for many Christian Democrats all over the world. In daily politics, it is not a defining feature. As seen from Brussels, until now the AKP has behaved as the party it claims to be: a party with liberal views on the economy and conservative views on social policy and values-related issues. The founders of the party have broken with their past views on Europe because they think that many pious Turkish Muslims will profit from the freedom of religion that comes with membership of the EU.[6]

That calculation got a strong blow, though, in 2005, when the European Court of Human Rights ruled that Turkish secular advocates had the right to ban the wearing of headscarves at universities as long as the present constitution is in place. It was a big disappointment for Prime Minister Erdoğan and other AKP leaders who had hoped for European support in getting rid of this ban.[7] According to some, after this ruling Erdoğan lost his strong commitment to Turkey's EU accession. This view simplifies things too much and puts too much emphasis on only one of the elements in the way the AKP looks at the EU project. It is also an example of viewing the rise of the AKP only through the prism of religion.

Transformation

The effort to define the AKP as a post-Islamist party is only one part of the story. While it is important as a means to silence some of the critics who claim that Erdoğan is the infamous Islamist wolf in democratic sheep's clothing, it must be noted that there is more to the party. The AKP is the political expression of a much broader rise of a new elite from Anatolia that is challenging the old guard in Istanbul and Ankara. Other very visible areas of contention are the economy and the media. In both fields, Turkey is in the midst of a struggle between old and new elites. The AKP is the political representative of a new elite that is pushing for power and influence in the economy and in society. Very successful Anatolian companies are supporting the AKP, hoping to get a bigger and better part of the deal in Ankara. The old oligarchs resist and use their contacts in the state apparatus to stop the emergence of these new power centers.[8] New media owners challenge the established ones and use their closeness to the AKP to put pressure on their old competitors. It is the uprooting of old patterns of power in the Turkish state and economy that made the AKP popular with many liberals and leftists who were sick and tired of the old establishment and considered the AKP as the best possibility to open up the country in many ways.[9]

In debates on the AKP and Turkey, this multilayered character of the transformation process is often overlooked. There is a strong tendency to focus solely on the political players and on the question of whether Turkey is becoming more religious or not under AKP rule. There is far less attention for the tough but often less visible fight that is taking place between old and new business conglomerates. What matters in Turkey is not only who manages to dominate the debate on ideas and attitudes but also which powers will get the biggest slice in the rapidly growing Turkish economy.

The inclination to judge the AKP on its commitment, or lack of, to the secular character of the Turkish Republic did dominate the first AKP term in power. In the debate on secularism. the AKP and influential liberals found each other on the same side of the argument . . . at least in the first years of AKP rule. The efforts of the AKP to redefine secularism were not always well planned and communicated. But many in Europe agreed with the analysis that secularism in Turkey had become a kind of religion with its own sacred rules. It was thus only natural that those dogmas were challenged by a party that represented those parts of Turkish society that were never fully convinced by the aggressive secular message they were taught in school and in the media. The call for a shift away from the particular Turkish version of secularism and toward a more passive version as practiced in most EU member states was understood and well received by Turkish and European liberals.[10] The problems started when the AKP was not able to explain clearly how its new model of secularism would look and how it wanted to cope with the inevitable pressures on secular lifestyles that would arise once religion was allowed to be more visible in society.

Elections in 2007

In July 2007, the AKP went for early elections after the parliament was not able to elect a new president. The AKP was unable to use its parliamentary majority to elect Foreign Minister Abdullah Gül as the president of Turkey because the Constitutional Court, in a highly disputed ruling, decided that such a vote could take place only in the presence of two-thirds of all members of parliament. Because the only opposition party of the time, CHP, refused to be present, the parliament could not elect a successor to the staunchly secular president Ahmet Sezer, and the AKP decided to call for new elections

The obstructionist policy of the CHP was part of a wider polarization in the country in the spring and summer of 2007. Millions took to the streets to show their anger and fear about Gül being elected as president, mainly because his wife wears a headscarf. On April 27, 2007, a message was published on the Web site of the General Staff of the Turkish Army clearly warning the AKP not to go too far in challenging the existing secular order. It was clear: millions of secular Turks, supported by the army, did not want Gül to become the new president.

The pressure on the AKP and its electorate totally backfired. In July 2007, the AKP won 47 percent of the votes, increasing its support by almost 12 percent. Few people, even within the AKP, had expected the party to do so well after five years in government. The main reason behind this huge electoral victory seems to have been that the economy had grown by 6 to 7 percent each year since 2002. Many Turks had benefited from the new possibilities and wanted to reward the AKP for its economic policies, which had created stability, growth, and low inflation after the financial disasters of 2001. On top of this general appreciation, the AKP managed to cash in on its less confrontational policy toward the Kurds (over 60 percent of voters in the southeast voted for the AKP) and on its pro-EU policies of 2003 and 2004 (winning over many liberals who were willing to overlook the slowdown of reforms in 2005 and 2006). Besides, both Kurds and liberals wanted to show that they strongly opposed the intervention by the army and voted for the party that the generals did not want to win.

After this big victory, hopes were again high that the AKP would return to the reform agenda. The party had announced before the elections that it would present a new, civil, and democratic constitution to replace the present one, which dates from 1982 and was drafted by the military after the 1980 coup. But the autumn of 2007 passed, and soon disappointment among AKP's pro-reform supporters set in.

Disappointment

The uncomfortable coalition between the AKP and the liberals broke down the moment the latter got the impression that in the end the AKP was interested only in making gains for its own electorate. The decision in January 2008 to make a deal with the Nationalist Action Party (MHP) in parliament to create a majority to lift the ban on wearing headscarves at universities was one of AKP's major strategic and tactical mistakes. There was and is broad support in Turkish society for lifting the ban at universities. But liberal support was always conditional on two things: lifting the ban should be part of an overall package of reforms aimed at improving the situation of several groups in society, and the government should make it clear from the start that it would do everything in its power to defend the rights of girls and women who did not want to wear a headscarf. Both conditions were not met in 2008. For many, it was the final proof that the reform-mindedness of the AKP had dwindled strongly since 2004 and that the second Erdoğan government was no longer interested in creating a broad movement in favor of structural reform of the Turkish state and society.

On top of the badly prepared and promoted legislation on headscarves, the trend of reforms coming to a halt continued in 2008. The government kept denying this development by adopting two lines of defense. First, there was the outright denial of a slowdown. Members of the government and AKP politicians stubbornly referred to the reform of the infamous article 301 of the Penal Code and the adoption of the Law on Foundations, which gave minority organizations the right to reclaim some lost property. If people were not really impressed by these signs of continued reforms, a second line of reasoning was used to convince these skeptics; its main argument concerned the case against the AKP in the Constitutional Court that forced the party to focus on its own survival. According to this logic, from April until August 2008 the AKP simply did not have the time and the energy to invest in further reforms. This argument was accepted by many in and outside Turkey. It was not purely accidental that during the closure case hardly anybody in Europe called on Turkey to return to the reform agenda. Everybody knew that this was not the time to do so. But that does not explain why after August 2008, when the AKP narrowly escaped closure, there was no restart either. The AKP needed a break in the middle of 2008 to get its act together again. The problem was that the European Commission and the European Parliament expected something in return for their unwavering support of the AKP during the closure case: a swift return to the energetic way the party had introduced reforms in the years 2003 and 2004. Only in the first months of 2009 did things start moving again. By that time, many had started to doubt strongly and openly whether the government and especially the prime minister were still really interested in EU accession.

Continuing Accession Issues

In order to evaluate the AKP's performance with regard to the EU accession process in its second term in power, we will now look into some of the issues that keep dominating the Turkey reports of the European Commission and the European Parliament. What did the governing party do after 2007 to respond to the repeated calls from EU institutions to radically change policy in order to solve some of the long-standing problems in Turkey that go to the heart of the Copenhagen criteria on democracy and human rights?

Freedom of Speech

Are the skeptics right in claiming that the changes to the often-criticized article 301 of the Turkish Penal Code in the spring of 2008 were not substantial at all? According to many human rights defenders, the full deletion of this article—which has been used to bring many writers and journalists, such as Orhan Pamuk, Elif Safak, and Hrant Dink, before court— would have been the best decision. Instead, after years of postponing the issue, the government took another line. "Insulting Turkishness" as a basis for prosecution was replaced by "insulting the Turkish nation." The good thing about this change is that it removed the extremely vague term "Turkishness," which had proved to be open to massive misuse and/or misinterpretation. The term "Turkish nation" is copied from the penal codes of several EU member states. For that reason, it is difficult for the EU to criticize the new formulation. It is slightly less vague but in itself still leaves much room for maneuvering by nationalist lawyers and prosecutors. That room was severely limited, however, by a second change, also copied from some EU penal codes: from now on the minister of justice has to give the green light for every new case that a prosecutor wants to open on the basis of article 301. Legal experts around Europe protested against this interference of the executive with the judiciary branch. It is indeed true that this change will never win a legal beauty contest, but it could be extremely effective in the hands of a liberal and reform-minded minister of justice.

Can both AKP ministers who have been in charge since the spring of 2008 be considered as such? The jury is still out. The minister first had to deal with a backlog of over nine hundred cases that had been tabled by assertive prosecutors before the article was changed in May 2008. The minister dismissed more then 90 percent of all these "old" cases. But almost eighty cases got the green light, meaning that even today people are brought before court, for instance, because they spoke out against the official Turkish version of the tragic events of 1915. This is hardly an impressive step forward in the direction of full freedom of speech. The picture is mixed because after May 2008 the minister of justice reviewed over two hundred requests by prosecutors, out of which he granted permission to eight criminal investigations (i.e., 4 percent of the cases referred to him) to continue on the basis of the new article 301.[11] An important positive example of the gradual shift away from repressing dissident voices was the decision not to allow the start of a court case against the initiators of the so-called Armenian apology campaign in the beginning of 2009.

The Turkish Penal Code, the Anti-Terror Law, and the Press Law still need a serious overhaul to ensure that freedom of expression is fully respected in Turkey in line with European standards. The government claims that it is in favor of more reforms, and even the main opposition party, CHP, which voted against the limited changes to article 301, would not openly argue against further reforms. It does not happen or happens too slowly because these reforms are seen as giving in to the EU. Unfortunately, it is still relatively easy for populist politicians to deny that more freedoms are in the interest of Turkish citizens independent of what the EU is asking for. They paint a picture of Turkey in which, without strong limitations on freedom of expression, it could easily turn into a country where everybody could start insulting everyone else. As long as that fear is still so strong, it will remain an uphill struggle for any government to make progress in this area. That is a pity for the people of Turkey. It also makes life difficult for the politicians and the journalists inside the EU who defend Turkish accession to the EU. For them and for their voters and readers, freedom of expression is the single most important yardstick for measuring progress in Turkey.

Civil–Military Relations

High on the to-do list of the European Union is changing the relations between the civil authorities and the Turkish military. The intervention of the army into politics is a major point of ongoing EU criticism. In no other EU member state could one imagine a press conference, given by a military officer (the chief of the General Staff), on the threats to secularism or the government policy toward the a minority group (the Kurds) being broadcast live on all major national (Turkish) television channels. The good thing for the AKP is that the EU demands to push back the role of the military more or less overlap with the party's traditional wish to end military tutelage. On first sight, this seems to be an issue where the AKP should not have too much trouble in complying with EU standards. But it has turned out to be more complicated than that.

In the first years of AKP rule, the military seems to have accepted that its visible and intense interference with politics had to be modified. In one of the EU-inspired reform packages, the structure and function of the National Security Council were changed. The NSC—consisting of the top military brass, the president, and the key government ministers—had always been used by the military to make its points clear on all issues that the army considered to be of importance for Turkey's security, in the broadest definition possible. That changed under the combined pressure of the EU and the AKP. The NSC was going to meet less, its secretary general would be a civilian, and, most important, in the future its decisions would really be advice to the government, not dictates as in the past. In 2003 and 2004, the government and the army clashed over the best policy on Cyprus and the UN plans to reunite the island. In the end, the chief of staff announced that, despite differences of opinion, the generals had allowed themselves to be overruled by the government. Turkey supported the Annan plan, thereby accepting the withdrawal of almost all Turkish troops. Many observers explain this phase of "controlled conflict"[12] by focusing on the personality of the then–chief of staff, General Hilmi Özkök, who was not in favor of openly confronting a government that had been, he acknowledged, democratically elected.

This willingness to look, be it grudgingly, for a compromise ended in 2006 when Özkök was replaced by General Yaşar Büyükanıt, who opted for a more confrontational line. After having stepped down, Büyükanit admitted, in 2009, that it was he who had written the so-called E-Memorandum, which was posted on the Web site of the General Staff on April 27, 2007, and was interpreted by many, at that time, as a barely concealed warning to the ruling party not to nominate Abdullah Gül for the presidency, and to the Turkish population not to vote for the AKP in the upcoming elections. The result of this interference in politics was additional support for the AKP in the July 2007 elections and, as a result of that, the election of Gül to the presidency in August.

The army had to lick its wounds, but the relations with the new, confident AKP government improved rapidly at the end of 2007 when Turkey made a deal with the United States on cross-border military operations in northern Iraq against the Kurdish terrorist organization the Kurdistan Workers' Party (PKK). On this issue, the army and the government agreed, and it gave both some breathing space after their clash in the summer of 2007.

The AKP did not use this moment of improved relations to continue with EU-backed reforms to strengthen civilian oversight of the military. As we saw, in 2008 the AKP was busy trying to survive a closure case brought against it at the Constitutional Court. But that year saw the start of two other phenomena that would rock civil–military relations much more strongly than any government reform had done up until then. In June 2008, the independent liberal newspaper *Taraf* published a leaked document and claimed that it was an "action plan" prepared by the General Staff to intervene in politics. It would be the start of a whole series of disclosures that would seriously harm the reputation of the armed forces. A second related development that put the army on the defensive was the start of the so-called Ergenekon case.

Ergenekon is an alleged criminal network accused of attempting to overthrow the AKP government and to instigate armed riots. Suspects include several retired generals and a former commander of the gendarmerie as well as ultra-nationalist journalists and lawyers. Dozens of people have been arrested, and many remain in jail while their trials progress slowly. It is the first case in Turkey to probe into coup attempts and the most extensive investigation ever on efforts to destabilize the democratic institutions. For most AKP-minded journalists and observers, the trial is the best illustration that finally the "untouchables" of the "deep state" no longer have complete impunity but can be brought before court. But there is also widespread criticism of the way the investigations are being done and of the fact that suspects are being held in custody on the basis of vague indictments or accusations based on flimsy evidence. Since 2008, many unsolved murders and other crimes from the past have been linked with the Ergenekon gang. Many Turks, let alone people living outside Turkey, have lost track of where the investigations are going and which new revelations, often linked to army officers, to believe.

Some observers have come to the conclusion that the whole Ergenekon trial is a well-organized effort by the AKP to destroy some of its harshest critics. They claim that there are no convincing proofs of the existence of a clandestine network and accuse the government of serious breaches of the rule of law in the course of the Ergenekon investigations.[13] Most Turks still tend to agree with the way the European Commission put it in its 2009 progress report: "The case is an opportunity for Turkey to strengthen confidence in the proper functioning of its democratic institutions and the rule of law. It is important that proceedings in this context fully respect the due process of law, in particular the rights of defendants."

There are many other aspects of civil–military relations that still need to be tackled. In 2009, for instance, the government tried to limit the role of military courts and made it possible for civil courts to put on trial military personnel who were suspected of serious crimes. The proposal was adopted by parliament but later, on the request of the main opposition party, annulled by the Constitutional Court as going against the provisions of the present constitution. Only a constitutional change can overcome that hurdle. Another point of criticism, both from European institutions and from civil society organizations in Turkey, is the lack of parliamentary oversight of the defense budget. Until now, no serious efforts have been made to overcome that defect.

The leaked coup plans and other documents, apparently originating within the army, raised the tensions between the AKP and the military in 2009. At the same time, there are strong indications that the present top military brass realizes that things have changed in Turkey, both in politics and in society, and that the army cannot use its old tactics any more.

The 2007 efforts to influence the elections backfired; after all the negative publicity, support for the army among the general population has gone down considerably. The General Staff seems to agree that some of the most extreme pro-coup elements need to be removed from the army and that military education needs a radical overhaul. If that really happens, the AKP would have hit two birds with one stone. It would have strengthened its own position in Turkey while complying with one of the key EU demands.

Alevis

One of the most sensitive issues for the AKP, a party deeply rooted in the traditional Sunni interpretation of Islam, is how to deal with the Alevis. An estimated 25 percent of Turks regard themselves as Alevis, a movement within Islam that is far removed from the Sunni "mainstream." The Alevis are extremely suspicious of the AKP, which they regard as exclusively representing the Sunni majority, who do not recognize the special character of the Alevis. The violent aggression against the free-thinking Alevis in the 1990s that cost scores of people their lives is still fresh in many Alevis' memories.

At the end of 2009. it was still unclear whether the initiatives by the government to look for a dialogue with Alevi leaders were genuine or not. Alevis had their voices heard more clearly in 2008 and 2009. but no major solutions to the old prejudices and problems have been found yet. Gestures have been made, talks have been held, but the main points of disagreement are still there. The government partly blames the Alevis for this lack of progress because the Alevi organizations are divided among themselves. That may be true on some issues, but they generally agree on their basic demands: make state-run religious classes noncompulsory; abolish the Religious Affairs Directorate, or fundamentally reorganize it; and recognize the *cemevis*, the Alevi places of worship. On more than one occasion, a solution for at least one or two of these demands seemed to be close. But it did not happen.

It is widely believed that when the government could manage to deal with the Alevi issue in a convincing way, it would show to many skeptics in Turkey and abroad that it is serious when it talks about equal rights for all Turkish citizens and respect for religious freedom—for that is what the Alevi demands boil down to. What is sought here is full implementation of the principles of "equal citizenship," so that all citizens can enjoy their fundamental rights and freedoms without being subjected to discrimination because of their religion, origin, language, or race. A breakthrough on this issue would also signal to all those who still believe that the AKP has the hidden agenda of Islamizing the country that this is not true. It would show that tolerance is not a faraway ideal in Turkey but could be a leading principle for practical politics in a multireligious society.

Kurds

The European list of problems that need to be solved before Turkey can join the EU is topped by the Kurdish problem. Approximately 20 million Kurds live in Turkey, mainly in the southeast of the country and in the big cities in the west. They speak a different language from the Turks, have a different culture, and suffer from socioeconomic deprivation. The official state policy, for decades, has been to deny these differences and problems and to forbid the use of the Kurdish language.

Long years of discrimination and repression of Kurds by the Turkish state led to a violent confrontation in the 1990s between the Turkish state and the PKK, a Kurdish guerrilla movement that resorted to terrorism to reach its aim of a separate Kurdish state. Almost 35,000 people were killed, mostly Kurds, and Turkey was heavily criticised for its use of indiscriminate force and its heavy-handed treatment of the civilian population in the southeast. The violence died down after the capture of PKK leader Abdullah Öcalan in 1999. Since then, many Kurds and Turks have been waiting for the leaders of their country to come up with structural reforms that would deal with the problems of cultural discrimination and economic underdevelopment that remain.

The AKP leaders never used the official harsh rhetoric about the Kurds that was so common among Turkish politicians of all other parties. During a visit in 2005 to Diyarbakır, the main Kurdish city in the southeast, Prime Minister Erdoğan recognized the existence of a Kurdish problem and opted for democratic—that is, nonviolent—methods of dealing with it. Together with some socioeconomic improvements under the first AKP government, this moderate approach helped the AKP win 60 percent of the votes in the southeast in the 2007 elections. It raised the expectations that finally a political solution could be found, especially because in the same elections, twenty independent Kurdish candidates managed to get elected. For the first time, a Kurdish nationalist party, the Democratic Society Party (DTP), was represented in the Turkish parliament.

But until the beginning of 2009, it seemed that after 2007 the situation had gone from bad to worse. The AKP and DTP, the two parties that had received almost all the votes in the southeast, did not manage to find a compromise. Soon the DTP was under threat of being disbanded by the Constitutional Court, which eventually happened in December 2009. (Former) DTP politicians face dozens of court cases. After years of only sporadic attacks, the PKK again started a campaign against the Turkish military. The army, with the agreement of the AKP government, reacted with cross-border raids into northern Iraq that were quite successful but have raised the terrorist's group profile and its popularity in the region. The DTP was not willing and/or able to distance itself clearly from the PKK and has therefore lost much of its support among Turkish liberals and intellectuals. The hope that the AKP would deal differently with the situation than other Turkish parties had went down dramatically.

All of a sudden in January 2009, however, was the launch of TRT 6, the first-ever twenty-four-hour television channel in Kurdish, and the announcement that soon the Kurdish language and culture would be taught at some state universities. A few months later, the government announced the so-called Democratic Initiative, aimed at finally solving the Kurdish problem and other democratic deficits. Prime Minister Erdoğan committed himself and his party to radical solutions that mirrored key Kurdish and EU demands. At the end of 2009, the problem was that after these announcements many meetings were organized and plans floated but no concrete proposal has been tabled. Nationalist opposition against the initiative was strong, in parliament and in parts of society. It seems that the AKP was having second thoughts and was afraid that pushing these reforms through parliament could damage its electoral prospects in 2011. Many in Turkey and Europe are afraid that, after raising expectations, the AKP is, again, not able to deliver, thereby missing the biggest opportunity so far to prove that it is really different in dealing with the ethnic complexities of Turkey.

Republican People's Party

One of the main problems for Turkey on its road to the EU is the fact that, since 2005, accession has become a controversial issue between the AKP government, on the one hand, and both main opposition parties, on the other. It is a situation that we seldom saw in other candidate states. In most countries that want to join the EU, there is a basic understanding between all major parties that EU accession is a national priority that should not be endangered by petty party politics. Parties do not challenge the basic premise of EU accession and ultimately support the reforms that are necessary to take their country into the EU. Not so in Turkey. The few reforms that the government has introduced since 2005 have not been supported by the main opposition party. The CHP voted against changing article 301 and the Law on Foundations. The CHP also made it clear that it is opposed to the Democratic Initiative and that it will vote against the protocols signed by the Turkish and Armenian governments in the autumn of 2009 that, when and if ratified, would mean a serious improvement in the relations between the two countries. Both initiatives were welcomed by many in the EU but were heavily criticized by the CHP and described as acts of treason. Invitations from the government to try to find a compromise on substantial changes to the 1982 Constitution fell on deaf ears.

The CHP still presents itself as a pro-European party, but the problem for the CHP in both Europe and Turkey is that few see the CHP as a supporter of European values. The party is seen as defending the status quo that will definitively not help bring Turkey into the EU.

Many on the left in Turkey hope that the CHP manages to free itself from the ambiguous position it got itself into. A party cannot convincingly claim to be in favor of EU accession and at the same time vote against the reforms that are necessary to reach that goal. Looking back at the confrontational strategy chosen by the CHP's leader, Deniz Baykal, after 2005 and at the ongoing attempts to block each and every government initiative to introduce EU standards in Turkey, it seems unlikely that the CHP will transform itself into a committed pro-European party soon, meaning a party that supports reforms and pushes other parties to introduce them more quickly and that stops using anti-Western and anti-European rhetoric because it realizes that it makes more sense for a social democratic party to try to win the future than to defend the past.

The result of the CHP's move away from EU-inspired reforms is that Turkey lacks a pro-European opposition party that could push the AKP to be more courageous and continue the reform process, even if specific measures might not be very popular among the population. Nobody expects the other opposition party, the nationalist MHP, to play that role. Because of its strong ties with the state institutions and its support among many AKP skeptics, the only party that, together with the AKP, could construct a broad pro-EU consensus in Turkish politics is the CHP. It would help Turkey to speed up its reforms, and it would remove an excuse for slowing down the process that is too often used by AKP officials.

Conclusion

The AKP's performance on EU accession since coming to power in 2002 has had several ups and downs. In order to make a proper evaluation, we must divide the period 2002 to 2009 into three parts.

In the first two full years of AKP government, 2003 and 2004, the party surprised many in Turkey and the EU. The reforms that had started in 2001 and 2002 under the coalition government led by Prime Minister Ecevit not only continued but accelerated in pace. The AKP was keen to show that fears of an Islamically inspired slowdown of reforms or even a backlash against EU accession were undeserved. The party had something to prove, and it successfully passed the test, helped by the only opposition party, the CHP, that supported the necessary changes in line with its traditional pro-European vocation. The reward for these united and convincing efforts came at the end of 2004, when the EU decided to start accession negotiations with Turkey in 2005.

However, the years 2005 to 2008 were marked by a surprisingly rapid slowdown in the reform process. There are several reasons that could explain the change. Since the start of the negotiations, opponents of Turkey's accession, both in Turkey and inside the EU, have become much more visible and vocal. The EU started looking increasingly inward after the defeat of the Constitutional Treaty in 2005. As a result, further enlargement of the EU has been put on the back burner, both in the minds and on the agendas of many Europeans. On top of that came the changing of the guard in key EU member states Germany and France. The new leaders of both countries broke with the pro-Turkey policy of their predecessors and spoke out clearly against Turkey's EU membership. Their very vocal opposition played into the hands of those forces in Turkey that were against reforms from the very start. It pushed the only opposition party of the time to change its pro-reform policy, hoping to benefit from its turn to nationalism at the ballot box. The failure of the EU to handle the Cyprus problem after 2004 only added to the perception among many Turks that they were the losers and that the EU would never deliver on its promises.

In such a situation, one needs courageous politicians who are willing to continue making the case for accession even if it is not very popular at that particular moment. After Gül became president in 2007, there was nobody in the government with enough vision and power to convince Erdoğan that it would make sense for the AKP to keep on pushing for accession. The prime minister himself has never been a convinced EU supporter, but he made the calculation in 2003 and 2004 that the reforms would pay off electorally. He was right. After 2007 he made another calculation, giving in to the inevitable tendency with every governing party to cling to power no matter what it takes.

It was only at the beginning of 2009 that the AKP leader seemed to realize that there are limits to this policy of indefinite postponement of necessary reforms. Finally, a full-time chief negotiator was appointed, the number of civil servants working on EU accession was increased, and an overall plan to implement EU rules and regulations was adopted. In the course of 2009, the government started several initiatives that, if successful, would silence the skeptics in Turkey and abroad who claim that the AKP has given up on reforms and on EU accession.

In the future, the Cyprus issue will play an important role in relations between Turkey and the European Union. The negotiations on Cyprus between the two communities either will produce a solution to the problems on the island or, if they fail, will make life very difficult for Turkey and the EU. Without a breakthrough, Cyprus will continue to block more than ten chapters in the negotiations between Turkey and the EU. How will the AKP react to that situation, knowing that giving in to the EU on Cyprus is extremely unpopular?

In the autumn of 2009, several reports were published by Friends of Turkey in Europe and the United States, warning the government that it cannot go on like this and that without changes, Turkey runs the risks of creating a serious crisis in its relations with the EU. For the moment, these warnings seem to have been effective. The government is showing signs of waking up. But it takes more to repair the damage that has been done by putting EU accession on the back burner for so long.

During seven years in power, the AKP has proved both its critics and its supporters wrong. The party is not a simple continuation of its predecessor, the anti-European Welfare Party. But neither is the AKP a convinced pro-European party that is willing to push for EU accession, no matter what it takes. The AKP policy toward EU accession is based on a careful calculation of the domestic costs and benefits. That policy has taken Turkey closer to the EU, but the unanswered question remains whether it will be enough to take Turkey inside the European Union.[14]

Notes

1. The survey in Germany was cited in *Der Spiegel*, October 2004. The survey in Netherlands was conducted by Dutch polling organization Peil van Nederland in October 2004; its Web site is no longer functioning.
2. Eurobarometer, June 2005, http://ec.europa.eu/public_opinion/index_en.htm (accessed April 2009).
3. M. Hakan Yavuz, ed., *The Emergence of a New Turkey: Democracy and the AK Parti* (Salt Lake City: University of Utah Press, 2006), and *Secularism and Muslim Democracy in Turkey* (Cambridge: Cambridge University Press, 2009).
4. Angel Rabasa and F. Stephen Larrabee, *The Rise of Political Islam in Turkey* (Santa Monica, Calif.: RAND, 2008); Gareth Jenkins, *Political Islam in Turkey: Running West, Heading East?* (New York: Palgrave Macmillan, 2008).
5. İhsan Dağı, *Turkey: Between Democracy and Militarism: Post-Kemalist Perspectives* (Ankara: Orion, 2008).
6. Dietrich Jung and Catharina Raudvere, eds., *Religion, Politics, and Turkey's EU Accession* (New York: Palgrave Macmillan, 2008).
7. Joost Lagendijk and Jan Marinus Wiersma, *Travels Among Europe's Muslim Neighbours: The Quest for Democracy* (Brussels: Center for European Policy Studies, 2008), 52.
8. Ziya Öniş, "Conservative Globalists Versus Defensive Nationalists: Political Parties and Paradoxes of Europeanization in Turkey," *Journal of Southern Europe and the Balkans* 9 (2007): 247–261, and "Conservative Globalism at the Crossroads: The Justice and Development Party and the Thorny Path to Democratic Consolidation in Turkey," *Mediterranean Politics* 14 (2009): 21–40.
9. Ümit Cizre, ed., *Secular and Islamic Politics in Turkey: The Making of the Justice and Development Party* (New York: Routledge, 2008).
10. Ahmet T. Kuru, *Secularism and State Policies Towards Religion: The United States, France, and Turkey* (New York: Cambridge University Press, 2009).
11. European Commission, *Progress Report on Turkish Accession to the EU* (Brussels: European Commission, 2009), 14.

12. William Hale and Ergun Özbudun, *Islamism, Democracy, and Liberalism in Turkey: The Case of the AKP* (New York: Routledge, 2009), 82.
13. Gareth Jenkins, *Between Fact and Fantasy: Turkey's Ergenekon Investigation* (Washington, D.C.: Central Asia–Caucasus Institute and Silk Road Studies Program, 2009).
14. Philip H. Gordon and Ömer Taşpınar, *Winning Turkey: How America, Europe, and Turkey Can Revive a Fading Partnership* (Washington, D.C.: Brookings Institution Press, 2008)

8

The "Turkish Model" in the Matrix of Political Catholicism

STATHIS N. KALYVAS

For a long time, especially the first two decades after World War II, the Kemalist model, epitomized by the establishment of a secular nation-state in 1923, was hailed as one of the most successful models for modernization.[1] In recent years, this first "Turkish model" has faded away and a new one gradually has taken its place. This "new Turkish model" is based on the combination of moderate Islamism, liberal reforms, and democratic consolidation.[2]

In this chapter, I ask two questions. First, what exactly does this new "Turkish model" consist of and what explains its emergence? Second, is it an outcome associated with causes that are idiosyncratic to Turkey, or can it be thought of, instead, as a generalizable manifestation of a broader political phenomenon? I argue that the Turkish model represents a particular type of interaction between religiously rooted politics and a process of liberalization and democratization. Although there are many elements that are specific to Turkey, I point out that this is not a new phenomenon. Rather, it shares several elements with an earlier and largely forgotten process of religious mobilization that took place in nineteenth-century Europe, epitomized by Catholic mobilization, the precursor of modern Christian Democracy.

What Is the "Turkish Model" and What Explains Its Emergence?

Since 2002, Turkey has been governed by the Justice and Development Party (AKP), a political party that has been described as both "pro-Islamic" and "Islam-friendly."[3] The AKP's birth was not easy: it emerged from the ashes of another Islamist party, the Virtue Party (Fazilet Partisi), which was banned by the Constitutional Court in 2001. It is worth noting that the AKP's founder and leader, Recep Tayyip Erdoğan, was imprisoned for "inciting hatred and enmity" and barred from running for the parliamentary elections of November 2002.[4] Indeed, this is a party with religious roots that has challenged the type of secularism prevailing in Turkey[5] and has sought to give religion a more prominent place in Turkish society. At the same time, several scholars have noted that the AKP also has been the vehicle through which a new class of upwardly mobile economic entrepreneurs with strong ties to the provincial towns and villages of Anatolia have mobilized the language of religion and Islamic identity to demand a bigger role in political affairs.[6] Seen from this angle, Islamic identity has acted more as a "lubricant" for mobilization than as its deeper cause.[7]

There has been a long and heated discussion about the exact place and meaning that religion holds for the AKP. It is clear, however, that the AKP has challenged the forceful secularism that came to be the cornerstone of Kemalism, and that it has been at the forefront of an effort to articulate a version of Islamic identity that reconciles it with social and political modernity. In spite of its Islamist coloration, the AKP has never attempted to implement a radical, anti-system set of policies that would undermine (rather than mitigate) the secular character of the Turkish state and challenge its democratic institutions. On the contrary, it can be argued that it has deepened these institutions by implementing a set of liberalizing political reforms mainly contained in the so-called harmonization packages, which were initially intended to satisfy European Union (EU) integration criteria. Despite ups and downs,[8] these reforms have resulted in a marked reduction of the role of the military in politics. It is in retrospect quite clear that the AKP has put Turkey on a path leading to a more liberal and democratic future. In other words, this party, with its "pro-Islamic and anti-Western roots, has ironically played a historically important role in consolidating democracy in Turkey and integrating Turkey into the EU."[9]

In turn, this process of political transformation has had a significant impact on the party itself. The party's identity and political discourse have shifted toward a more pronounced emphasis of themes such as democracy, human rights, and the rule of law—the AKP has been "metamorphosed," concludes Berna Turam.[10] Indeed, this transformation has elicited apprehension among the more hard-core elements of the party, who see it as "having moved away from its 'roots and habits' towards 'mundane vocations and expectations.'"[11]

All in all, then, the combination of Islamist moderation and the deepening of democratic institutions justifies references to a new "Turkish model," one characterized by a process of twin political transformations: of the state and of the party. Turam explains these transformations as the outcome of a "politics of engagement" between the two.[12] And yet this is more of a description than an explanation. The real challenge consists of explaining the emergence of this "politics of engagement," which entails a type of strategic interaction whereby the outcome may be systematically optimal irrespective of the initial preferences of the actors involved.

It is well known that the Turkish state had harbored a strong distaste for religiously rooted mobilization in politics; it has also been able to send clear signals about the cost of such anti-system politics.[13] This was the case, most notably, with the so-called soft military coup of 1997, which resulted in the banning, the following year, of the Welfare Party (Refah Partisi) and, in 2001, of the Virtue Party. The interaction with the state shaped an entire generation of Islamist politicians, who came to interpret the Refah debacle in particular as a waste of resources, opportunities, and hope. As a result, they came to discard the "essentialist and dogmatic" aspects of the Refah discourse, with its pronounced anti-system and anti-secular attitudes, and embarked instead on a pragmatist course of action by promoting "a discursive denial" of their "Islamist pedigree" and the adoption "of a moderate and non-religious discourse in its place."[14] This was true for both Erdoğan, whose trajectory went from confrontational to cooperative positions, and for Fethullah Gülen and his grassroots movement.[15] Gamze Çavdar summarizes this process by describing it as one of political learning;[16] there is little doubt that it has been motivated by strategic considerations about costs and rewards. At the same time, it also must be recognized that the guardians of the Kemalist order got pulled into an incrementalist process from which it quickly became too difficult to remove themselves.[17] A key reason is undoubtedly the "shadow presence" of the European Union.[18] The

European integration process constrained the state elites in how far they could go with repression, while simultaneously supplying the AKP with a convenient set of benchmarks for institutional reforms that constrained the power of the traditional power centers, and especially the military.[19]

Is the "Turkish Model" Idiosyncratic?

What has been happening in Turkey since 2002 contains several elements that are specific to it; after all, Kemalism was distinctively Turkish. Nevertheless, this process is hardly unique to Turkey when viewed in the context of a broader historical perspective.

I have argued elsewhere that the relevance of political Catholicism extends beyond the boundaries of the European nineteenth century and that it is especially pertinent today.[20] Formulated in ideal-typical terms, what I call the "Christian Democratic experience" embodies the trajectory of a mass political movement, primarily Catholic in its confessional orientation, which emerged in an institutional context that was not yet fully democratic, with the aim of challenging the liberal and secular character of European political modernity. In many ways successful, this movement ultimately contributed to the consolidation of the modern liberal democratic order. In fact, so effective were European Christian Democratic parties in reinforcing the political order they initially challenged that they ended up completely forgetting their anti-liberal political origins. Told in a nutshell, and coupled with the parallel Social Democratic experience,[21] this is the story of the astonishing capacity of democratic institutions to absorb their enemies, while expanding. But is it reasonable to extend the Christian Democratic experience to non-European and non-Christian contexts, and especially the Muslim world? A closer look into that experience helps address this question.

The Catholic politics of Europe during the second half of the nineteenth century can be boiled down to five key elements: (1) mass mobilization, (2) an anti-system political discourse, (3) the combination of an appeal to religious sensibilities coupled with a political message of economic inclusion, (4) the modernization of religious practices, and (5) the ultimate moderation of Catholic parties and the democratization of the political institutions within which they operated.

First, the mobilization of European Catholics took on a pronounced grassroots character, initially located outside the narrow political arena and within what we would call today civil society. The collective action problem was solved through the deployment of a wide range of selective incentives centered primarily around the effective, local provision of a variety of services, ranging from social services (hospitals, clinics, legal-aid societies), economic activities (banks, credit and investment houses, insurance companies), or educational initiatives (schools, child-care centers, youth camps)—all widely publicized by dense networks of religious publishing and broadcasting. Catholic activists were able to build real counter-societies (known as "subcultures" or "milieus"), which were later incorporated into the Catholic political parties. In the process, they were also able to set examples of successful management, typically contrasted to the ineffective or corrupt state efforts.

Second, religious mobilization in Europe relied on an "anti-system" discourse—where "anti-system" does not necessarily correspond to "revolutionary." The Catholic movement criticized existing political institutions and their underlying secular and liberal character without, however, calling for a revolution. Today, the association between Catholicism and democracy appears to be so natural that a mention of the deeply aliberal character of their precursor movements comes as a great surprise. And yet, even a cursory look at the infamous *Syllabus Errorum*, pronounced by the pope in 1864, gives pause. There, the pope denounced concepts such as freedom of speech, freedom of the press, freedom of conscience and religion, the legal equality of cults, the sovereignty of the people, the doctrine of progress, the separation of state and church, liberalism, and the modern conception of civilization. He condemned as a grave error the belief that a regime that did not repress the violators of Catholic religion could be good. This critique of the liberal and secular order was crucial in energizing and mobilizing the Catholic masses across Europe.

Third, religiously oriented appeals combined with the activation of new social cleavages centered around the political mobilization of primarily petit bourgeois, urban and rural sectors that felt politically excluded and economically marginalized. This is why, and in contrast to socialist mobilization, Catholic movements became primarily cross-class movements. The social heterogeneity of the emerging parties reflected their cross-class basis; their ability to weave together disparate, or even competing, social groups became their linchpin, one that affected their political platforms for many decades. Viewed from this perspective, religion provided a language for the articulation of political and economic claims.

Fourth, Catholic mobilization in Europe did not just activate traditional religious identities. Rather than advocate only a return to premodern practices of religion, as often portrayed by their political adversaries, Catholic movements updated and modernized what it meant to be religious. For example, the revival of piety that took place in the context of this mobilization was accompanied by what at the time were modern forms of political activism that ended up undermining the traditional relations both between clergy and laity and between higher and lower clergy. Seen from this perspective, Catholic mobilization was not a mere manifestation of religion in politics; it amounted to a long-term transformation of religious practices.

Finally, the anti-liberal dimension of Catholic mobilization was eventually toned down and effectively reversed, once Catholic parties became integrated into the political systems of their countries. While these parties moderated, they contributed to the democratization of their countries. New political and social groups were integrated into the liberal institutions, and both political moderation and democratic institutions acquired a self-enforcing dynamic that had been lacking up to that point. What is remarkable is that this outcome was achieved less as a result of a process of independent ideological adjustment and more out of self-interested actions resulting from the process of political participation: democracy made democrats, rather than the other way around.

The emergence of Islamist movements in the Muslim world supplies us with many parallels to the Catholic political revival in nineteenth-century Europe, in spite of its variation across countries.[22] The Islamist movement constitutes a recent and modern phenomenon that became a potent political force during the 1970s and 1980s, primarily through the channel of mass mobilization. Using both mosques and modern communications technology to propagate their message, several Islamist movements crafted an electoralist strategy (where this option was available to them) and combined it with a grassroots strategy, weaving the fabric of a veritable counter-society based on a variety of local groups. In turn, this mass mobilization was based on a critique of authoritarian practices and corruption, but also the spread of secular and Western ideas. Searching for the social bases of this discourse, one uncovers broad social coalitions that range from the urban poor to the middle classes, and that encompass small businessmen, low-level state functionaries, shop owners, lawyers, and teachers. Furthermore, most Islamist movements do not just advocate a return to traditional religious practices. They have blended new and modern forms of organization based on the primary role of social and political action in urban settings with selected elements of Islamic tradition. The striking parallels between nineteenth-century Catholic mobilization and contemporary Islamist mobilization echo Ahmet Kuru and Alfred Stepan's critique of essentialist generalizations about the supposed impact of Islam on politics.[23]

In spite of the striking parallels between Catholic and Islamist movements, a key difference immediately jumps out. Especially in the Middle East, Islamist movements appear to have failed to transform themselves and to transform the political systems in which they emerged. On the one hand, many Islamist movements have radicalized rather than moderate; on the other hand, most of these political systems have become even more autocratic. Obviously, this outcome is overdetermined: unlike western Europe, which was engaged in a process of democratization, many Muslim countries were autocratic to begin with; unlike western Europe, which was industrializing, many Muslim countries appear mired in political and economic stagnation; European countries also lacked the legacy of colonization that shaped many Muslim countries; and despite a rhetoric that could be bombastic, Catholics did not stray away from peaceful politics—there was no Catholic equivalent of violent jihadism.

Nevertheless, at the core of the difference between Catholic and Islamist movements lies the absence of even a limited democratic option in many Muslim countries: competitive elections have been unavailable.[24] It is this absence, equivalent of the use of a stick without a reward, that has often fueled a vicious cycle whereby Islamist movements radicalize and authoritarian regimes justify further repression. Herein, I think, lies the broader significance of the Turkish case. As in the European case, the Turkish state credibly foreclosed the most radical options while allowing for a democratic opening that in turn spun off a virtuous cycle of Islamist moderation and democratic transformation based on mutual revision, adaptation, and accommodation.[25]

This raises the question of whether the Turkish model can be generalized to the rest of the Muslim world. Some authors have argued that the Turkish experiment cannot be replicated in other Muslim countries because either Turkey is seen as possessing a uniquely accommodating Muslim culture or Atatürk's heritage of authoritarian modernization and the secularist republic is equally unique.[26] Once, however, the Turkish model is juxtaposed to the European Catholic experience of the nineteenth century, it ceases to appear unique or totally idiosyncratic.

Keeping in mind that the situation in Turkey retains a degree of fluidity,[27] here is, then, the core message conveyed by the new Turkish model: liberalization, democratization, and inclusion are more likely where states provide rewards for moderation while sanctioning anti-system behavior, and where Islamist movements are included in the competitive political arena as players with a real chance of achieving a lasting political impact. Given the exciting possibility of an Arab democratic spring, Turkey reminds us that a combination of sticks for extremism and rewards for participation offers a path toward the construction of new democracies.

Notes

1. Bernard Lewis, *The Emergence of Modern Turkey* (New York: Oxford University Press, 1961); Sibel Bozdoğan and Reşat Kasaba, "Introduction," in Sibel Bozdoğan and Reşat Kasaba, eds., *Rethinking Modernity and National Identity in Turkey* (Seattle: University of Washington Press, 1997), 3. For a useful overview of Kemalism, see M. Şükrü Hanioğlu, "The Historical Roots of Kemalism" (chap. 2, this volume).

2. Gamze Çavdar, "Islamist New Thinking in Turkey: A Model for Political Learning?" *Political Science Quarterly* 121 (2006): 477.

3. Berna Turam, *Between Islam and the State: The Politics of Engagement* (Stanford, Calif.: Stanford University Press, 2007), 3; Ümit Cizre, "Introduction: The Justice and Development Party: Making Choices, Revisions, and Reversals Interactively," in Ümit Cizre, ed., *Secular and Islamic Politics in Turkey: The Making of the Justice and Development Party* (New York: Routledge, 2008), 1. For an (ultimately unconvincing) argument denying the Islamic character of the AKP, see M. Hakan Yavuz, "The Role of the New Bourgeoisie in the Transformation of the Turkish Islamic Movement," in M. Hakan Yavuz, ed., *The Emergence of a New Turkey: Democracy and the AK Parti* (Salt Lake City: University of Utah Press), 2.

4. İhsan D. Dağı, "The Justice and Development Party: Identity, Politics, and Human Rights Discourse in the Search for Security and Legitimacy," in Yavuz, ed., *Emergence of a New Turkey*, 88.

5. Ahmet T. Kuru, *Secularism and State Policies Toward Religion: The United States, France, and Turkey* (New York: Cambridge University Press, 2009).

6. Yavuz, "Role of the New Bourgeoisie," 5.

7. Ibid., 6.

8. Joost Lagendijk, "Turkey's Accession to the European Union and the Role of the Justice and Development Party" (chap. 7, this volume).

9. Dağı, "Justice and Development Party," 104.

10. Turam, *Between Islam and the State*, 139.

11. Cizre, "Introduction: The Justice and Development Party," 2.

12. Turam, *Between Islam and the State*, 134.

13. Çavdar, "Islamist New Thinking in Turkey," 486.

14. Cizre, "Introduction: The Justice and Development Party," 4–5; Sultan Tepe, "A Pro-Islamic Party? Promises and Limits of Turkey's Justice and Development Party," in Yavuz, ed., *Emergence of a New Turkey*, 114.

15. Turam, *Between Islam and the State*, 135.

16. Çavdar, "Islamist New Thinking in Turkey," 480; Ahmet T. Kuru, "Globalization and Diversification of Islamic Movements: Three Turkish Cases," *Political Science Quarterly* 120 (2005): 254.

17. On the specific modalities of this process, see William Hale and Ergun Özbudun, *Islamism, Democracy, and Liberalism in Turkey: The Case of the AKP* (New York: Routledge, 2009).

18. Çavdar, "Islamist New Thinking in Turkey," 496.

19. Lagendijk, "Turkey's Accession to the European Union."

20. Stathis N. Kalyvas and Kees van Kersbergen, "Christian Democracy," *Annual Reviews of Political Science* 13 (2010): 183–209; Stathis N. Kalyvas, "Religious Mobilization and Unsecular Politics," in Thomas A. Kselman and Joseph Buttigieg, eds., *European Christian Democracy: Historical Legacies and Comparative Perspectives* (Notre Dame, Ind.: Notre Dame University Press, 2003), 293–320; "Commitment Problems in Emerging Democracies: The Case of Religious Parties," *Comparative Politics* 32 (2000): 379–399; "Democracy and Religious Politics: Evidence from Belgium," *Comparative Political Studies* 31 (1998): 291–319; and *The Rise of Christian Democracy in Europe* (Ithaca, N.Y.: Cornell University Press, 1996). The most fruitful comparison is between the Turkish case and the Catholic movements and parties of pre–World War II Europe, rather than the institutionalized post–World War II Christian Democratic parties, as attempted by William Hale, "Christian Democracy and the JDP: Parallels and Contrasts," in Yavuz, ed., *Emergence of a New Turkey*, 66–87.

21. Adam Przeworski, *Paper Stones: A History of Electoral Socialism* (Chicago: University of Chicago Press, 1988); Roberto Michels, *Political Parties* (New York: Free Press, 1966).

22. Kalyvas, "Commitment Problems in Emerging Democracies"; Kuru, "Globalization and Diversification of Islamic Movements"; Mona El-Ghobashy, "The Metamorphosis of the Egyptian Muslim Brothers," *International Journal*

of Middle East Studies 37 (2005): 373–395; Melani Cammett and Sukriti Issar, "Bricks-and-Mortar Clientelism: Sectarianism and the Logics of Welfare Allocation in Lebanon," *World Politics* 62 (2010): 381–421.

23. Ahmet T. Kuru and Alfred Stepan, "*Laïcité* as an 'Ideal Type' and a Continuum" (chap. 4, this volume).

24. Indeed, El-Ghobashy provides evidence of a similar trajectory in Egypt that was ultimately foreclosed by the regime:

> Setting out to win Egyptian hearts and minds for an austere Islamic state and society, Hasan al-Banna's Society of Muslim Brothers was instead irrevocably transformed into a flexible political party that is highly responsive to the unforgiving calculus of electoral politics. The Muslim Brothers have left no political opportunity untapped, plunging with gusto into the vote-seeking game, pushing other political forces and the state to take seriously what began as a farcical margin of electoral competition in the 1970s. The case of the Ikhwan confirms that it is the institutional rules of participation rather than the commandments of ideology that motivate political parties. Even the most ideologically committed and organizationally stalwart parties are transformed in the process of interacting with competitors, citizens, and the state. Ideology and organization bow to the terms of participation." ("Metamorphosis of the Egyptian Muslim Brothers," 390)

25. Yavuz, "Role of the New Bourgeoisie," 2; Turam, *Between Islam and the State*, 134; Çavdar, "Islamist New Thinking in Turkey," 479, 493. Note also that the Turkish model addresses Eva Belin's reverse concern, that theories of religious mobilization are contingent on characteristics unique to the Catholic Church, as discussed in "Faith in Politics: New Trends in the Study of Religion and Politics," *World Politics* 60 (2008): 315–347.

26. Yavuz, "Role of the New Bourgeoisie," 2; Çavdar, "Islamist New Thinking in Turkey," 478.

27. Ergun Özbudun, "Turkey—Plural Society and Monolithic State" (chap. 3, this volume).

Selected Bibliography

Abu Rabi, Ibrahim, ed. *Islam at the Crossroads: On the Life and Thought of Bediüzzaman Said Nursi*. Albany: State University of New York Press, 2003.

Ahmad, Feroz. *The Making of Modern Turkey*. New York: Routledge, 1993.

Akan, Murat. "Twin Tolerations or Siamese Twins? Kemalist Laicism and Political Islam in Turkey." In Douglas Chalmers and Scott Mainwaring, eds., *Institutions and Democracy: Essay in Honor of Alfred Stepan*. Notre Dame: Notre Dame University Press, 2011.

Akbulut, Zeynep. "Banning Headscarves and Muslim Women's Subjectivity in Turkey." Ph.D. diss., University of Washington, 2011.

Akdoğan, Yalçın. "The Meaning of Conservative Democratic Political Identity." In M. Hakan Yavuz, ed., *The Emergence of a New Turkey: Democracy and the AK Parti*, 49–65. Salt Lake City: University of Utah Press, 2006.

Aktürk, Şener. "Regimes of Ethnicity: Comparative Analysis of Germany, the Soviet Union/Post-Soviet Russia, and Turkey." *World Politics* 63 (2011): 115–164.

Akyol, Taha. *Ama Hangi Atatürk*. Istanbul: Doğan, 2008.

Arslan, Zühtü. "Conflicting Paradigms: Political Rights in the Turkish Constitutional Court." *Critique: Critical Middle Eastern Studies* 11 (2002): 9–25.

Aydın Cemil. *Politics of Anti-Westernism in Asia: Visions of World Order in Pan-Islamic and Pan-Asian Thought*. New York: Columbia University Press, 2007.

Azak, Umut. *Islam and Secularism in Turkey: Kemalism, Religion, and the Nation-State*. New York: Tauris, 2010.

Barkey, Karen. *Bandits and Bureaucrats: The Ottoman Route to State Centralization.* Ithaca, N.Y.: Cornell University Press, 1997.

——. *Empire of Difference: The Ottomans in Comparative Perspective.* New York: Cambridge University Press, 2008.

Başgil, Ali Fuat. *Din ve Laiklik.* 1954. Reprint, Istanbul: Yağmur, 1977.

Belge, Ceren. "Friends of the Court: The Republican Alliance and Selective Activism on the Constitutional Court of Turkey." *Law and Society Review* 40 (2006): 653–692.

Berkes, Niyazi. *The Development of Secularism in Turkey.* 1964. Reprint, New York: Routledge, 1998.

Bottoni, Rossella. "The Origins of Secularism in Turkey." *Ecclesiastical Law Journal* 9 (2007): 175–186.

Bozarslan, Hamit. "Islam, laïcité et la question d'autorité dans l'Empire ottoman et en Turquie kémaliste." *Archives des sciences sociales des religions* 125 (2004): 99–113.

Bozdoğan, Sibel, and Reşat Kasaba. *Rethinking Modernity and National Identity in Turkey.* Seattle: University of Washington Press, 1997.

Braude, Benjamin, and Bernard Lewis, eds. *Christians and Jews in the Ottoman Empire: The Functioning of a Plural Society.* 2 vols. New York: Holmes and Meier, 1982.

Burdy, Jean-Paul, and Jean Marcou. "Laïcité/Laiklik: Introduction." *Cahiers d'études sur la Méditerranée orientale et le monde turco-iranien* 19 (1995): 5–34.

Çarkoğlu, Ali, and Binnaz Toprak. *Değişen Türkiye'de Din, Toplum ve Siyaset.* Istanbul: TESEV, 2006.

Çavdar, Gamze. "Islamist New Thinking in Turkey: A Model for Political Learning?" *Political Science Quarterly* 121 (2006): 477–497.

Çetin, Muhammed. *The Gülen Movement: Civic Service Without Borders.* New York: Blue Dome, 2010.

Çınar, Menderes, and Burhanettin Duran. "The Specific Evolution of Contemporary Political Islam in Turkey and Its 'Difference.'" In Ümit Cizre, ed., *Secular and Islamic Politics in Turkey: The Making of the Justice and Development Party,* 17–40. New York: Routledge, 2007.

Cizre, Ümit. "The Anatomy of the Turkish Military's Political Autonomy." *Comparative Politics* 29 (1997): 151–166.

——, ed. *Democratic Oversight and Reform of the Security Sector in Turkey.* Berlin: Geneva Center for the Democratic Control of Armed Forces, 2007.

——. "Parameters and Strategies of Islam–State Interaction in Republican Turkey." *International Journal of Middle Eastern Studies* 28 (1996): 231–251.

——, ed. *Secular and Islamic Politics in Turkey: The Making of the Justice and Development Party.* New York: Routledge, 2008.

Dağı, İhsan D. "The Justice and Development Party: Identity, Politics, and Human Rights Discourse in the Search for Security and Legitimacy." In M. Hakan Yavuz, ed., *The Emergence of a New Turkey: Democracy and the AK Party*, 88–106. Salt Lake City: University of Utah Press, 2006.

Davison, Andrew. *Secularism and Revivalism in Turkey: A Hermeneutic Reconsideration*. New Haven, Conn.: Yale University Press, 1998.

Erdoğan, Mustafa. *Demokrasi, Laiklik, Resmi İdeoloji*. Ankara: Liberte, 2000.

Evin, Ahmet, and Metin Heper, eds. *State Democracy and the Military in the 1980s*. New York: de Gruyter, 1988.

Göle, Nilüfer. *The Forbidden Modern: Civilization and Veiling*. Ann Arbor: University of Michigan Press, 1996.

——. *İslam ve Modernlik Üzerine Melez Desenler*. Istanbul: Metis, 2000.

——. "Secularism and Islamism in Turkey: The Making of Elites and Counter-Elites." *Middle East Journal* 51 (1997): 46–58.

Gülalp, Haldun. "Globalization and Political Islam: The Social Base of Turkey's Welfare Party." *International Journal of Middle East Studies* 33 (2001): 433–448.

Hale, William, and Ergun Özbudun. *Islamism, Democracy, and Liberalism in Turkey: The Case of the AKP*. New York: Routledge, 2010.

Hanioğlu, M. Şükrü. *Atatürk: An Intellectual Biography*. Princeton, N.J.: Princeton University Press, 2011.

——. "Blueprints for a Future Society: Late Ottoman Materialists on Science, Religion, and Art." In Elisabeth Özdalga, ed., *Late Ottoman Society: The Intellectual Legacy*, 27–116. New York: Routledge Curzon, 2005.

——. *A Brief History of the Late Ottoman Empire*. Princeton, N.J.: Princeton University Press, 2008.

——. "Garbcılar: Their Attitudes Toward Religion and Their Impact on the Official Ideology of the Turkish Republic." *Studia Islamica* 86 (1997): 133–158.

——. *Preparation for a Revolution: The Young Turks, 1902–1908*. New York: Oxford University Press, 2000.

Heper, Metin. *The State Tradition in Turkey*. Walkington: Eothen Press, 1985.

Hurd, Elisabeth Shakman. *The Politics of Secularism in International Relations*. Princeton, N.J.: Princeton University Press, 2007.

Inalcik, Halil, and Donald Quataert, eds. *An Economic and Social History of the Ottoman Empire, 1300–1914*. Cambridge: Cambridge University Press, 1994.

Kaplan, Sam. *The Pedagogical State: Education and the Politics of National Culture in Post-1980 Turkey*. Stanford, Calif.: Stanford University Press, 2006.

Karpat, Kemal. *Ottoman Population, 1830–1914: Demographic and Social Characteristics*. Madison: University of Wisconsin Press, 1985.

——. *The Politization of Islam: Reconstructing Identity, State, Faith, and Community in the Late Ottoman State*. New York: Oxford University Press, 2001.

Kasaba, Reşat, ed. *The Cambridge History of Turkey*. Vol. 4, *Turkey in the Modern World*. New York: Cambridge University Press, 2008.

Kayalı, Hasan. *Arabs and Young Turks: Ottomanism, Arabism, and Islamism in the Ottoman Empire, 1908–1918.* Berkeley: University of California Press, 1997.

Kazancıgil, Ali, and Ergun Özbudun, eds. *Atatürk: Founder of a Modern State.* London: Hurst, 1981.

Kılınç, Ramazan. "History, International Norms, and Domestic Institutional Change: State–Religion Relations in France and Turkey." Ph.D. diss., Arizona State University, 2008.

Kösebalaban, Hasan. "The Impact of Globalization on Islamic Political Identity." *World Affairs* 168 (2005): 27–37.

——. *Turkish Foreign Policy: Islam, Nationalism, and Globalization.* New York: Palgrave Macmillan, 2011.

Küçükcan, Talip. "State, Islam, and Religious Liberty in Modern Turkey: Reconfiguration of Religion in the Public Sphere." *Brigham Young University Law Review* 2 (2003): 475–506.

Kuru, Ahmet T. "Globalization and Diversification of Islamic Movements: Three Turkish Cases." *Political Science Quarterly* 120 (2005): 253–274.

——. "Passive and Assertive Secularism: Historical Conditions, Ideological Struggles, and State Policies Towards Religion." *World Politics* 59 (2007): 568–594.

——. *Secularism and State Policies Toward Religion: The United States, France, and Turkey.* New York: Cambridge University Press, 2009.

Lagendijk, Joost, and Jan Marinus Wiersma. *Travels Among Europe's Muslim Neighbours: The Quest for Democracy.* Brussels: Centre for European Policy Studies, 2008.

Mardin, Şerif. *The Genesis of Young Ottoman Thought: A Study in the Modernization of Turkish Political Ideas.* 1962. Reprint, Syracuse, N.Y.: Syracuse University Press, 2000.

——. "The Just and the Unjust." *Daedalus* 120 (1991): 113–129.

——. *Religion and Social Change in Modern Turkey: The Case of Bediüzzaman Said Nursi.* Albany: State University of New York Press, 1989.

Navaro-Yashin, Yael. *Faces of the State: Secularism and Public Life in Turkey.* Princeton, N.J.: Princeton University Press, 2002.

Öniş, Ziya. "Conservative Globalists Versus Defensive Nationalists: Political Parties and Paradoxes of Europeanization in Turkey." *Journal of Southern Europe and the Balkans* 9 (2007): 247–261.

Oran, Baskın. *Türkiye'de Azınlıklar: Kavramlar, Lozan, İç Mevzuat, İçtihat, Uygulama.* Istanbul: TESEV, 2004.

Ortaylı, İlber. 1983. *İmparatorluğun En Uzun Yüzyılı.* Istanbul: Hil.

Özbudun, Ergun. *Contemporary Turkish Politics: Challenges to Democratic Consolidation.* London: Rienner, 2000.

Özbudun, Ergun, and Ömer Faruk Gençkaya. *Democratization and the Politics of Constitution Making in Turkey.* Budapest: Central European University Press, 2009.

Özbudun, Ergun, and Serap Yazıcı. *Democratization Reforms in Turkey, 1993–2004*. Istanbul: TESEV, 2004.

Özyürek, Esra. *Nostalgia for the Modern: State Secularism and Everyday Politics in Turkey*. Durham, N.C.: Duke University Press, 2006.

Parla, Taha, and Andrew Davison. *Corporatist Ideology in Kemalist Turkey: Progress or Order?* Syracuse, N.Y.: Syracuse University Press, 2004.

Sarıtoprak, Zeki, ed. "Special Issue on Bediüzzaman Said Nursi." *Islam and Christian–Muslim Relations* 19 (2008): 1–147.

Somer, Murat. "Moderate Islam and Secularist Opposition in Turkey: Implications for the World, Muslims, and Secular Democracy." *Third World Quarterly* 28 (2007): 1271–1289.

Stepan, Alfred. "The World's Religious Systems and Democracy: Crafting the 'Twin Tolerations.'" In *Arguing Comparative Politics*, 213–253. New York: Oxford University Press, 2001.

Tarhanlı, İştar B. *Müslüman Toplum, "Laik" Devlet: Türkiye'de Diyanet İşleri Başkanlığı*. Istanbul: AFA, 1993.

Taşpınar, Ömer. "The Old Turk's Revolt: When Radical Secularism Endangers Democracy." *Foreign Affairs* 86 (2007): 114–130.

Tezcür, Güneş Murat. *Muslim Reformers in Iran and Turkey: The Paradox of Moderation*. Austin: University of Texas Press, 2010.

Tuğal, Cihan. *Passive Revolution: Absorbing the Islamic Challenge to Capitalism*. Stanford, Calif.: Stanford University Press, 2009.

Turam, Berna. *Between Islam and the State: The Politics of Engagement*. Stanford, Calif.: Stanford University Press, 2006.

Uğur, Etga. "Intellectual Roots of 'Turkish Islam' and Approaches to the 'Turkish Model.'" *Journal of Muslim Minority Affairs* 24 (2004): 327–345.

White, Jenny B. *Islamist Mobilization in Turkey: A Study in Vernacular Politics*. Seattle: University of Washington Press, 2003.

Yalman, Nur. "Some Observations on Secularism in Islam: The Cultural Revolution in Turkey." *Daedalus* 102 (1973): 139–168.

Yavuz, M. Hakan. *Islamic Political Identity in Turkey*. Oxford: Oxford University Press, 2003.

Yavuz, M. Hakan, and John L. Esposito, eds. *Turkish Islam and the Secular State: The Gülen Movement*. Syracuse, N.Y.: Syracuse University Press, 2003.

Yükleyen, Ahmet. *Contextualizing Islam in Europe: Turkish Islamic Communities in Germany and the Netherlands*. Syracuse, N.Y.: Syracuse University Press, 2011.

Zürcher, Erik Jan. "Ottoman Sources of Kemalist Thought." In Elisabeth Özdalga, ed., *Late Ottoman Society: The Intellectual Legacy*, 13–26. New York: Routledge Curzon, 2005.

——. *Turkey: A Modern History*. New York: Tauris, 2004.

Contributors

Karen Barkey is professor of sociology and history at Columbia University. She is the author of *Bandits and Bureaucrats: The Ottoman Route to State Centralization* and *Empire of Difference: The Ottomans in Comparative Perspective*, which won awards from the Comparative Historical Sociology section of the American Sociology Association and the Politics and History section of the American Political Science Association.

Ümit Cizre is professor of political science at Istanbul Şehir University. She is the author of *The Politics of the Powerful* (in Turkish) and the editor of *Secular and Islamic Politics in Turkey: The Making of the Justice and Development Party* and *Democratic Oversight and Reform of the Security Sector in Turkey*.

M. Şükrü Hanioğlu is Garrett Professor in Foreign Affairs and chair of the Department of Near Eastern Studies at Princeton University. He is the author of *Atatürk: An Intellectual Biography*, *A Brief History of the Late Ottoman Empire*, *Preparation for a Revolution: The Young Turks, 1902–1908*, and *Young Turks in Opposition*.

Stathis N. Kalyvas is the Arnold Wolfers Professor of Political Science and director of the Program on Order, Conflict, and Violence at Yale University. He is the author of *The Rise of Christian Democracy in Europe* and *The Logic of Violence in Civil War*, which won awards from the American Political Science Association and the European Academy of Sociology.

Ahmet T. Kuru is formerly postdoctoral scholar and assistant director of the Center for the Study of Democracy, Toleration, and Religion at Columbia University, and currently associate professor of political science at San Diego State University. He is the author of *Secularism and State Policies Toward Religion: The United States, France, and Turkey*; his dissertation on this topic received the award for best dissertation from the Religion and Politics section of the American Political Science Association.

Joost Lagendijk was a Dutch politician from Green Left, a member of the European Parliament, and chair of the Delegation to the European Union–Turkey Joint Parliamentary Committee. He currently resides in Istanbul, conducts research at Sabancı University, and is a columnist for the newspaper *Zaman*.

Ergun Özbudun is professor of law and political science at Bilkent University, Ankara. He is the author of *Contemporary Turkish Politics: Challenges to Democratic Consolidation*, co-author of *Islamism, Democracy, and Liberalism in Turkey: The Case of the AKP*, and co-editor of *Atatürk: Founder of a Modern State*.

Alfred Stepan is the Wallace Sayre Professor of Government; director of the Center for the Study of Democracy, Toleration, and Religion; and co-director of the Institute for Religion, Culture, and Public Life, all at Columbia University. He is the author of *Arguing Comparative Politics* and co-author of both *Problems of Democratic Transition and Consolidation* and *Crafting State Nations: India and Other Multinational Democracies*.

Index

Made in the USA
Lexington, KY
23 July 2014